Ting Tangs, Trebles and Tenors

A collection of historical notes, anecdotes and customs about
some of the bells, belfries and bell-ringers of East Derbyshire
and West Nottinghamshire.

Written and Compiled by
Glyn Holdgate

1999

British Library Cataloguing in Publication Data.
A catalogue record for this book is available
from the British Library.

ISBN 0 9535472 0 5
Published by:
Glyn Holdgate
11 Spanker Lane
Nether Heage, Derby DE56 2AT

Print Management, Typesetting & Design by

MOORLEY'S Print & Publishing
23 Park Rd., Ilkeston, Derbys DE7 5DA
Tel/Fax: (0115) 932 0643
using data from author's disc.

Printed and bound at Redwood Books

CONTENTS

Preface.   6

1   Campanology ... What's it all about?   8
    Three centuries of Bell-ringing in East
    Derbyshire and West Nottinghamshire.

2   Bellfounders. Local craftsmen bequeath their legends.   19

3   Heathcotes of Chesterfield. Bellfounders 1476 - 1647.   27

4   Bellfounders of Nottingham;   32
    Selyoke to Hedderly via Mellor and Oldfield.

5   Belfry Jingles, Rhyme, Verse and Hymn.   39

6   The Belfries of:-
    St. Martin, Alfreton, Derbyshire.   47
    All Saints, Ashover. Derbyshire.   54
    St. John the Baptist, Ault Hucknall. Derbyshire.   67
    St. Peter, Belper, Derbyshire.   74
    St. Werburgh, Blackwell, Derbyshire.   78
    St. Mary & St. Laurance, Bolsover, Derbyshire.   82
    St. Mary and All Saints, Chesterfield, Derbyshire.   87
    St. Bartholomew, Clay Cross, Derbyshire.   100
    St. Mary, Crich, Derbyshire.   104
    St. Helen, Darley, Derbyshire.   110
    St. Mary the Virgin, Denby, Derbyshire.   113
    St. Mary, Edwinstowe, Nottinghamshire.   117
    St. Lawrence, Heanor, Derbyshire.   121
    All Saints, Heath, Derbyshire.   125
    St. Wilfrid, Kirkby in Ashfield, Nottinghamshire.   128
    S.S. Peter and Paul, Mansfield, Nottinghamshire.   133
    St. Edmund, Mansfield Woodhouse, Nottinghamshire.   139
    St. Giles, Matlock, Derbyshire.   142
    Holy Cross, Morton, Derbyshire.   146
    St. Lawrence, North Wingfield, Derbyshire.   155
    S.S. Peter and Paul, Old Brampton, Derbyshire.   164
    St. Matthew, Pentrich, Derbyshire.   167
    St. Helen, Pinxton, Derbyshire.   172
    St. Michael, Pleasley, Derbyshire.   176
    All Saints, Ripley, Derbyshire.   179
    St. Leonard, Scarcliffe, Derbyshire.   184
    St. Helen, Selston, Nottinghamshire.   187
    St. Leonard, Shirland, Derbyshire.   195
    St. Michael & All Angels, South Normanton, Derbyshire.   202
    All Saints, South Wingfield, Derbyshire.   207
    St. Mary Magdalene, Sutton in Ashfield, Nottinghamshire.   214

St. Andrew, Swanwick, Derbyshire. 220
St. Katherine, Teversal, Nottinghamshire. 229
St. John the Baptist, Tibshelf, Derbyshire. 233
S.S. Peter and Paul, Warsop, Nottinghamshire. 239
All Saints, Wingerworth, Derbyshire. 244

7   The Decade next before the Millennium. 247

Bibliography. 256

ILLUSTRATIONS Photographs

Denby, Crich, Chesterfield. i
Ault Hucknall, Pentrich, Blackwell. ii
Clay Cross, Heath, Kirkby in Ashfield, Swanwick. iii
North Wingfield, South Normanton, South Wingfield. iv
Bolsover, Old Brampton, Edwinstowe, Mansfield Woodhouse. v
Matlock, Morton, Pleasley, Shirland. vi
Alfreton, Belper, Heanor, Ripley. vii
Mansfield, Sutton in Ashfield, Scarcliffe, Warsop. viii
Pinxton, Selston, Tibshelf, Teversal. ix
Wingerworth, Ashover, Darley. x
Bells at rest. xi
The Bell Chamber. xii
The lie of the clapper. xiii
Ancillary bell parts. xiv
Ting Tangs and Tower Clock. xv
Bell maintenance. xvi
South Normanton Ringers. xvii
Swanwick and Ashover Ringers. xviii
Alfreton Ringers. xix
Ringers meet in Teversal Belfry. xx
Association members gather at Ashover and Selston. xxi
Ringers of Sutton in Ashfield and Warsop. xxii
A 1952 ringing tour and a 1953 wedding peal. xxiii
Tuition sessons at Alfreton and South Wingfield. xxiv
Selston Ringers - a decade apart. xxv
The Ringers of S.S. Peter and Paul, Mansfield. xxvi
The Annual Ringing Outing. xxvii
New Treble cast for Kirkby in Ashfield. xxviii
Cutting the Centenary Cake. xxix
Centenary Dinner. xxx
Forty years apart. xxxi
Bedfordshire Tour. Chesterfield's Ringers 1900. xxxii

ILLUSTRATIONS within the text.

A new belfry door, Alfreton.   1
IHC The mark of George Heathcote.   7
The Ringers' Card of 1887.   14
Samuel Midworth and John & Ebenezer Smith, Bellfounders.   22
The Heathcotes of Chesterfield, Bell-marks.   31
The mark of Robert Mellor.   38
St.Martin's Guild, Alfreton ,1892.   53
Some bell-marks found on Ashover bells.   66
The Logo of a local Bell-hanger, Frederick Pembleton.   73
The old Weathercock at Crich.   109
1915 Balance Sheet of the East Derbyshire Association.   116
Certificate of Merit.   132
George Heathcote's 16th century inscription.   141
The Belfries of Morton and North Wingfield.   154
North Wingfield's inscription stone.   163
Removal of pre-reformation bell at Pinxton.   175
Sir A.P. Heywood, Bart.   183
The mark of Robert Crowch at Shirland.   201
1876 Peal recorded in Shirland Belfry.   201
All Saints Church, South Wingfield.   213
Stone commemorates building of Swanwick Belfry.   228
Peal board records first peal rung on Swanwick bells.   228
Inscription on third bell at Teversal.   232
Easter 1889, Report of the Association.   237
The Ringing World.   246
Sutton Scarsdale's PH mark.   254

Outer cover: "Calling ye folk to church on time." From a watercolour by the author.

Preface

The writing of Ting Tangs, Trebles and Tenors, came about by accident. In 1987, as Honorary Secretary to my local Association of Church Bell Ringers, which happened in that year to reach the centenary of its founding, I had become involved in researching into its past history. Over the previous forty years, I had also slowly assembled a private collection of notes on the history of local bells and belfries, and was able to use some of the material. Having this, together with innumerable anecdotes I had gathered from many sources, plus my first hand experience of Change Ringing in the area over the period, and access to the records of the Association, I was able to write a number of short articles for the occasion. In addition, I assembled an exhibition depicting one hundred years of the Association's history. This exhibit made a tour of many local libraries and churches during centenary year.

I soon realised that my store of material exceeded that which could be used within the scope of the centenary exhibits and its articles. Also, such was the interest shown at the time, that I was further encouraged to continue collecting my anecdotes and snippets of history. Now, fifty years have past since I first took to the art and science of bell-ringing, and I have come to realise that in this ever changing world of ours it might not be too bad a thing to commit some of my collection to print. If for no other reason than to simply try and ensure that a very small part of a purely English tradition is truly recorded.

In writing this account I have made a sincere attempt to bring together a little of the history and life of just thirty-six of England's five thousand belfries. A fascinating few.

Geographically these belfries span an area from the Derbyshire Peak District, eastward, to the Sherwood Forest area of Nottinghamshire. Today, they straggle into two counties and into two dioceses, Derby and Southwell, this uniquely places the activities of local bell-ringers in two provinces of the Anglican Church, namely Canterbury and York. . It just so happens that for over a century these belfries have formed the nucleus of what is now the East Derbyshire and West Nottinghamshire Association of Church Bell Ringers. In many of these belfries, records show that the bells have been rung regularly throughout several centuries to inform parishioners of, and to mark, both local, civic, national and ecclesiastical occasions. Not forgetting, of course, the ringing taking place week by week, for the Sunday services of the Church that all ringers' serve.

It is therefore the simple act of unselfish dedication, by a handful of local bell-ringers, that I wish to place on record and to whom I dedicate this work. Alas, most will not even be mentioned by name, nor perhaps will their skills be noted, other than in general terms, but, whoever they may be, it is truly about their unstinting dedication to the art and science of bell-ringing, throughout past centuries, that I aim to portray in every part of this story.

Whilst accuracy has been my prime objective I am well aware that no sooner will the ink be dry than out of some woodwork of these towers and spires will emerge items of history and ringers' anecdotes that I have missed. In defence, I can only say how delighted I will be at seeing such an emergence, for it is and was the very fascination of this ever-recurring fact that prompted me to collect and compile this account in the first place. The sheer history of the bells, the towers, the spires, the bell-ringers never failed to amaze me as it unfolded, and I trust that you, the reader, will obtain some measure of this amazement and enjoyment.

In this ever-changing world my story is something of a timewarp and for that very reason I sincerely trust you will obtain great pleasure from reading about the workings and activities of what in reality is just a handful of England's beautiful and active belfries.

Glyn Holdgate, July 1998.

"To call ye folk to church in time   - we chime.

When mirth and joy are on the wing   - we ring.

At the departure of the soul   - we toll."

1. CAMPANOLOGY

What's it all about?
Three centuries of Bell-ringing in East Derbyshire and West Nottinghamshire.

To stand alongside the Fabrick Rock above the village of Ashover, and look from this vantage point, down into the village, on a fine clear evening in summer, when the sound of the bells of the parish church is being carried aloft on a gentle breeze, must truly be one of the most tranquil of English scenes.

Change ringing as practised on the church bells in England is something very much taken for granted by all who hear it, yet it is very much missed when the bells of our churches lay silent. It is true to say that everyone has, at sometime in their lives, been dictated to by the sound of bells. The school bell, perhaps a fire bell, the early morning alarm bell and the telephone bell are but a few examples. Most people love to hear the sound of properly rung church bells - a few don't. Most people can associate the ringing of church bells with some event in their lives, such as a wedding, or in celebration of some great national occasion. Down the ages, royal weddings, births and coronations have been marked by the ringing of peals. Then, there is the sombre mood, created more frequently in former years, by the tolling of the passing bell, or the half-muffled peal heard upon the death of a loved one. Yes, bells are one of life's outward signs. To the faithful of course, they are primarily a call to the house of God for prayer.

From early days man has wanted to express his emotions over joy, sorrow, fear and anger and throughout history bells have helped to fulfil this purpose.

We find in the Bible only two references to bells. In Exodus, we learn that the skirt of the robe of Aaron, as he entered and left the temple, was trimmed with pomegranates alternating with gold bells. And, Zachariah, in telling of the annual pilgrimage to Jerusalem, refers to the bells of the horses as being inscribed, "Holy to the Lord". The purpose of attaching bells was to attract attention in order that people would bear witness. Just as the bells that ring forth from our parish church towers today proclaim Christ's Gospel to all who hear them.

In medieval England, every town had its chiming bells announcing the time of day and marking the allotted time for prayer. Later, the jangling of several bells being chimed simultaneously became a normal form of expression and used for celebrating a victory or some event of national importance.

As the shape of the bell evolved and grew in size it became necessary to find suitable housing for them. The local church tower was most suitable, if not the only place capable of holding bells. So, we find that ecclesiastical buildings became the custodian of bells. Ringing continued, as from earlier days, to commemorate secular events alongside the marking of religious festivals and the ringing for the divine services of the church.

During the Reformation period the use of bells in public worship and for liturgical purposes was forbidden and during this period many bells were confiscated for the value of their metal.

The Puritan movement was also hostile to bell-ringing and so we find the ringer and the church becoming estranged. Ringing was hard work, but it gave enjoyment, especially to the healthy young man seeking an energetic outlet. This was deemed by the Puritans as a sinful act who at best would only allow a single bell to be chimed on a Sunday, and then strictly only to call worshippers to service. This situation meant that bell-ringing had to be undertaken for secular use only or to cease altogether. It did not cease. This very unsatisfactory state continued in many rural parishes until well into the nineteenth century when it became essential that some form of status within the church be afforded the bell-ringer.

Compatible with this period changes had taken place with regard to the hanging of bells. Early bells had been chimed by means of a rope and lever. This allowed just enough swing of the bell for the clapper to strike. In the course of time the lever gave way, first to the quarter wheel and then the half wheel. This enabled the bell to be swung higher.

By the seventeenth century the full wheel was in use and this allowed the bell to be raised full circle. With the mouth uppermost, or as is termed in ringing parlance, 'raised' or 'rung up'. The ringer was now able to hold the bell momentarily in the inverted position before reversing the movement and in so doing create an orderly and controlled timing of the striking. When used in conjunction with the other bells this produced sequence ringing. It was but a short step to introduce bells tuned to produce the musical scale and when these were rung in order the 'Round' was born. This was indeed a breakthrough, for instead of the hitherto jangle, the bells were rung in order down the musical scale. Beginning with the striking of the small Treble Bell, the highest note, and ending the round with the deeper note of the large Tenor Bell striking last.

It was not long before the ringer, tired of this repetitive set sequence, began experimenting by changing the striking order of one pair of bells. This was done on the audible call of the appointed leader, known as the conductor, and this form of ringing became known as Call Changes or Churchyard Bob. A popular and exacting manner of bell-ringing still very much favoured in the west of England to this day.

As the skill of the team progressed with regard to handling the bells and striking after each other in good rhythm, call change ringing was developed into change ringing, known as the Hunt.

To Hunt, each bell takes its allotted space in the musical scale. Let us assume we are ringing the third bell and that all five bells in our tower are ringing. Bear in mind, that at each pull of the rope the bell turns through a vertical three hundred and sixty degrees, before, at the next pull of the rope, reversing to its original position. These two strokes are known as the 'Handstroke' and 'Backstroke' respectively. Each bell moves in turn, first from handstroke to backstroke to produce one round or change. They all then return from backstroke to handstroke to produce the second round or change and continue alternating the two stokes.

Taking our bell, the third to strike when ringing in rounds, we go into changes at the handstroke next after the conductor's command. Even numbered bells move by one place at each stroke toward the front, known as the lead, and the odd numbered bells move by one place at each stroke toward the back, known as behind. We, number three, being an odd numbered bell, move into the place of the fourth bell, who being an even numbered bell, takes our place in thirds. Similarly at this first change the treble and second have transposed whilst the fifth bell remains behind. But, in the second change, which is at backstroke, the second bell remains at lead whilst the other two pairs, treble and four and three and five transpose. By transposing the first two pairs of bells at each handstroke and by transposing each of the latter pair of bells at each backstroke you will find that by starting from rounds 12345 the exercise will return to rounds in ten changes thus:-

<u>12345</u>
21435
24153
42513
45231
54321
53412
35142
31524
13254
12345

And so from these basic changes the exclusive form of English bell-ringing was born.

One promoter of English Change Ringing was undoubtedly Fabian Stedman, a printer of Cambridge who was born in 1631. He introduced various peals for ringing on five and six bells, printed them on slips of paper and distributed them about the country. Stedman, a ringing method (or tune) named after him is still very popular with ringers to this day. It is also considered one of the most musical of methods.

As already mentioned, in rural parishes, to a greater or lesser degree, the estrangement between church and ringer continued well into the middle of the nineteenth century. Then came reform. It was masterminded by the clergy and the ringers together and so we witnessed the setting up of territorial societies modelled

10

upon the old craft guilds. Some were introduced as isolated societies centred at one tower, usually a cathedral or the large town church were there was already installed a peal of six, eight or possibly ten bells. These tower guilds were self-sufficient and in the main only fraternised with ringers from other towers of similar standing. They did much in the way of composing new change ringing methods. Method, by the way, is the ringers' term for a different sequence of changes, a new tune or a piece of music so to speak. Two such methods, with local overtones, spring to mind, Duffield, a principal method and Killamarsh Treble Bob. Tower guilds adopted good guidelines. This organised growth led to the adoption of the ringer by the church which rightly meant that bells already installed in church towers were once again used for their rightful purpose. The marking of religious festivals and the calling of the faithful to worship, whilst at the same time, continuing to commemorate civic and national events.

In the villages, where life developed at a slower pace, many of the parish churches possessed only a single bell and it was rare to find peals of over four bells. But, since the restoration of the Monarchy under Charles II there had been a steady introduction of new bells into our village churches and by the middle of the nineteenth century rings of five and six bells were becoming common place. With this increase in the number of bells grew a greater interest in change ringing. The time was therefore right for organising teams of bell-ringers within the church and to afford them a status parallel with that of the office of organist, chorister, server and sidesman. Campanology was now an honourable pursuit.

Five local clergymen were the first to grasp the benefits to be gained from forming a local organisation. They were, the Rector of Ashover, Rev. J.B. Nodder; Rector of South Normanton, Rev. J.C. Massey; Vicar of Clay Cross, Rev J. Oldham; Rector of Old Brampton, Rev. G. Shipson and the Vicar of Crich. Together with their bell-ringers they deliberated upon the feasibility of forming an Association and organised exploratory meetings. These meetings culminated with a meeting in the Parochial Schools at Clay Cross on 29th October 1887 and the founding of the East Derbyshire Association of Change Ringers.

A strong need was felt at this meeting that an Association was urgently needed locally to bring together bell-ringers of the villages. In fact, the first rule adopted by them defined that only towers with six bells or fewer be admitted members. Such was felt the need to cater primarily for the village church and ringer.

This point proved interesting as time went on and as the number of bells in some towers was augmented. By the time Alfreton augmented to eight bells in 1899, to become the Association's first peal of eight bells, the rule had been discarded. But, it is fair to state that throughout the history of the Association the ringing of five bells, termed Doubles, and six bells termed Minor, has dominated. Of the thirty-six towers in the Association's area today there are only fifteen with peals of eight bells.

Although at the time of writing there is an idea mooted that Ashover may augment to a peal of ten. Should this come to fruition, then only time will tell if it is indeed wise for a village to saddle itself with the burden of maintaining and ringing this number of bells week in and week out, year in and year out, for the services of the parish church. If it is not practical, and the bells only get rung by visiting bands of ringers, then surely the situation is that of returning bells back to pleasure use only.

One of the main benefits in forming the Association may be deduced from the original list of objectives:- 'The chief object of this Association is the promotion of Belfry Reform, as it is obvious that a great deal of good may be accomplished thereby, and having been established, it directs its attention, among other points, to the following, viz:-

1. The observance of good and peaceable behaviour in the belfries of our Churches, as being an integral part of the Church, and therefore consecrated to the services of God, while the bells and ringers are intended to be exercised equally with the organ and choir for His glory and worship.

2. To refrain, as far as possible, from using the bells on the Lord's day, except for the services of the Church.

3. To obtain full recognition of the ringers' office as essentially a branch of the Church's work, that they and their services (which demand much time, skill, and mental labour) may be placed upon a true and acknowledged basis.

4. To cultivate the Art of Change Ringing, by frequent meetings in various centres for friendly peal ringing; and to provide, at a reasonable cost, instructors for those who may require them.

As a means of securing the above objects, the Association provides a medium for bringing into closer relationship, one with another, the Clergy, Churchwardens and others interested in the objects for which the East Derbyshire Association of Change Ringers has been established; and it is earnestly trusted that all such will hasten to join its ranks, and increase its influence, as its operations cannot be conducted without incurring considerable expense."

Within two years, on Easter Monday, 1889, forty five members from Clay Cross, North Wingfield, Ashover, Old Brampton, Crich and South Normanton met at Clay Cross and were joined by ringers from Heath, Bolsover and Ault Hucknall for the first recorded Annual Meeting of the Association. It was reported that three previous Meetings had been arranged in an attempt to promote interest in the district about the newly formed East Derbyshire Association of Change Ringers. Each member received a printed copy of the Objects and Rules of the Association in what was termed 'The Ringers' Card', which clearly states on the front cover, 'For cultivating the Art of Change Ringing and Belfry Reform'.

A century later the phrase, 'Belfry Reform', strikes a note of terror in the minds of present day bell-ringers and one wonders why such a phrase was used so prominently. The plain fact being that such reform was needed in many local belfries at that time.

Throughout years of neglect the base of our towers had become dumps for unwanted items which in many cases had been left to gather mildew and rot. Very few churchgoers took the trouble to visit the tower and were even less likely to climb the dark spiral stairs to examine what was aloft. Here louvres were often missing and decayed giving access to everything on the wing. Huge mountains of twigs forming the nests of Jackdaws were commonplace. Bats hung from rafters, and owls made their home in the dark niches, regurgitating the remains of feasts upon bell and frame. The whole scene of a neglected belfry is deplorable. Added to this 'natural' scene was to be found cascades of candle tallow, broken stays and odd lengths of rope and other debris, rusty, empty and half empty containers used to carry grease for the bells, rags, etcetera, etcetera.

The following contemporary report taken from 'Bell News', a bell-ringers weekly journal of the time, and published some twelve years after the founding of the Association clearly illustrates the point about belfry reform :-

"Belfry Reform at Horsley, Derbyshire.

On Saturday, September 17th, 1898 the Horsley company had their photographs taken, standing in a group near the belfry door. The number of bells at Horsley is five, and there are a like number of ringers. They are the first local band of change ringers at the above place. Considerable improvements have been made of late at Horsley, change-ringing taking the place of Churchyard Bob. The ringing chamber has been put into nice order; the walls, thanks to the Vicar, have been wood- panelled all round; lamps taking place of candles. The refuse has been cleared out from beneath the bells, and wire netting put over the sound holes, and over all, right up the spire, to keep out the birds. There is also a proper set of muffles, thanks to Mr. Harry George, who kindly presented them, and also instructed the company in the Art of change-ringing. They possess a set of handbells, fifteen in number, subscribed for by the parishioners, for use of the ringers."

Another aspect to merit affiliation to an Association is raised when we look at St. Martin's, Alfreton. A tower in which there had been a peal of five bells since 1780. There had been an active band of ringers at Alfreton for some years but upon the founding of the Association they showed no interest in affiliating for a period of some ten years. Then, in 1897, a new treble bell was installed to make a ring of six bells. This sparked off new interest and the ringers, keen to obtain the best from their new six, joined the Association in a search to further their change-ringing practice and gain additional skills in the ringing of new methods alongside other ringers.

As additional bells were placed in towers, isolated groups of ringers became commonplace. Ringers were being encouraged to fraternise with ringers from neighbouring towers. This brought an increasing desire among them to try and master the complexities and techniques of ringing new and as yet untried methods

EAST DERBYSHIRE

Association of Change Ringers,

FOUNDED OCTOBER 29TH, 1887,

For Cultivating the Art of Change Ringing and Belfry Reform.

———

President : Rev. J. C. MASSEY, Rector of South
Normanton.

Vice-President : Rev. J. B. NODDER, Rector of Ashover
Parish Church.

Committee : Formed of two Probationers and Ringers
from each Belfry.

Honorary Treasurer : Rev. JOS. OLDHAM, Rector of Clay
Cross Parish Church.

Hon. Secretary : Mr. JAMES GREEN, 141, High
Street, Clay Cross.

———

The Belfry is part of the Church, and is consecrated to the
service of God.   The Bells are instruments of Sacred Music.
The office, therefore, of ringer is a holy one, and should ever
be performed in a reverent manner.

———

CLAY CROSS :

H. WALKER, PRINTER AND STATIONER.

Frontispiece taken from the original Ringers' Card.
It was issued to 45 Founder Members from the belfries of
Clay Cross, North Wingfield, Old Brampton, South Normanton
And Crich, setting out the objects and rules of membership.

14

and by so doing extend their skill. A local association for ringers was in demand and claimed to be a very worthwhile project.

By the turn of the century bell-ringers from seventeen towers had affiliated bringing the membership to one hundred and thirteen. This brought some eighty-eight bells within the care of members. Of the new towers affiliating since 1889 were the ringers from Shirland, 1893; Ripley, Wingerworth and Morton, 1895; Alfreton, 1897 and Pentrich 1899.

The East Derbyshire Association of Change Ringers was not and has never been a large organisation. It is not even a leader in the realms of campanology, but, in its small and quiet way, it is a 'grass roots' society. Always a nursery for the budding bell-ringer, and always offering opportunity to the novice to gain experience through practice. Many a leading ringer has exploited his or her basic skill through membership. One yardstick by which societies are rated is taken from the number of peals of 5040 changes that are rung and recorded by each society. Members of the E.D.& W.N.A. have rung few by comparison with some guilds, just over two hundred or on average two a year. But, members have faithfully rung regularly for the Sunday services of the Church, for the Church's festivals and special services throughout each year. Many a bride and groom has been publicly heralded by bells ringing on their wedding day and numerous days of national rejoicing and indeed sadness has been noted by members ringing the bells of our local parish churches.

In addition to ringing, they have diligently attended to the maintenance of the bells, bellframes and ropes, kept the fabric of the towers in good order. Several generations of members have given freely of their time and talents in this way, many of them without consideration of the cost to themselves or their families in order that the bells in just a few of England's towers and steeples may continue to ring forth in this most English tradition.

Not all bell-ringers are keen to join an association and this is no different now than it was a century ago. Ringers at Morton obviously had reservations about joining the Association in the early days. On several occasions they were singled out for a special invitation to join. They hosted members at a meeting in 1891 and later raised some proposition regarding proposed membership through their secretary, Mr. E.A. Pickwell, but in spite of this contact and dialogue the first members from Morton did not materialise until 1895. Two years later a meeting scheduled for Morton was cancelled and transferred to Alfreton. At this meeting a letter was read from the Rector of Morton, Rev. J.W. Maltby, expressing regret that his ringers could not see their way clear to remain members. It was to be a further nine years, 1906, before the ringers of Morton re-affiliated.

In 1891 a proposition that an amalgamation be effected with the Old East Derbyshire Association, which operated in the north east of the county and bordering onto Sheffield and Rotherham, brought division between the sixty-six

15

members attending. After strong discussion, a vote was taken and the proposition lost. But this was by no means the end of the matter. Over several years correspondence flowed between secretaries. Some of it reaching the columns of Bell News and Ringers Record as late as 1897.

The reasons for or against the amalgamation of the two Associations is not recorded in detail in the minutes but what does seem a trifle odd is why, with the existence of the Old East Derbyshire Association, the forty-five founder members forming the new organisation in 1887 chose almost the same designation. The matter was finally laid to rest by a large majority at the 1897 A.G.M. when it was agreed not to amalgamate.

The first interest shown toward peal ringing was in 1893 when member towers were asked to keep records of any peals they rang. It was also agreed that 'New men' be elected as members before attempting to ring a peal. Alas, if any peals were rung at this time no records remain as the first record of a peal being rung for the Association was at Bolsover on January 26th, 1901. This peal, rung by the local band, was of 5040 changes of Plain Bob Minor. The occasion was unfortunately saddened by the death of H.M. Queen Victoria who had died four days earlier on January 22nd. As a token of respect the peal was rung with the bells deeply muffled and being rung slowly, as befits such a sad occasion, it took three hours and three minutes to complete.

A popular custom amongst ringers at this period was to ring date touches. Two examples are recorded at South Normanton. In 1880 when the same number of changes of Grandsire Doubles was rung followed ten years later by the ringing of 1890 changes of the same method.

For the benefit of the non-ringer the meaning of the term, "Peal" is for the bells to be rung continuously in excess of five thousand different changes. An "Extent" is the maximum permutation on any given number of bells. Using six bells, in a sequence termed, 'Minor', seven hundred and twenty changes are produced in the extent. In order to accomplish a recognised peal on six bells it is therefore necessary to ring seven of these extents consecutively and without a pause. This produces a peal of 5040 changes. On a higher number of bells the required 5000 changes is produced within the permutation.

Mention has already been made as to the ringing of five bells producing 120 changes and being termed Doubles, and on six, Minor. To ring seven bells is termed Triples and on eight, Major. For bells numbering nine to twelve we have Caters, Royal, Cinques and Maximus. An extent of Triples produces 5040 changes whilst the additional bell, eight, produces 40,320 changes. A recognised peal takes between two hours and thirty minutes and three hours and ten minutes to complete dependent upon the number of bells and the weight of them.

Realizing just what the dedicated ringer gives in time and talent is not always appreciated, and it was to some extent the very essence of this unselfish and generous giving that the founders of our associations and guilds wished to place on a proper basis. They sought to bring the ringer, through the body of an Association, into the true realms of being a church worker.

It was normal practice for members up to a decade or so ago to arrange Sunday Service Ringing to take place for thirty minutes prior to Matins and Evensong with additional ringing for festivals. Early morning ringing on Easter Day and Christmas Day commenced at six thirty and often on Christmas Eve the bells would be rung either prior to the Midnight Mass or earlier in the evening, depending upon the liturgical requirement in practice. New Year's Eve ringing was popular, with several of the local incumbents being known to provide refreshment, either in the form of supper, or 'eats in the belfry'. Confirmation services, harvest and patronal festivals were also occasions when the bells were rung.

In any progressive band of ringers the practice of new methods and the teaching of learners is left to the mid-week practice and only the best ringing that is attainable by the band is rung prior to services. That at least is the ideal way. But, as anyone who has tried his or her hand at bellringing will recall, many hours of diligent practice are required to achieve a reasonable standard. It is estimated that well under ten per cent of new recruits reach the standard of competence whereby they become useful members of a good team and even fewer attain competence at peal ringing. Of these only a few go on to become good conductors of peals.

Fortunately, campanology can and does accommodate ringers of all grades. A ringer can attain a level of competence which is both useful to the team and enjoyable to the ringer and there are several side avenues to explore along the way, maintenance, rope splicing and teaching learners to mention but three.

The maintenance of the bells is a very important factor in any belfry and to the ringer willing and able to undertake this work there is endless scope for gaining satisfaction. Many of our churches have tower clocks which need constant attention. In fact a whole chapter could be written on the clocks to be found in our churches ranging from the ones which strike only each hour to the fascinating tune playing systems similar to that at St. Peter's, Mansfield.

Returning for a moment to our vantage point alongside Fabrick Rock and looking eastward over the plain toward and beyond the Nottinghamshire border it is possible to locate, on a clear day, seventeen of the Association's member towers. Some are silhouetted against the eastern sky whilst others lurk in the valley that was once, and not too long ago, dotted with innumerable coal mines. Others lie behind us, over the hill, and one, Crich, stands sentinel to the south and surveying, as we do, this tiny area of England whose towers and bells have been entrusted to the safe keeping of members for the past century.

In fact, bellringing locally can be traced back over two further centuries. The reader will find included a brief history of local bellfounders in Chesterfield; Nottingham and elsewhere which take us back three centuries. At Crich, it is known that at least one bell has hung in the tower for over seven hundred years, for the first record of a bell being at the church dates from 1280. Many old churchwardens accounts relate items paid for the upkeep of bells, bell-fittings and for the ringing of bells down the ages but nothing is known of local bell-ringers by name before 1688 when it appears that local ringers began to fraternise.

At Ashover at this period Leonard Wheatcroft was Parish Clerk and he later became noted for his writings about local events. In his writings are several items relating to bells and bellringers. The earliest being in verse gives the names of twelve bell-ringers who visited North Wingfield Church and rang the five bells on May 29th, 1688. The ringers were Henry Royles, Robert Mottershaw, George Brent, John Pendleton, William Mottershaw, Tommy Clay, John Marsh, William Ashmore, John Breilsford, Edward Clay, John Wheatcroft and Will Browne.

Among other writings of Leonard Wheatcroft can be found further verses recording visits to Ashover by the bell-ringers of Shirland, on Lady Day, March 25th, 1689 and the ringers of South Wingfield, on April 9th, 1696.

To commemorate the tercentenary on May 29th, (Oak Apple Day) 1988, simultaneous Quarter Peals were rung by Association members at Ashover and North Wingfield. The ringers were:- at Ashover, Adrian Dempster (Conductor), John Thorpe, Glyn Holdgate, Wendy Heading, Peter Taylor, Pauline Taylor, Eric Sterland and Edward Dakin. North Wingfield, David Lester (Conductor), Margaret Wright, Maurice White, Karen Jeffrey, Terry Jeffrey, Frederick Flint, John Underwood and Frederick Pembleton.

2. BELLFOUNDERS

Local craftsmen bequeath their legends.

Of the two hundred and forty bells, that are in the care of the ringing members of the belfries under review in this book, almost all of them bear an inscription. In age they span almost five centuries, ranging from pre-reformation bells to bells of modern casting. They were cast by a variety of bellfounders. Some came from local foundries in Chesterfield, Mansfield, Nottingham, Sheffield and Derby. Whilst others were cast at Loughborough, Birmingham, Gloucester, Wath on Dearne, Downham Market and at Whitechapel and Cripplegate in London. With the exception of the foundries in Loughborough and Whitechapel none are in business today.

Of the two bellfoundries carrying on business at the present time I will say very little. Both firms, John Taylor and Co (Bellfounders) Ltd., The Bellfoundry, Loughborough, and the Whitechapel Bell Foundry Ltd., Whitechapel Rd., London E1, need little introduction, as both have a long history of bell founding and are responsible for many bells of quality that have done yeoman service over a long period in local towers.

John Taylor & Co. have retained the family name throughout their business activities, whereas the foundry at Whitechapel has been known by several titles since commencing business over four hundred years ago, in 1570. This makes them about the eighth oldest firm in the world according to a recent survey. Lester & Pack, C. & G. Mears, Mears & Stainbank are just three of those names and will be referred to occasionally in later text. A whole book could be devoted to each of the two foundries, and whilst I would like to acquaint the reader further with an account of their history, this must be sacrificed in favour of including an account of the history of now extinct local foundries, whose work, I feel, is very much in need of being recorded. I have further included a glimpse of the founders from further afield; who have in the past, cast the odd bell to hang in belfries in the area.

Nottingham was a centre for bell-founding for over four hundred years from 1376 until about 1795. It was carried on by several families. The Selyokes, Mellors, Oldfields and Hedderlys and it is from these families that many of our older local bells originate.

There were however several smaller local founders and to whom a few of our bells are lasting reminders. Ebenezer Smith cast a bell for Ashover at Chesterfield in 1814. Thomas Wheeldon of Derby cast a bell for Kirkby in Ashfield in 1813 and Samuel Midworth in 1831 cast a bell at Mansfield for the new tower at St. Peter's Belper. Later in that century Naylor, Vickers & Co., of Sheffield introduced steel bells, but, without doubt the prominent local bellfounders were the Heathcotes who cast bells in Chesterfield from about 1476 until 1643, and who together with the Nottingham founders are the subject of separate chapters.

We are introduced to the other Chesterfield founder when we read the inscription on the "Bonaparte Bell" at Ashover, for we find inscribed:-
"The old bell rung the fall of Bonaparte, and broke, April 1814.
J. and E. Smith, Chesterfield B.F."
The inscription on this bell is unique inasmuch that no other bell can be found that records the abdication of Napoleon.

Napoleon I (Bonaparte) (1769-1821), French Emperor and General was forced by the Allies to abdicate on April 11th, 1814 and retire to Elba. On this news reaching Ashover the bells of the parish church were rung and from the inscription we can assume that by some misfortune an accident happened causing damage to this bell. Several theories can be offered which would result in the bell cracking or breaking but as theory could not prove what actually happened they are better not uttered. Far better to stick to the fact that after ringing for the victory the bell was found to be broken.

Within weeks, the bell was taken out of its frame and removed to the foundry of John & Ebenezer Smith at Chesterfield for re-casting. An item in the Church-wardens Accounts, dated June 17th, 1814, must refer to this bell. 'To Geo Bamford and assistants to Gett the Bell drawne up... 5 shillings' (25p) and, 'to Mathew Bower for assisting ... 1s.6d' (7½p). Whether this payment included the cost of transporting the bell to Smith's foundry is not mentioned.

The following year, April 16th, 1815, we again find in the Churchwardens Accounts reference to this bell. This time in payment of liquid refreshment. 'Ale at John Marsden at Pulling up the bell ... 4s.6d' (26p). Then on May 4th, John Wright was paid £2.14.11½d (£2.54) for hanging the bell and so in just over a year the bell was recast and returned to the tower.

The foundry of John and Ebenezer Smith was situated in Brampton. Today the memory of this concern is kept in the names of two buildings incorporated in the Wheat Bridge Mills of Messrs. Robinsons of Chesterfield, Canon Mill and Griffin Mill and in the name of a nearby public house, The Griffin Inn. The whole complex being known in the late 18th. century as The Griffin Foundry of John and Ebenezer Smith and Company.

The Smith family had for many years been connected with the cutlery trade in Sheffield. William is known to have had a Cutlers Mark in 1614. John Smith was Master Cutler in 1722 and his eldest son John (II) continued the family cutlery business and ironworks situated on The Moor in Sheffield.

After his father's death in 1753, John (II) employed his brothers William and Ebenezer, both bachelors, together with three of his four sons, John (III), William and Joseph. The fourth son, born in 1756, and named Ebenezer, after his uncle, was trained for the Ministry and went to live in London. He later returned to Chesterfield to assist in the management of the firm shortly before his father's death in 1784. William died four years after his father in 1788 and Joseph remained in the family cutlery business, living in Sheffield. He was Master Cutler in 1796. He died in 1804. So, following his father's death we find the brothers John (III) and Ebenezer managing the Chesterfield Foundry Complex.

In 1775, when the Smiths came to Brampton, the main road to Baslow that we know today did not exist. The only way west from Chesterfield being the road now known as Wheatbridge Road. This led to Old Brampton and was little better than a cart track. Brampton, as we know it, did not exist either, it was just a few scattered cottages over an area known as Brampton Moor, and separated from the old borough by land belonging to the Maynard family on either side of the road now known as West Bars. Lying between Wheatbridge Road and the River Hipper was the Forge Mills, the Griffin Foundry, with its iron furnaces just across the river adjoining Shemwell's Corn Mill. This area, although outside the borough, was Chesterfield's industrial centre in the closing years of the eighteenth century.

Smith's were not in the business of casting bells. However, whilst researching I found that the Ashover 'Bonaparte Bell' was probably the third bell to be cast at the foundry. They cast a bell now hanging in Parwich Church Tower which bears the inscription 'Smith & Co, Chesterfield 1804'. In 1812 they cast a bell for Clowne bearing the inscription 'E. Smith, Chesterfield', but this bell, like the one at Ashover, was later recast thus leaving the only known bell cast by Smith's, and still ringing out over Derbyshire to be the one at Parwich.

It is also quite probable that their connection with the Ashover bell came about through the good offices of Joseph Thompson a leading engineer living in Ashover. Thompson worked closely with Smith's, as his father Francis Thompson had done until his death in 1809. It is also interesting that in 1833, when Smith's closed down, it was Joseph Thompson who purchased the Forge, and stock, and continued manufacturing.

The Smiths however were leaders in their field and primarily responsible for the introduction of coke-blast furnaces into Derbyshire. They were the pioneers on which the reputation of Derbyshire foundry iron was made and later borne by names like Staveley, Clay Cross, Butterley and Stanton. Their works included furnaces and foundries at Brampton, Duckmanton, Calow and a branch at Manchester. At their peak they employed 1200 men.

In 1787 the partners were described as Ironfounders, Forgers of Iron and Whitesmiths. No mention of bellfounding?

The famous Pentrich pumping engine which remained in use at Pentrich Colliery for over 125 years, carries on its cylinder "Smith & Co., Chesterfield 1791". It was

Samuel Midworth, Bellfounder, Mansfield.
Early in the 19c Samuel Midworth had a foundry in Leeming St. Mansfield and was known as an Iron Founder and Brass Cock Manufacturer. He is known to have cast several bells, amongst them a treble for Warsop in 1812 and a single bell for St. Peter's, Belper. This bell, cast in 1831, he installed in the new (1824) tower at a cost of £160. It was reputed to be of a very fine tone. Later it was removed to make way for a peal of six and the one at Warsop was recast. The inscription is of a bell he cast for Skegby in 1830.

> ❦ **GOD SAVE HIS CHURCH**
> MIDWORTH
> MANSFIELD
> ANNO DOMINI.1830

John and Ebenezer Smith, Brampton, Chesterfield.

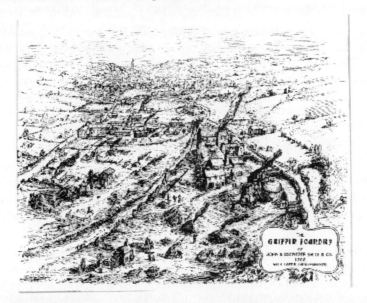

The Griffin Foundry of John and Ebenezer Smith was extensive, as this fine sketch by Hadyn Jensen illustrates. Smiths were renowned for the pioneering of constructional castings, fire-grates and mountings and parts for pumping engines. In 1814 a bell at Ashover broke ringing the downfall of Napoleon and was recast by Smiths. They cast a few other bells, among them one for Clowne and a single bell for Parwich in 1804. Ebenezer (inset) returned from London in 1784 to assist in managing the business after his father's death. His brother John died in 1814 and he in 1827 and the whole complex was sold in 1833.

designed by Francis Thompson, Engineer of Ashover and now has an honoured resting place in the Science Museum in London.

They also specialised in stoves for heating purposes. Chesterfield Parish Church was for many years warmed by two of their ornamental stoves which in 1820 cost £50 each.

Another important product which Smith's pioneered was cast iron columns for supporting floors in multi-storey buildings. Strutt's of Belper used large numbers of these when building their West Mill in 1793. Whether any sections for bell frames was manufactured is not known.

Not a lot is known of John Smith either. Other than at the age of 47 in 1775 he acquired a furnace, foundry and boring mill at Brampton with the intention of developing the Newcomen Engine.

At this time, the American War of Independence raged and France, Spain and Holland became in conflict with Britain. This undoubtedly led to the casting of cannon at the Griffin Foundry.

Ebenezer was a man of deep religious conviction and a man of forceful character. He was educated for the Nonconformist Ministry and in London became assistant preacher to Dr. Gifford at Eagle Street. He was in line to succeed Dr. Gifford but in renouncing the doctrine of the Trinity was thrown out of that connection.

Moving with several other followers who shared his principles he set up meetings in various other premises and raised a congregation.

He remained with them for only a few years before returning to Chesterfield, as already mentioned, prior to his father dying in 1784.

In 1777 he married Elizabeth Cater of London, and had a very large family of eighteen children, six boys and twelve girls of whom only nine reached adult age.

On his return to Chesterfield the family lived in Wheatbridge House, adjoining the works. He died on Tuesday, 8th. May 1827 at the age of 70 and is buried in Old Brampton churchyard. His grave being adjacent to the east window.

His brother John predeceased him in 1814, the year the Ashover bell was recast in the foundry.

By 1816 the Company had fallen on hard times and found it necessary to ask Lord Fitzwilliam to postpone his demand for royalties, not due until the following spring, "as the great scarcity of money and decline of business renders our situation truly embarrassing at present." A year later they were asking the rating authority to lower their assessment. This decline continued until 1833 when the foundry was sold to Joseph Thompson.

By coincidence the churchwardens at Ashover kept Smith's waiting for their money for over eighteen months, finally paying for the recasting at Christmas 1816. An entry in the accounts reads "1816 Exmus, Paid Mr. Smith for repares of a Bell that wass Brok when ringing for Good News £25.13.9d"(£25.66 approx.). So, the exercise of breaking, recasting and rehanging the Ashover "Bonaparte" bell cost a total of £28.19.8½d to complete.

In Mansfield at the same period Samuel Midworth had an iron foundry. The Directory of 1832 lists Samuel Midworth as Iron Founder and Brass Cock Manufacturers. The foundry was situated in Leeming Street on a site where the library now stands. Midworth lived in Gilcroft House and the name of Blind Lane close by was later changed to Midworth Street.

Four bells are known to have been cast by Midworth between 1812 and 1841. His first known bell was a treble, cast for Warsop in 1812 to make a peal of four bells. Later, in 1830 he cast a treble for Skegby and in the following year cast and installed a bell for the newly erected tower of St. Peter's, Belper, at a total cost of £160. Ten years later he cast the second bell for the church at Arnold.

The bell at Warsop was recast in 1913 and the bell at Belper was discarded in favour of a peal of six steel bells supplied by Naylor, Vickers & Co., of Sheffield in 1861.

Naylor, Vickers & Co. were pioneers of steel bells between 1855 and 1860. It is estimated that they cast over three thousand steel bells of varying size. One bell weighed almost five tons, took 176 crucibles of steel, a process which occupied eleven minutes.

These bells of steel were a drastic departure from the conventional bell which is made of bell-metal, a mixture of 78% copper and 22% of tin.

In 1858 they cast a peal of six bells for Eastwood which were believed to have been the first peal of steel bells to have been hung in England. Further peals were placed in the newly built tower at Bamford and at St. Marie's (R.C.) Church in Sheffield. The bells at Eastwood and Belper were replaced early this century by bells of conventional metal. During 1998 the Bamford bells are due to be replaced by bells cast of conventional bell-metal.

At Kirkby in Ashfield we have a bell, cast in Derby, by Thomas Wheeldon in 1803 which fortunately has not been recast. Little is known of this founder with the exception that in 1818 he also cast a bell for the village of Meerbrook in Staffordshire.

Mention must now be made of Warners who in 1857 cast the peal of six at Clay Cross, James Barwell of Birmingham, who in 1876 recast the second bell of five at Darley, and Thomas Hilton who in 1774 recast the sixth of the old peal at Chesterfield.

The six bells first hung in the then new tower at Clay Cross in 1857 were cast by John Warner and Son. John Warner set up business as a Bell and Brass Founder at a house known as The Three Bells and a Star, in Wood Street, Cheapside, London, in

1763. Tomson Warner, a brother joined John in the business after serving an apprenticeship as an Ironmonger at Amptill in Bedfordshire. Between 1763 and 1782 they moved premise to Fore Street, Cripplegate, London.

Eventually, the partnership was dissolved, Tomson remaining in Fore Street as a bellfounder and John going to Fleet Street where he carried on business, also as a bellfounder, under the name of John Warner and Sons. Tomson Warner's eldest son was named John after his uncle and through him the business descended to grandson Robert Warner.

Prior to 1850 all Warner bells were cast in sand which limited the size to less than fifteen inches in diameter but Robert Warner introduced the casting of larger bells. Locally, at West Hallam there are three bells cast by him in 1876, and in 1860 a peal of five bells he cast for Winster.

Thomas Hilton of Wath on Dearne, Yorkshire was casting bells from 1774 until 1809. In 1774 he recast the sixth bell in the old peal at Chesterfield Parish Church. By 1794 the firm was known as Walker and Hilton. They supplied bells into Lincolnshire and a feature of their smaller bells was that they were narrow in the crown and waist.

In 1782, Edward Arnold of St. Neots cast a peal of six bells for Staveley and the single bell for Cromford in 1796. In 1784 he opened a foundry in Leicester. This is established by the inscription upon the treble bell at Doveridge cast in 1796. In 1792 he cast two bells for Hartshorne. During this period of having two businesses he apprenticed Robert Taylor who later succeeded to the business. The Taylor family moved to Oxford, and then to Devon for a short period, before returning to Oxford and eventually settling in Loughborough to become world famous as John Taylor & Co.

James Harrison was the second son of a carpenter Henry Harrison, of Wragby near Pontefract, Yorkshire and was born in 1697. In the same year the family moved to Barrow on Humber. By 1763 James was in business as a bellfounder and had been joined by his son Henry. Although they had been building bellframes for many years, it is thought they did not cast bells until about the time of his marriage in 1758. About 1770, some four years after his father's death, Henry opened a foundry in Barton on Humber.

Henry had five sons, of whom two; William and James became involved with the foundry. William's connection was brief, although his name does appear as the founder of bells in Lincolnshire and he left Barton to live in Liverpool. Upon the death of their father about 1784, the foundry passed into the hands of James.

Derbyshire bells cast by James are the six for Norton in 1810. In 1812 he augmented his 1803 peal of six at Castleton into a peal of eight and at Glossop he was responsible for six bells, four of which are dated 1816 and two dated 1815.

James Harrison died in 1835 and was considered quite a character to the point of being eccentric in habit. It is said that his calculations were made mentally whilst remaining in a bed which he had erected in the foundry. Upon reaching his conclusion he would jump from the bed exclaiming, 'I have got it! I have got it!', and would then proceed with his plans. He cast his bells in cellars several feet below ground level and, it is said, often in the dead of night because any sound, such as a cock crowing or an ass braying would be communicated to the bell as the metal set. Another theory which James laid great stress upon and for which he strived was that all bells had more metal in them than necessary and thereby, in his opinion, the tone of the bell would be considerably improved.

After James's death the foundry which stood on the west side of Brigg Road, Barton, near the Market Place was demolished to make way for a house and wheelwright's shop but some of the cellars used by James for casting bells were incorporated into the new building.

Several other founders have made singular visits to Derbyshire towers from time to time to hang their bells. Some of them represented very ancient bellfoundries such as Samuel Smith of York who in 1705 hung a new treble in the tower at Tideswell.

Bellfounding at York can be traced back to 1327 when Richard Tunnoc a Bellfounder was M.P. for the city. The Bellfounder's window in York Minster is to his memory. Other York founders were William Seller, Edward Seller and James Smith father of the founders of Tideswell's treble.

From Downham Market came bells supplied by William Dobson to Ashbourne, Tissington and Brailsford. In 1833 this foundry passed into the hands of Thomas Mear of London.

Numerous other bellfoundries existed up and down the country. Some flourished for short periods, others for several generations but quite often all that remains of their activities are a few letters and numerals inscribed, if we are lucky, alongside another, and much later, founder's mark on the bells themselves. Thus we have simple proof of man's skill and labour: a few marks depicting a lifetime's work.

3. HEATHCOTES OF CHESTERFIELD

Bellfounders, 1476 – 1647

The name of Hethcote appears in Chesterfield records from as early as the reign of Edward 1V (1461-1483). In 1476 John Hethcote, mercer, granted land to William Withil of Brampton, smith, and in 1480, he was a Capital Burgess. His name also appears attesting charters, either alone or in company of Ralph Hethcote, as late as 1512. The family undoubtedly took a leading position in the town at this period

Over matters of business and in positions of trust they were associated with the family of Foljambe. Henry Foljambe, then Lord of Walton, acted as Trustee for the Hethcote family in 1502 in an important charter amongst the Hardwick Charters. It is in this deed that Richard Hethcote is described as an Alderman. In the same year Ralph Hethcote, potter, and John Hethcote, mercer, both of Chesterfield were witnesses. The use of 'potter' in describing the occupation of Ralph Hethcote is of interest. At this period the word potter was used in connection with the making of brazen pots. As with the Oldfield's of Nottingham, it is thought that the casting of bells constituted only part of their total business at this time.

It is most probable that the family had come to Chesterfield from the Peak District and were originally connected with Tideswell, although it is possible that Ralph Hethcote was born in Charlesworth, in north west Derbyshire. For, after his death a chantry was founded there, within the parish of Glossop, by his beneficiary William Woolley of Riber, near Matlock. "In the early part of the reign of Henry VIII, William Woolley of Riber in the Parish of Matlock, left certain lands in Chesterfield, Newbold, Tapton and Dronfield (which lands had been given to him by Ralph Hethcote, bell-founder of Chesterfield), to provide a priest to say mass for his soul, and for the souls of his benefactors in the chapel of Charlesworth. The land was left by William Woolley to Otwell Needham of Thornsett, and to Thomas Poynton, Vicar of Glossop, as trustees of the charity". The vicar Thomas Poynton died in 1551.

Three of these parcels of land appear to have been purchased in 1480 by Ralph's brother Richard from Thomas Hampton of Leicester and James Hethcote senior for the sum of forty marks. The extent of the transaction being one messuage, eight acres of land, nine acres of pasture, in Chesterfield, Tapton and Newbold. It is interesting to note that in his will of January 15, 1518 Richard styles himself brazier and mentions his brother Ralph as bellfounder. It is difficult to establish the various member lines of the family at this period, as they were fond of repeating a limited number of Christian names of which Ralph was favourite. As our concern is with the bell-founding members let it suffice to mention that at the time of Ralph the bellfounder, there was in Chesterfield, another Ralph, a butcher, for they both act as witnesses to a deed dated 1516.

Returning to the previous generation we establish that Thomas Hethcote had two sons: Richard, the Alderman and Ralph the bellfounder. About 1487 Richard Hethcote was associated with John Thomson in a trusteeship. John Thomson being a brazier of Chesterfield with two daughters, Ellen and Elizabeth. Brother Ralph married Ellen Thomson. Ellen's sister by coincidence married a James Hethcote, but whether there was any relationship between Ralph and James is not known nor is it our concern, for it was Ralph and Ellen who were the undoubted founders of the line of Hethcotes who, for four generations, were established in Chesterfield as braziers and bellfounders. They had a large family of ten children, John, William, Thomas, George, Rowland, Ralph, Christian, Johan, Anne and Margot.

As a tradesman of considerable importance Ralph Hethcote became an Alderman of Chesterfield and a man of substance. Early in the reign of Henry VIII (1509-1547) Ralph was found at the head of a list of gentlemen of Scarsdale who advanced loan money to the King. The sum advanced by him was 53s.4d (£2.67p) with few others advancing more than 40s (£2.00p) and only six persons in the whole of the Hundred of Scarsdale advancing more than his four marks, notably Foljambe, Varley, Revel, Mering, Leke and Eyre. So it is clear that Ralph Hethcote was one of the more substantial people of the county.

Ralph was quite young when he made his will in 1502 for he especially makes provision, that 'If any of my sonnes wyll be a priest, I wyll that he be sent to the schole till he be able, and then his part of land to be divided among the other'. It is possible that William availed himself of this, and was the Sir William Heathcott sometimes called vicar, but more correctly one of the Stipendiary Priests of Chesterfield. Although, it should be noted, James Hethcote and Elizabeth Tomson had a son William, who may also have been the one to secure this position.

Note also, how, at this time, a variation in the spelling of the surname Hethcote comes into general use. We see above Hethcot, Heathcott, and shortly we will find Heathcote becoming the adopted spelling.

Of the land and properties belonging to Ralph little is known other than items mentioned in his will. To Thomas he left a house and land at Tapton, Chesterfield. To Rowland he left two shops and land in Chesterfield and to Ralph he left 'Broadmeadow House Close and grounds that butts on the water of Rodder.' Presumably the river Rother. Each of the four daughters received ten marks.

Ralph Hethcote is credited with using as his mark the Fylfot Cross which he placed within the capital letter of his inscription. His mark can still be found on the old fifth bell at Matlock and on the third bell at Teversal. From the illustration it will be noticed that the pagan symbol of the Fylfot Cross used by Ralph almost five centuries ago is more easily recognised by recent generations as the Swastika and used by the Hitler regime during the Second World War.

Although the will of Ralph was drawn up in 1502 the inventory of his goods appears not to have been taken until 1525 after he died. A release from Ralph Hethcote, Bellfounder, to his son George Heathcote, of houses and lands in Chesterfield and Tapton in 1524 substantiates this as the possible date of his death.

Undoubtedly George Heathcote, the fourth son but the third son mentioned in the will of his father Ralph, was a bellfounder and succeeded to the business. For, in his will, dated August 4th, 1558 he says, "I give and bequethe to Ralph Hethcote my sonne and Heyre all my lands and also I bequethe to the same Raffe my sonne all my moldes and Towles, all my Brass and Bell metell and all other things in my workhouse apperteyning to my Occupation for and in recompence of a certaine summe of moneye which I the said George doe owe unto him".

George used an elaborate shield design for his bellmark but was careful to incorporate the fylfot cross. His mark can be found on the third bell at Mansfield Woodhouse and on the second and third bells at Beeley. The eighth bell of the old peal at Chesterfield also carried his mark.

George's wife Margaret was left his dwelling house at Saltergate-head. In addition to Ralph they had four sons George, John, Thomas and William and four daughters. The second son, George, was a draper in Chesterfield.

This brings us to the third generation bellfounder Ralph Heathcote who died in 1578 and was buried at Chesterfield on 31st, March. In his will he leaves his son Godfrey executor. Besides Godfrey, the eldest son, there was George, Thomas and Francis and two others, John and William who died in infancy. They had two sisters Elizabeth and Margaret. Ralph's distinctive bellmark omitted the use of the fylfot cross in favour of a coronet. The third and fifth bells at Baslow bear his mark.

Godfrey Heathcote carried on the bellfounding business through into the seventeenth century. Godfrey was baptised March 21st, 1558 and married three times. His first wife Anne, who died in 1605, left several children. In the same year he married Anne Allen, widow of David Allen a surgeon of Chesterfield. His third wife was Frances Crawshawe. This third marriage took place in 1625 when he was Mayor of Chesterfield. There were no children by his second or third marriages but by his first wife Anne he had two sons, Godfrey and Ralph and four daughters. He reintroduced the fylfot cross, placing it on a simple shield and incorporating his initials GH above as his mark, and it is to Godfrey that most of our old surviving Heathcote bells belong.

It is probable that Godfrey, the eldest son of Godfrey the bellfounder, died in his father's lifetime. This would account for the omission of his name in his father's will of 1638. Ralph Heathcote, second but eldest surviving son of Godfrey the bellfounder, was sole executor to his father's will when proven in 1643. Ralph carried on the business, possibly in partnership with his father, and was living in 1647 when all traces of bellfounding ceased. He designed a mark similar to that of his father but using his own initial.

Ralph was baptised on 27th, May 1592 and was twice married. First to Katherine who died in 1630 and was buried with a son on 1st May. And, secondly to Mary Brailsford of Ankerbold, in North Wingfield, who died in 1654. By his first wife Katherine he had five children of whom only two survived childhood. Dorothy, baptised 19th October 1618 and who married Alexander Nodder of Handsworth-Woodhouse on 29th November, 1638, and Godfrey, baptised 11th June, 1620, married Mary Stacey who survived Godfrey when he died in 1651.

With Godfrey, the bellfounder's, death about 1643 and Ralph, the partner's, sometime after 1647, when they ceased in the business of casting bells, a period of one hundred and seventy one years of bellfounding in Chesterfield was brought to a close.

Further representation of the family devolved on Ralph Heathcote the only son of Ralph by his second wife Mary Brailsford who took his degree of B.A. in 1654-5 and his M.A. in 1662, at Magdalen College, Cambridge. He became Rector of Staveley in 1662 and died there in 1715. He married three times but had only one son, Ralph, by his first wife Grace Bateman of Hartington, whom he married in 1663.

Their son, Ralph, was baptised at Staveley on 3rd, November 1664, educated at Cambridge and became Rector of Morton in 1710. He died there in 1738. He had married Elizabeth West, of Aston, in 1695. They had a family of eight children. Ralph the eldest was born in 1697, educated at Cambridge and succeeded his father as Rector of Morton and died there in 1765. A descendant, also named Ralph, became Vicar of Tibshelf in 1817.

The second son of Ralph Heathcote, who became the first Rector of Morton, Godfrey, was a prominent attorney in Chesterfield and was for twenty years chief steward and auditor to three successive Dukes of Devonshire. On a pillar at the entrance of the chancel of Chesterfield church can be found an inscription to his memory.

Several bells, cast almost four centuries ago by Godfrey, can be found in local churches, at Alfreton, Ashover, Denby, Heanor, Heath, Baslow, Barlborough, Bonsall, Horsley and Whitwell. A favourite inscriptions of his was 'Gloria in Excelsis Deo' and, 'I sweetly tolling men do call, To taste on meats that feed the soule'. Ralph (III) was responsible for casting bells at Teversal (3rd), Scarcliffe, Hathersage, Dronfield and Shirley. And a few of Heathcote's bells in general are scattered across the rest of Nottinghamshire and into Lincolnshire.

The Heathcotes of Chesterfield
Bellfounders from about 1476 until 1647

Ralph Heathcote, son of Thomas Hethcote, Brazier and Bellfounder.

Married Ellen Tomson, eldest daughter of John Tomson of Chesterfield, Brazier.
Ralph Heathcote's will dated 1502. Inventory 1525.
(Note alternate spelling of surname adopted by Ralph.)

George Heathcote fourth son of Ralph Heathcote, Brazier and Bellfounder (1525-1558).
Alderman of Chesterfield 1545.
Like his father, George continued to use the fylfot cross within his founder's mark. It is thought that the introduction of this mark derived by modification of part of the family coat of arms.
The fylfot cross is also an ancient pagen symbol.

Ralph Heathcote, eldest son of George.
Brazier and Bellfounder (prior 1558-1577).
Buried at Chesterfield, March 31, 1577/8.

Ralph discontinued using the fylfot cross in favour of placing a crown above his initials.

Godfrey Heathcote, eldest son of Ralph.
Brazier and Bellfounder.
Baptised March 21, 1558/9.
Several times Mayor of Chesterfield.
His will proved 1643.
Godfrey reintroduced the fylfot cross as his mark. He placed 'Gloria in Excelsis Deo' on his bells, introducing the fylfot cross within the letter G.

Godfrey Heathcote, eldest son of Godfrey. Swordschleifer (sword grinder) and bellfounder? Pre-deceased his father but living in 1628 and died 1635.

Ralph Heathcote, second but eldest surviving son of Godfrey.
Baptised May 27, 1592. Bellfounder.
Known to be living in 1647 when all traces of bellfounding ceased.

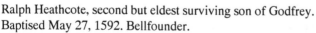

Like his father, Ralph used a plain shield with his initials and the fylfot cross.

4. THE BELLFOUNDERS OF NOTTINGHAM

Selyoke to Hedderly, via Mellor and Oldfield.

We now turn to bellfounding in Nottingham, which was established over three centuries and probably for a much longer period. From 1488 until about 1785 a continuous history of casting bells in the city can be traced, and during one period of fifty years, 1499 to 1548, two distinct bellfoundries were in business.

It is also quite probable that bellfounding was carried on in Nottingham in the middle years of the fourteenth century for we find at Norwich that a William Brasyer de Nottingham was admitted to the freedom of that city in 1376. In all probability he is identical with William de Norwyco an ancestor of the Brasiers, a well known family of bellfounders in Norwich and therefore it can be assumed that William learnt his trade in Nottingham before moving and taking up residence in Norwich.

Records show that in 1488 Richard Mellor was carrying on business as a 'bellyetter' or bellfounder in Nottingham. It is possible that he succeeded into the business of William Langton. Langton had gone into business with Richard Redeswell about 1437 but this partnership lasted only a few years because on 14th December 1440 Langton alone sued a surety on behalf of a potter in his employ. November 1467 saw Langton as a witness in an enquiry as to boundaries but after that date no further trace of him is recorded.

Richard Redeswell, on the other hand, had in December 1433 withdrawn an action taken for trespass against a Kimberley man, John Borley. Redeswell it appears possessed a close, 'whereupon and wherein he made bells' and complained that Borley had caused damage by treading down the ground by three cart loads of sea coal and other materials making it 'so that he was not able to make the aforesaid bells there'.

The last bellfounder, George Hedderly, left Nottingham for America about 1790, so it would appear that bells may have been cast in Nottingham for well over four centuries.

The piecing together of the history of bellfounding in Nottingham is a lengthy process and worthy of longer and more in depth research. But, for our purpose, we begin by looking back to the end of the fifteenth century and to one Richard Mellor of Castle Gate, Nottingham.

We find the surname of Richard Mellor described in several aliases, Mellours, Mellows, Mellers, Mellors, all of them synonymous, with some having the name spelt minus the letter 's', whilst his kinsman at Leicester was known as Miller.

Richard Mellor it is known was carrying on business as a bellyetter as early as 1488 for a grant was made to him of a house in Castle Gate, Nottingham in that year.

He seems to have been a man of some wealth, and held a leading position in the city, being Mayor on two occasions, 1499 and 1506. It is thought probable that the family derived their name from the village of Mellor in the Peak District of Derbyshire.

Bellyetter was the usual term applied to the bellfounder's trade at this time and is the origin of the surname Billiter. Later, in 1539, we find the word potter used when describing the trade of Henry Oldfield who is also well known for his casting of bells in Nottingham.

Richard Mellor's wife, Agnes, is well known as the foundress of Nottingham Free School. In 1508, Agnes is described as a widow in Richard's will. This was proved at York and names Agnes as his executrix.

After Richard's death Agnes took vows and became known as 'Dame', then in 1513 she founded and endowed the Grammar School in Stoney Street. In her will, proved in 1514, she made the bequest 'To the reparation of twenty of the poorest churches where my said husband in his life made any bells, to every church 6s.8d'.

Richard Mellor's will mentions three sons and a daughter. He left property at Arnold to Thomas. To Robert, his successor, he left his house, six thousand pounds of copper and all the instruments belonging to his trade. His son Richard was then at Oxford, and was bequeathed the sum of £20 in addition to a house on Long Row. His daughter, Margery's inheritance is not known.

Returning to the will of Dame Agnes. She gave to William Millers, son of William Millers of Leicester, and most probably a nephew, the sum of ten marks. This William Millers of Leicester is most probably the younger brother of Richard Mellers, of Nottingham and the same William Millers, Bell Heytaur whose will was proved in 1507 at Peterborough. His widow, Margory, afterwards married Thomas Newcombe and from this union the Leicester Bell-foundry descended after passing, for a short time, through the hands of Thomas Bett who was Margery Newcombe's third husband.

Robert Mellor succeeded in 1507 to the bellfoundry business. He married Juliana Mapurley, heiress of the ancient family that takes its name from the then hamlet of Mapperley near Ilkeston. They had one daughter, Elizabeth, who married Humphry Quarnby, of a Derbyshire family, who in turn succeeded into the foundry business. Robert Mellor was Sheriff of Nottingham in 1511 and Mayor in 1521 and died in 1525.

Their son-in-law, Robert Quarnby succeeded to the Mellor family business and took a leading roll in the city. He was four times Mayor and in 1562 chosen as M.P. for the borough. On 26th January, 1567/8 he married Frances the daughter of Henry Dand a bellfounder, and later a partner in the rival Nottingham bellfoundry belonging to Henry Oldfield.

After the dissolution of the religious houses, the Commissioners return mentions selling Quarnby a small bell that had belonged to the Grey Friars in Nottingham.

Later in the century Robert Quarnby entered into a partnership with his father-in-law, Henry Oldfield the senior of an equally prosperous family of bellfounders whom it is known had co-existed in Nottingham at least since 1539 for Margory Mellors mentions Henry Oldfield in her will as being a 'potter' living in Lister Gate.

Before moving on from the Mellors, it is interesting to note that within the scope of this book we will be looking at a number of bells cast by them in Nottingham for example the treble of the old four bells that were destroyed by fire in 1897 at Bolsover. At Morton, Shirland, Scarcliffe and Denby are to be found bells cast by them with a dozen others scattered throughout Derbyshire towers.

It is very likely that two bellfoundries existed in Nottingham for many years. As already mentioned the Mellors and Oldfield foundries competed for at least fifty years. It is thought that the Mellor foundry was situated in what is now Parliament Street at Bellfounders Yard which was in 1785 used by the Hedderly family who had followed on casting bells there after the Oldfields. At that time the Hedderlys firmly believed that bellfounding had been continuously carried out at the site for upwards of three hundred years.

It is known that Henry Oldfield lived in Lister Gate in 1539 and it is thought the family hailed from the Congleton area of Cheshire. This would suggest that Oldfield being the 'new boy' established his original business in a newer part of town and possibly only moving into the Mellor premises after becoming a partner with Robert Quarnby. To some extent, this is conjecture, but not without foundation inasmuch that Robert Quarnby, at that time, was leading a very busy life in politics at the personal expense of bellfounding. Whilst Henry Oldfield, being of a different nature, was seeking only to follow his craft. Also, the Mellors had been favoured with a period of opulence and splendour following the Wars of the Roses, whilst Oldfield met with less prosperous times. This gives reasons for Quarnby and Oldfield to join in partnership and for Oldfield to move into the premises of Mellor from where the Oldfield family carried on business until 1747/8 when the Hedderlys became the leading bellfounders of Nottingham using the same premises.

Fascinating as it is, it is probable that two bellfoundries also existed in Nottingham long before the Mellor-Oldfield overlap in the middle of the sixteenth century. We have the Selyoke family casting bells from 1499 until 1548. Richard Selyoke and his son John enrolled a deed in the borough court and in 1548 one of them became Mayor which suggests they were not in the employment of Mellors. Could it be that our man from Congleton, Henry Oldfield took over the Selyoke business, - after all, he was living in Lister Gate in 1539?

Before picking up the Oldfield story I want to turn back to the fourteenth century.

In Norwich there was, for many years, a famous family of bellfounders named Brasiers who trace their ancestors back to one William de Norwyco. In all probability he is identical with William Brasyer de Nottingham, bellfounder, who was admitted to the freedom of Norwich in 1376. One can therefore assume that William Brasyer de Nottingham learnt his trade in Nottingham before migrating to Norwich. Thus indicating that bellfounding has been in existence in Nottingham since the middle of the fourteenth century.

The Oldfield family carried on bellfounding in Nottingham for close on two hundred years. Many of their bells are still in existence in our belfries. We have mentioned Henry Oldfield living at Lister Gate in 1539 and migrating from Cheshire. This Cheshire connection is further strengthened when in 1545 he and his servant John Stockes were given an agreement by the churchwardens of Mottram in Longdendale, Cheshire to purchase a tenor bell.

In 1558 Henry the son of Henry Oldfield was living in Bridlesmith Gate, Nottingham and by 1572 was carrying on a thriving business, not only providing bells for local churches, but installing them in churches throughout the country. Henry Oldfield (II) became the first to add the date to his inscriptions. Possibly using the same mark as his father which was a square depicting a cross of Calvary and displaying the initial 'H' on the left and 'O' on the right of the cross. Over the initials he placed a crescent and star respectively. Occasionally the emblem was embellished with a crown. In 1590 Henry Oldfield, always known as the elder, died and is buried in St. Mary's Church, Nottingham, as was his son Henry when he died on 23rd January, 1619/20.

At this period the Oldfield family history becomes somewhat hazy. There is little doubt that the bellfounding business was thriving and that they had in their employ Henry Dand who cast many bells. But, we also find mention of another Henry Oldfield who we find married twice. He had five children by his first wife. Two daughters both named Mary of which only the youngest survived infancy. Of the three sons Richard, Robert and P (name unknown) all of whom were known to be bellfounders. Of Henry (III) all we know is that he was buried alongside both his wives at St. Peter's Church, Nottingham.

Henry Dand is reputed to have eventually become a partner with Henry Oldfield (II) and his daughter, Frances, who married Robert Quarnby, also became a partner with Oldfield. It was this union which brought together the two Nottingham bellfounders.

Henry Dand cast many bells. At Sutton in Ashfield the second of the old peal of six bells carried upon its waist the shield of Mellors but with the initial 'H' and 'D' flanking it. This could of course mean that Dand recast one of Mellors' bells. His initials also appear on other bells as on the trebles at Mansfield Woodhouse and Denby. The Denby initials, in Lombardic capital letters, also flanking the mark of Mellor. Whilst at Mansfield Woodhouse on the waist of his treble bell we find his initials 'H' and 'D' are elaborately ornamented. The former with a lion's head, and the latter with a spear piercing the heart. In 1591 he cast a bell for Shrewsbury

Abbey Church and later in 1597 he was fined at Nottingham Sessions for not attending at church.

Another employee of Oldfield was George Lees who married Ellen Oldfield in January 1590. George was travelling foreman and the branch manager at Congleton. A document in the Congleton Records dated 1595 relates to Henry Oldfield of Nottingham maintaining two bells he had placed in the church there. But no mention is made of them having a foundry there. On the waist of the fourth bell at St. Peter's Church, Mansfield, cast in 1611, can be found his initials. George Lees died in 1619.

Later in the seventeenth century another founder occurs, and who is thought to have been in the employ of Oldfield's namely, William Noon. William Noon is known to have cast the treble and second bells for All Saints Church, Derby, which became in 1927, our Cathedral. In 1686 he also cast a bell for Heanor. At the age of 91 years William died on 13th August 1732 and a memorial to his memory was erected in St. Mary's Church, Nottingham.

Returning to 1620 and the Oldfield family we find George who headed the business for sixty years, until his death in 1680. He married Elizabeth Green at St. Mary's, Nottingham in 1622 and they had a large family. George used the same mark as his father, Henry. He simply cut out the initial 'H' and substituted 'G'.

His business activity covered the Commonwealth period and the restitution of Charles II to the throne, and many of his inscriptions bear the date 1660 or 1662. He favoured the use of small Roman capitals with a narrow border between each word. The third bell at Sutton in Ashfield is a rare casting of his, from the Commonwealth period dated 1656.

Among George Oldfield's large family was a son, also named George. He was also a bellfounder but died before his father in 1660. In his will he gave a legacy of 5 shillings to Hugh Oldfield, but does not show him as a relative. In 1663 his sister, Alice, married this Hugh Oldfield. Hugh died in 1672 leaving an infant son named George. Alice carried on the business for her infant son after her father's death in 1680 and ceased from this date to put any name, mark or stamp on any bell cast at the foundry. Eventually George (III) took over the business until he died in 1741 when his son, also named George (IV) carried on bellfounding until his death in 1747/8. He was buried in St Mary's Church, Nottingham. His family consisted of daughters and so the foundry passed out of the Oldfield family after over two hundred years.

We now come to the third family of bellfounders to continue the trade in Nottingham, the Hedderlys.

The Hedderlys began their business in Bawtry and Derby long before Thomas took the business into Nottingham where it is known he was casting bells in 1742. It is interesting to note that although he placed his name upon the bells he did not add the word 'Nottingham' to any inscription until after the death of George Oldfield (IV) in 1747/8. Thomas died in 1778 at the age of 66 years.

Daniel Hedderly moved from Bawtry to Nottingham and his initials 'D.H.' are found inscribed on a bell at East Drayton, Nottinghamshire dated 1744. What relationship existed between Thomas and Daniel or the unfortunate Thomas who died of apoplexy in 1785 I have not established. But after the sudden death of Thomas some seven years after the death of the first Thomas in 1778 the business passed into the hands of a younger brother George.

It was during George's term in business that an advertisement was issued informing that bellfounding had been carried on at the "Old Bellfoundry in Parliament Street for upwards of three hundred years". Towards the close of the century and in consequence of some family disagreement George emigrated to America and the foundry closed.

Having briefly sketched the history of three of the leading Nottingham bellfounding families, Mellor, Oldfield and Hedderly and taken a brief glimpse at William Brasyer, Richard Redeswell, William Langton, Henry Dand and William Noon we must return to the year 1499 and Richard Selyoke.

It is known that Richard Selyoke was Mayor of Nottingham in 1497,1498 and again in 1505 and that Richard Mellor was Sheriff in 1472, Chamberlain in 1484 and Mayor in 1499 and 1506. We have read of the foundry of Richard Mellor and learned that a bellfoundry was already in being in Nottingham prior to his arrival, this older foundry being in the hands of Richard Selyoke and dating back to the fourteenth century. Very little is known of the Selyokes other than Richard was succeeded by his son John who became Mayor in 1548 at the same period that Humphrey Quarnby was four times Mayor before becoming Member of Parliament.

From this fact, showing that members of both families were prominent citizens of Nottingham at one and the same time, suggests clearly that two prosperous bellfoundries flourished in the city. For, had one been in the employ of the other it is doubtful if the one employed could have achieved a leading position of Mayor.

So, for a period of fifty years two bellfoundries existed in Nottingham. But where were they situated? Narrow Marsh and in the rear of Long Row in Bellfounders Yard have been put forward. But, who was at which? Charles Dearing in his History of Nottingham suggests that in 1641 two old and one new foundry existed. On the Session Roll of Nottingham for the year 1574/5 are two presentments of Henry Oldfield which are by no means creditable to him or his family. But, for our purpose they serve to give the locality of the foundry at that time. "Henrye Oldefellde bellfounder of the Long Row". This or the back part of it became known as Bellfounder's Yard with a foundry there until just before the nineteenth century.

In the Transactions of the Thoroton Society, Vol XXXV1 1932 "An Itinerary of Nottingham" by J Holland Walker, "Bellfoundry". 'King Street and Queen Street represent that curious V-shaped slice of slum property which was called the "Condemned Area" and which was all swept away about 1888. It was a most unhygienic and immoral neighbourhood and nothing good could be said of it. It took about three years to clear and King Street was formed upon it and opened on June 22nd, 1892. But while clearing away much that was undesirable, certain interesting features also disappeared, for example, the modern General Post Office stands on the site of Mellor's bell foundry where the fortune was made which was so nobly expended in founding the High School".

One other bellfounder who had his origins in Nottingham remains; Abraham Rudhall. He left Nottingham in 1684 and began business as a bellfounder in Gloucester. It is known that a foundry had been established in Gloucester during the early part of the fourteenth century and had flourished under John of Gloucester and later Sandre of Gloucester. Whether Rudhall took over the existing foundry or opened a new one I have not established.

Abraham Rudhall used a distinctive mark incorporating a bell flanked by his initials. About 1831 the foundry passed from the hands of John Rudhall, the last of the Gloucester bellfounders, into the firm of Mears whose foundry you will recall is at Whitechapel, London.

Derbyshire bells cast at the Rudhall foundry were three bells for Brailsford in 1717, a treble for Repton in 1721, a treble and sixth bell for Ilkeston in 1732 followed in 1733 by a complete peal of six bells for Chapel en le Frith. St. Peter's, Derby commissioned a third bell from Rudhall in 1738 and in 1749 Ilkeston followed up their previous order with the addition of a fourth bell. But the latest work of Rudhall's in Derbyshire was the peal of six bells for Hayfield in the Peak District.

There is little doubt that before the ink is dry further evidence will emerge to prove or otherwise the remarks already written about this interesting group of Nottingham bellfounders. Undoubtedly, if the subject were widened to take in all the bells within the Dioceses of Southwell and Derby, new facts would most certainly emerge. Such facts would be warmly received by the author, who on this occasion has limited his research to within the confines of a small Association of Church Bell Ringers' area. In fact, the thirty six belfries at which members of the East Derbyshire and West Nottinghamshire Association of Church Bell Ringers, past and present, have rung and maintained the bells, clocks and belfries throughout the past century.

5. BELFRY JINGLES, RHYME, VERSE AND HYMN

Offerton kettles,
Pentrich pans,
Shirland brave ringers
And Morton ting tangs.

Today, it is hard to imagine that anyone could possibly get lost within a few miles of home. Yet, before the enclosure of land took place toward the end of the seventeenth century getting lost, especially at dusk, was a commonplace event in rural areas.

With unmade roads travelling was at any time hazardous. After nightfall it must have been somewhat impossible and many local parishes have stories to relate of parishioners becoming lost in this way and of being guided to safety by the sound of their village bells.

For this very reason many places arranged for the curfew bell to be rung between Michaelmas and Lady Day (September 29th and March 25th) to which many churchwardens accounts relate. There were several reasons for ringing curfew. It was the time when fires in the home needed to be dowsed and the time when property and person be made secure. In Chesterfield curfew was rung to inform the French Prisoners of War out on parole that they should return to their quarters. But, to the homeward bound the curfew was often a guide as the darkness of night descended, and several are the legacies left by thankful travellers for the continuance of this service in perpetuity.

At Scarcliffe the curfew rings every year for three weeks on each side of Christmas in memory of Lady Constantia. It is said that the lady and her small child were lost in the forest hereabouts, overcome with weariness and cold they heard the curfew bell ringing at Scarcliffe and were guided safely home. In gratitude she left five acres of land to the church, the money raised annually from its rent to provide for the ringing of the curfew for ever.

There is no doubt that late evening travellers could recognise the bells of their own parish by their individual pitch and tone. Hence the various rhymes that have been passed on from generation to generation, the one above having local overtones. The old Rykneld Street ran to the west of Pentrich, Alfreton (Offerton), Shirland and Morton and the bells of each of these parishes would be heard distinctly from along its route.

In 1738 we find in the churchwardens accounts at Shirland, "Item, Paid ye clerk for ringing Curfur 5s.0d"(25p). At the same church within living memory the Angelus or Noon Day bell was regularly rung, and back in 1745, the churchwardens accounts show 5s.0d being paid to James Radford for ringing this same twelve o'clock bell.

At Chesterfield Parish Church each Shrove Tuesday the Pancake bell is rung.

Most bells bear inscriptions. Usually naming the founder, often the incumbent and the churchwardens and frequently a verse. These are often poignant if only the parishioner was readily aware of their content. The seventeenth century was a great period for these inscriptions. The following one was very popular and appears on bells at Alfreton, Ashover, Crich and Warsop. "All men that hear my mournful sound repent before you lie in ground".

A bell of the old peal at Chesterfield and bells at Ashover and Mansfield remind all who hear that 'I sweetly tolling men do call To taste on meats that feede the soule'. Another seventeenth century bell at Ashover warns, 'My warning sounde doth warning give That men cannot heare always live'. Whilst at Blackwell, Ault Hucknall, Kirby in Ashfield, Matlock, Shirland, Sutton in Ashfield and the fourth bell of Chesterfield's old peal was the reminder, 'Jesus be our spede'. At Alfreton the purpose of the fourth bell is, 'To the glory of God I sing and triumph to the King, the marriage joys I tell and tolls the dead man's knell'. Similarly at Edwinstowe we find, 'My sound it is all men to call, To serve the Lord, both great and small', and at Heanor, 'I toll the time that dul evill is to such as lived amisse, But sweete my sound seems unto them that hope for joyful bliss'. This latter is an inscription of Hedderly and according to a note in his pocket book the word 'dul evill' is an error in the casting and should read 'dismall'.

Many bells have inscriptions that refer to their donor. As at Mansfield, St. Peter's, 'At proper times my voice I'll raise and sound to my subscribers praise'. Texts and lines from Psalms are not uncommon as on the tenor bell at Sutton in Ashfield, 'Blessed are the peacemakers for they shall be called the children of God', and in the same tower the seventh bell says, 'Thine o Lord is the greatness and the power and the glory and the victory'. At North Wingfield the treble and second bells, added in 1902, are inscribed, 'O come let us sing unto the Lord', and 'My song shall be of mercy and truth'. Whilst at Matlock we are reminded to live well and welcome death, 'I unto those that liveth well, Do toll their welcome passing bell'.

These are but a few of the many inscriptions cast upon the bells of England and which are to be found locally, but, before we leave them, let us again visit the belfry of St. Peter's, Mansfield where the tenor bell originally cast in 1610 says,

> 'Tow summons by this bell we have
> One to the church, one to the grave'

Then, in 1948 when it was recast the following was added,

> 'This third year of the Atomic age
> A day of doubt
> Men's hearts failing them for fear
> Still we ring out
> That all the voice of God may hear.'

Turning the clock back three hundred years we find among the writings of Leonard Wheatcroft of Ashover verses describing a visit to North Wingfield of twelve bell ringers on Oak Apple Day, 29th May, 1688. It is the earliest record known locally which gives the names of the ringers.

> 'You gentlemen of Derbyshire, that minding are to ring
> If you'll be pleas'd to stay a-while, then you shall hear me sing.
> It is a song both new and trew, I boldly dare it say,
> At Wingfield it was done of late, the twenty nine of May.

> Ther's Henry Royles the parish Clarke, and Robert Mottershaw
> Besides ther is full half a score: i'll name them all a row.

> George Brent, he's one that's fast i'th heft
> And does observe his place:
> So will stiff John - Pendleton,
> The third bell bravely grace.

> The next is William Mottershaw,
> Who can the first bell toule,
> So can my little Tommy Clay,
> The pretty loving soule.

> John Marsh I know's a pretty man,
> And very well can ring:
> But William Ashmore far exceeds:
> He can the fifth bell swing.

> John Brelsford often rings behind;
> (He will pul far apart.)
> Besides, there's honest Edward Clay
> Will make his bell to start.

> John Wheatcroft for the second bell
> He'll ring it pretty trew:
> So will Will. Browne; I hold a crown
> He rings as well as you.

> And now you see my bretheren all,
> How well we do agree,
> To ring, and sing, and glass our King,
> And make us to agree:

> And when we drink a merry pot,
> We non of us may quarrel;
> But all agree to pay the shot,
> And broach the other barrel.

> Now here's a glass unto the soul,
> That did these lines invent:
> We'll make our bells most bravely troule
> To give him good content.

> We'll turn them up unto the height
> Each man shall own his string
> And hear we'll meet each Thursday night
> A merry peal to ring.'

This was sung to the tune "The Sparring of the Door." I am gratefully indebted to a former Rector of Ashover for allowing the use of all the quotations from Leonard Wheatcroft's writings which appertain to bells and ringers. They constitute the earliest known surviving record relating to bellringers locally.

The following Lady Day, 1689, a similar song again from the hand of Leonard Wheatcroft was composed in honour of a visit made to Ashover by the bell-ringers of Shirland and Higham. This time the tune is 'Lovely Nancy,' or 'smiling Francis'.

> 'You gentlemen of Derbyshire
> That minding are to hear me sing,
> I earnestly do you desire;
> That to my church you'll come and ring;
> Then your names and fames shall flourish
> Vp and down the Countery,
> And the Clerke of Asher parish
> Will thank you for your company.

I'll tell you now a pretty story,
If you'll be pleased a while to stay:
'Tis for the honour and memory
Of the Blessed Lady Day.
There were five young men came unto me
Desiring me to let them ring,
Who afterwards did kindness show mee
When they had handled each a string.

The first was Wright by name and nature,
He did ring the treble bell:
As for the rest, I will not flatter,
They far all others did excell.
Winfield men did ring most bravely,
And did behave themselves right well,
But Shirland men did far excell them,
As that heard can justly tell.

The second was a pretty young man
They say his name is Harry Lees
He followed bravely like a strong man
For two long hours he did not freeze:
They all did sweat from top to toe
I did observe them all so well:
And he's to blame that says not so;
I'm sure all others they excell.

Little Farmery did him follow
Scorning to o'erthrow his bell
Then after him an Heir did 'sallow' ('sally')
His name as yet I will not tell.
There was no teaching in their ringing
Each one had his part so true
I can no longer forbear singing
To give every man his due.

Mr. Miles for tenor ringing
I'll advance him very high:
And George Wright for gallant singing,
Few or non can say him nay,
Heire sang neatly, Lees completely
When-as we drank their Highness health
With Devonshire's, and Dallamotts,
Brave soldiers for our Commonwealth.

Now here's a glass to all true ringers
That live in city or in Towne,
With all my heart i'll drink to swingers,
If it costs me half a crowne.
For I doe love all good ringers,
Let them come from sea or shore,
And he that loves not merry singers,
I pray you-put him out the door.'

A footnote says 'heir' was most probably Mr. Revell of Ogston Hall. The 'string,' of course, is the rope and the 'sally' refers to the woollen tuft woven into the bell-rope and used by the ringer as a handgrip. These are often striped red, white and blue but can also be found in plain colours.

Some seven years later on 9th April, 1696, he again composed a song in favour of a visit by South Wingfield's ringers in which he mentions them by name in the second verse.

"Stout Mikell he shall lead the treble:
Brave Sidbury shall ring as true:
And honest Thorp he scorns to brable,
Nor Master Halton, - give him's due.
Clarke-son I hope (he) will not faile you,
For I am sure I know him well.
These five ringers are brave singers
Or they their changes could not tell."

Later, comes a fragment evidently relating to the same :-

"The fourth was Master John by name
Who rang in ample manner
I'll praise him ever for the same
He lives at Winfield Manner
He stood so straight, and rung so right
The like I never see
Brave Halton he shall have my voat
For he's brave companee."

Coupled with this verse we find at South Wingfield that six bells have existed in the tower since 1736. John Halton referred to in the above verse rang at South Wingfield and died in 1740. The fifth and the tenor bells both have reference to John. The fifth, cast in 1698, carries the inscription, "John Halton caused this ring of bells to be cast." Whilst the tenor cast in 1736 is inscribed, "Gloria Deo In Excelsis Johannes Halton Donavit".

Leonard Wheatcroft was a man of many talents and as Clerk he kept a very tight rein on the ringers at Ashover where on the 5th. November each year any young men wishing to become bell-ringers were required to diligently read and observe the Clerk's orders.

You noble ringers that at Random run
Observe your orders, and your forfits shun.
If here you enter, and intend to ring
Be sure you do observe here everything.
First doff your gloves, your spurs and hat,
Else twopence due to th' clerk for that.
Next, be you wise, and strive not to excell:
There's twopence due if you throw o'er a bell.
Also in setting, if you miss then I
Will have one farthing, if I do stand by.
When you ring changes, for each fault you make,
One farthing more you shall unto the stake.
Again I say, he that doth break a rope or wheel
Shall pay his stake and I will mend it well.
And if he will by force enter my steeple
He shall be lashed in sight of all the people.
And if you leave your ropes upon the ground,
Or wet or dirt on them, you shall be bound.
If in the church you do tobacko take,
You shall for every pipe one penny stake:
It is against the commons of this nation;
Besides it is a very ugly fation (fashion).
If any in our company sit down
He shall pay part, or I shall call him 'clown':
Tis all our minds to give him one glass
To which he's welcome, and so let him pass.
Each Monday night, I'd have th'old ringers ring,
And every Thursday, the young ones have their swing.
There's one thing more you Ringers must remember
That to our landlord, yes, we must be kinder;

Thats when we've money given us for ringing
They may have parts by turns else needs have flinging.
Three, and a shot-pot, is our due to have:
He that saith 'no,' the rest will call him knave.
Be all agreed;- assent and consent granting,
And on my part, there shall be nothing wanting,
And to conclude,- I wish you strength - And hope
A store of money: but, beware the rope.

By me Leonard Wheatcroft, Clerke.

The Twelve Articles for all Ringers to be sworne vnto :-

1. Ffirst, you are to be diligent and obedient vnto your Clerke, Giving him half a duzen of ale at your entrance.
2. You are to be carefull you doe not foule the Church for Displeasing ye sexton.
3. You are to observe all the times herafter nominated; that is to say, for the first yeare, you are to help ring the first and second peales every Sunday or Holy-day at 7 and 8 o'clock in the morning.
4. At nine o'clock to be ready to ring the sarmon-bell, and chime all in.
5. You are to be carefull and knit up your roapes when you have done that they be not troden under foot.
6. He that is last sworne, is to be monitor taking notice of all misdemeners.
7. He that is second sworne is to carry the Keyes when they goe to ring for pleasure, and take care that all be made sure.
8. He that is third sworne, is to turn the Rope when a bell is thrown over.
9. He that is fourth sworne, is to fetch all things necessary, as fire and candles.
10. He that is fifth sworne, is to observe the Boyes and Girls that they doe no mischeefe in the church, nor amongst the bells or ropes.
11. You are all to observe all the foregoing orders before mentioned, and to avoyde all quarreling in the church or churchyard whatsoever.
12. He that sweares aney oath in the church must and shall pay his two pence to the poore man's box or else forfit his part of Ringing money for one month next ensuing.

Leonard Wheatcroft obviously ruled the ringing and the ringers of Ashover with a rod of iron. He also was an entrepreneur. As an innkeeper he provided the place and through his verse and the bellringers, the entertainment ensueing most probably provided some of his income. Either way, he was a man of vision, and his notes of the happenings of his time are an enjoyable insight into the village's history. We shall meet up with him again when we look in more detail at Ashover's bells.

Almost three hundred years later at Crich the ringers honoured the tower captain, Frank Ashman, at Christmas, 1968 by composing the following ode. For several years it was displayed in the ringing chamber.

"To :- 'The Ash'.

A New Crich Bellringers Carol for Christmas, 1968.

1. Up in Belfry, Gaffer stands,
Rope end dangling from his hands.
Sez:- "Peter D., you stupid clod
I called a single not a bob."

2. Pips shirt tail gets caught in rope,
Up to heaven, thats what we hope,
It seems the lord is on his side,
Down he comes, t'was quite a ride.

3. Trebles going, trebles gone,
Pooh rings this, he is a one,
When on form and he lets ding
Glasses steam up, we can't ring.

4. Three quarters up, three quarters down
Mick T. knows these and goes to town
A sense of smell as out Mick Tom,
When trebles going he's soon gone.

5. The Bullbridge whisperer knows his stuff,
Tell all, else their Gen is Duff,
Ashman calls, "Please belt up Pont".
Can be clearly heard from font.

6. Rop pulls up with mighty force,
Tries to ring up in plain course.
Specs come off and land on ground
Back from plain course into round.

7. Carol service, so we learn,
Lesson reading, but whose turn.
Steve nips off, not fast enough,
Ash sez:- "Steve please do your stuff".

8. During holidays we have Nick,
Sometimes brings to Church, "His Chick".
She puts us off and makes Frank frown
Get five-six up mixed up with down

9. This Christmas we shan't have –"The Ash",
Without him we shall have a bash,
Poor old Frankie's on "The Club",
Hope he can manage his Christmas pud.

10. The ode is ended, and it tells
The story of the Crich Church Bells.
One bloke we ringers have to thank,
It's Ashman, Merry Christmas Frank."

Bellringing is often undertaken by successive members within a family and at Crich is a tablet, on the wall of the ringing chamber, that proves the point when taken in context with the ode above and the ringer, Frank Ashman.

East Derbyshire and Nottinghamshire Association
of Church Bell Ringers
On Saturday, January 26, 1929, in two hours, 59 minutes,
at the Church of St Mary.
A Peal of Grandsire Triples, 5040 Changes, being Thurston's Five Part.

Geoffrey Ashman	Treble	William E. Drake *	5
Wilfred H. Buxton	2	Joseph Lord	6
Frank F. Hill	3	Herbert G. Fretwell	7
William A. Parsons	4	Edger Ashman	Tenor

First peal on the bells since recasting and augmentation.
* First peal. Conducted by Joseph Lord.

Finally, and before we go on to look in detail at the history of individual belfries let us meditate upon the words of The Ringers' Collect, followed by The Ringers' Hymn, written by the Rev. W.G. Bridge, together with the Charge to all Ringers. They are all taken from the East Derbyshire and West Nottinghamshire Association's printed Order of Service, and published over fifty years ago. The Order of Service was compiled by John W. England, a ringer and Captain of St. Michael's, Belfry, South Normanton, a Diocesan Reader and a former Honorary Secretary and President of the Association.

The Ringers' Collect:

Gracious Lord, source of all skill and beauty, Who hast entrusted to us Thy servants the ringing of Thy bells that they may be used as a call to worship, grant to us the needful skill and grace for the faithful performing of our art. Through Jesus Christ our Lord. Amen.

The Ringers' Hymn:

O God, Who madest time and space
And needest not a dwelling place;
Yet for the need of Christian lands
Dost hallow temples made by hands.

Grant to us ringers, one and all,
Whom to thy service thou dost call
That, with the skill that comes from Thee,
We may Thy faithful servants be.

And grant, O Lord, the ringers' call
On heedful ears may ever fall.
That with the faithful, in each place,
We, too, may kneel to seek Thy grace.

To God the Father, God the Son,
And God the Spirit, Three in One,
Laud, Honour, Might and Glory be
From age to age, eternally. Amen.

The Charge to all Ringers:

Go ye forth into the land; wheresoever ye shall ring let the music of your bells proclaim the Gospel to all people. Sound your rounds and changes unto the Glory of the Lord and not unto men. Know ye that at all times ye exercise your art only to serve the Lord.

The sacred bells of England!
How gloriously they ring;
From ancient tower and steeple,
For Cottager, for king!
We love to hear their voices
While o'er the fields we roam,
And, answering, we enter
Our Father's earthly home.

The Belfry of St. Martin, Alfreton

Two coming of age bells. Rare Bell-founder's mark. Diamond Jubilee bell recast after only two years. St. Martin's Guild formed in 1892. Two practices each week.

There is no better place to view this church and tower than from the gate as we enter the churchyard. The western tower rises majestically beyond the porch. Supported by diagonal buttresses it carries an embattled parapet with four crocketed pinnacles. In the main, the tower we see dates from the fifteenth century. The base is much older. The fine tracery of the four louvred bell chamber openings is of the Decorated period and a single clock dial adorns the south face.

On the west side we find comparatively new oak doors. These were hung about 1973 to replace old and rather ill-fitting doors and are the gift of the then churchwarden and his wife, Mr. and Mrs Arthur Kirk. The doorway, however, is ancient work, note its dripstone and terminals. The huge west window above allows ample light into the ringing chamber.

Passing inside through the west door, we find on our left a very old door giving access to the tower. This door is most probably the oldest timber artefact to be found in the tower and could be all of six hundred years old. This ground floor was, until about 1960, when a new choir vestry was built to the north, used by the choir for robing. Passing into the nave through the door in the screen turn and look at the tall narrow arch. This is known as a stilted arch and quite uncommon. Notice that the point from which the arch begins to curve is well above the line of the capitals and does not curve immediately off the capitals as found in most arch construction. Both capitals have mouldings showing nail-head ornament but under this ornament on the north side capital is a well defined cable pattern. It could be of the very early English period but there is also a theory that it may not be as old as its style. It is known that a Derbyshire mason used the nailhead design well into a later period.

Now to the bells. We know that from 1687 there has been a peal of three bells. In 1780 the bell given in 1687 by John Turner of Swanwick was recast and two more bells added to make a peal of five. These remained ringing until 1897 when a treble bell was added to commemorate the Diamond Jubilee of Queen Victoria. Then in 1899 two further treble bells were added in order to complete the octave.

The two 1899 bells are hung in a metal frame of their own. This is above the oak frame in which the other six bells are hung. These two bells were the gift of Charles Palmer Morewood, Patron, at that time, of St. Martin's. They were given to mark the coming of age of his two children, Clara and Rowland. The work was put in hand early in 1899 and the bells were cast and hung in the tower and ready for ringing by early autumn, although Clara and Rowland's birthdays did not fall until December and January respectively. However, the bells were dedicated on

Wednesday, October 4th 1899, at the Harvest Festival Service. On the Saturday following, about forty ringers attended an invitation meeting at which they rang the bells to numerous touches and in a variety of methods. Alfreton being truly introduced to the science of Triples and Major Change Ringing Methods that day. They were entertained to a substantial tea, provided by the Vicar, Rev. A.C. Beckton, at the George Hotel. After this meeting the new bells were put into 'cold storage' until the following January. They are inscribed :-

Treble   Laus Deo
Given by C.R. Palmer - Morewood
in Commemoration of the 18th birthday
of his daughter Clara
Dec. 21st. 1899.

2nd.   Laus Deo
Given by C.R. Palmer - Morewood
In Commemoration of the 21st. Birthday
of his son Rowland
Jan. 9th 1900.

Two years previously, in 1897, a treble had been added to the old five by Messrs Carr of Smethwick, Birmingham. This bell commemorated the Diamond Jubilee of the reign of Queen Victoria, but when the augmentation to a peal of eight was carried out in 1899, John Taylor & Company, of Loughborough, had to recast this bell in order to obtain an octave in the key of F#. The inscription on what is now the third bell was faithfully reproduced and reads :-

3rd.   Gloria in Excelsis Deo.
Victoria Regina et Imperatrix 1897.

One hundred years previously, in 1780, a treble and a tenor bell had been added to the old peal of three. But, in order to make an harmonious five, the treble of the old three needed to be recast. Again the inscription of the original 1687 bell, given by John Turner, was faithfully reproduced by Thos. Hedderly of Nottingham in two lines of Roman capital letters. From the inscription on the new treble and tenor of 1780 we find the cost was met by subscription. The prime mover in raising the subscription appeal was George Bonsall and a monument to him is on the west wall of St Mary's chapel.

4th.   The churches praise I sound always.
Raised by subscription, 1780.
Thos. Hedderly, Founder, Nottingham,

5th.   The gift of John Turner, Esq., of Swanwick, 1687
and recast, 1780 Thos. Hedderly, Nottingham,
Founder. Tho. Haslam, Churchwarden.

We now come to the oldest surviving bell in the tower. The legend on the sixth bell is finely worked in Lombardic capitals. Below, on a shield, is the founder's mark, a Fylfot cross surmounted on the right side by the letter 'H'. This mark is that of the Heathcotes, Bellfounders of Chesterfield. It is unusual inasmuch that no initial appears opposite the 'H' within the shield. The inscription "Gloria in Excelsis Deo IHC" was used by Godfrey Heathcote, baptised 1558/9 and whose will was proved in 1643. However, he had two sons, Godfrey and Ralph, both became bellfounders but Godfrey died before his father leaving Ralph who carried on the business until 1647 when all traces of bellfounding ceased at their foundry in Chesterfield. Ralph used the same mark as his father Godfrey but placed his initial 'R' on the left side above the fylfot cross whereas his father placed 'G'. The absence of this initial on the sixth bell makes the mark unique. The bell however must have been cast in this period, prior to 1647 but later than 1577 when Ralph, Godfrey Senior's father died. For we know that Ralph Snr. used a different mark prior to 1577, a square shield with a crown surmounting his initials. Today this bell is the subject of a preservation order issued by the Council for the Care of Churches.

6th.   Gloria in Excelsis Deo ihc.

7th.   I.I.R.H. All men that heare my mournfull sound,
repent before you lye in ground. R.H. G.B. C.M. 1627.
Recast by J. Taylor and Co.

This bell was recast in 1881 and the inscription faithfully copied in one line of Gothic script with the initials below. Who the original founder was is not known, nor are the people who have their initials inscribed. Could it be the Vicar and Churchwardens? Maybe not, as the vicar from 1618 until 1629 was the Rev'd. Ralph Rodes.

We now come to the tenor, cast in Nottingham by Hedderly in 1780 it weighs 13cwt. 3qrs. 13lbs. and is $43^{13}/_{16}$ inches in diameter. For our younger readers this is approximately 679.45kg and 112cm. The following inscription is in Roman capital letters and occupies two lines round the haunch of the bell.

Tenor   To the glory of God I sing and triumph to the King.
the marriage joys I tell, and tolls the dead man's
knell. Raised by subscription, 1780. Tho.
Hedderly, Founder, Nottingham.

Fixed adjacent to the east window of the bell chamber is a small "Sanctus" bell measuring fourteen inches in diameter and dating probably from about 1750. It is without inscription. For many years this bell had no rope attached but in 1971 it was made to operate by means of an electrical device enabling it to be chimed from within the chancel at the elevation of the host in the Eucharist.

A small clapper was found among the debris being cleared from the bell chamber in 1970 and is thought to have once belonged to this bell. This bell was known also as the "Parson's Bell" and it was customary for it to be chimed for five minutes before service.

Ringing was extremely well organised at the turn of the century with the ringers having formed their own St Martin's Guild as early as 1892. By 1899 and the addition of two trebles to complete the octave there were ten regular members of the band.

On July 13th, 1901, eight members of the team rang their first peal, 5040 Changes of Bob Triples. A plaque in the ringing chamber records this achievement.

The ringer of the third bell was Fred Watkinson who became a most able ringer and performed the duties of Guild secretary for fifteen years until he removed to Sheffield in 1917. He conducted his first peal in 1903 and was responsible for arranging twenty-five peals on the bells of which he conducted eighteen. All are recorded by the Midland Counties Association.

One of the peals, on Thursday, March 31, 1910 was a peal of 5040 Changes of Grandsire Triples. This peal was rung with the bells half-muffled as a tribute to the late Charles Rowland Palmer-Morewood Esq. Patron and donor of the two treble bells. The ringers, all of Alfreton, were Arthur Kenworthy, Frederick Benbow, John Hall, Samuel Porter, George Pipes, William Allsop, Fred Watkinson (Conductor) and Arthur Bentley. Within six weeks, the bells were again rung in a peal. This time the bells were deeply muffled (each side of the clapper) in respect of the memory of his late Majesty King Edward VII. A footnote says, "this peal was rung at a slow pace, taking three hours and ten minutes to complete on Saturday, May 7, 1910. By comparison the Morewood peal took three hours and one minute to complete whereas today an open (no muffles) peal averages under three hours".

When in 1943 the ringing of church bells was resumed following the wartime ban the tower once again became active and it was during this period that ladies were introduced into campanology at Alfreton. The prime mover being Thomas W. Hopson who had been a member of St Martin's Guild since 1912.

On the evening of Tuesday, June 24, 1958 a Quarter Peal of 1260 Changes of Grandsire Triples was organised to be rung on the bells prior to an Alfreton Deanery Service to commemorate the Lambeth Conference of that year and the visit to the Church and Deanery of three bishops. It was agreed to hold a procession through the town from St Chad's Mission, Mansfield Road to St Martin's. Everything was planned for the procession to arrive at a given time and for the bells to be ringing as the procession approached St. Martin's. However, in order to create an impressive impact through the town it was agreed the procession move at a slow pace. The result was that it arrived at St. Martin's very much later than the appointed time and in consequence the ringers completed their Quarter Peal of Grandsire Triples and then had to keep the bells ringing for a further hour whilst the procession actually arrived in church. It was quite a hot June evening! The ringers, drawn from the Alfreton Deanery, were A.S. Smithson, E.G. Holdgate, W. Swain, W. Riley, B.A. Richards, A.E. Wheeler, E.J. Sterland and R.J. Stretton.

Returning to the year 1892 the St. Martin's Guild of Change Ringers adopted and had printed a set of rules. A few copies printed on green cloth card still survive. These were based upon the ones in use at Nynehead in Somerset and had been introduced by the Vicar.

One interesting item is that the ringers had a two-tier system of duty. The ordinary duty being that they ring for Morning and Evening Prayer each Sunday, and on Christmas Day and Easter Day they ring early peals not later than 6.30a.m. They must also ring a midnight peal at New Year's Eve. Under the heading of "Special duty", came ringing for weddings and civic occasions. This was at the discretion of the President for which the ringers were paid four shillings (20p) per bell. The first band recorded was Rev. L.B. Lee, Curate, Hon Sec.; John Burnham, Treasurer; John Clay, leader; John Brookes, T Barratt, Mr Pipes, J. Hutchinson, J. Johnson, G. Cook and H. Fell.

In 1893 the second annual meeting was held at the vicarage when it was reported that receipts for the year amounted to £9.18s.8d which was duly shared by the six full members. Five years later £15.10s.2d had been received this was again shared leaving just 1½d in the kitty. Two practice nights were held at this period. Saturdays at 7p.m. for full members and Mondays at 7.30p.m. for all. It is interesting that Monday is still the accepted practice night. There was quite a waiting list of would be probationer ringers at this time. If only it was so today?

The ringers presented the Vicar with a brass dinner gong in 1902 as a token of their esteem. Two years later a set of leather muffles was purchased for £2 of which the Vicar gave 7s.6d toward them. These were used for the first time on the day the Bishop died. The Churchwardens agreed to pay £5.19s.9d for a set of nineteen handbells and to have a cupboard built in the ringing room for them. This was situated on the sill of the large west window of the ringing room and comprised numerous compartments and a hinged cover. It was removed about 1970 at the time of the last restoration work upon the bells.

An interesting note in 1905 brought praise from the Vicar, who, to quote, "Was proud of the ringers, for unlike other parishes where they cause much annoyance and trouble the St. Martin's band did not".

Five peal attempts were made in 1907. An Easter Monday peal of Grandsire Triples came to grief after one and a half-hours when the rope of the third bell broke. Another attempt on April 9th was successful. In September a peal was lost through two of the ringers changing their coursing order. On November 9th a peal was lost due to bad striking but the final blow was on December 14th when a very well struck peal was lost due to the Vicar hammering on the underside of the ringing chamber floor, just five minutes before it was due to finish and with over three hours continuous ringing already achieved. A parallel incident happened some years ago when a visiting team were ringing a peal of Cambridge Surprise Major. The ringing started at 3p.m. when after almost two hours the lights in the tower suddenly went out. A master switch in church had been turned off by a flower lady as she left, as twilight fell it seemed inevitable that the peal must be abandoned but fortunately the ringers were able to attract the attention of two visitors who after a time were able to restore the lights. The peal was brought round in three hours and twelve minutes.

Royal occasions have been marked by the ringing of St. Martin's bells. On the occasion of H.M. The Queen's Silver Jubilee in 1977 a Quarter peal of Stedman Triples was rung on the bells as part of a programme of ringing organised to coincide with her visit to Derbyshire in July. A peal was rung on the bells by the local band to commemorate the wedding of H.R.H. Princess Anne to Captain Mark Phillips on November 23, 1973. The bells have rung out at Coronations down the years and in 1911 at the Coronation of George V the ringers actually received £2 for their efforts.

The bellframe was causing concern in 1929 by rocking somewhat. This was eventually attended to in 1931, then thirty years later whilst being rung for Evensong one Sunday the seventh bell shed its bearing and dropped within its frame. Fortunately it wedged itself within the frame in the process and thereby saved a more serious accident. This was a fateful blow to ringing at Alfreton and became the main reason for the bells remaining silent for a period of eleven years.

Then in 1970 a most generous offer was made by the Misses Ivy and Winnie Cluley to offset the expense of rehanging the seventh bell and having an overhaul of the other bells. This they wished to undertake in memory of their late parents. The work was undertaken by John Taylor & Co. of Loughborough and completed in January 1971.

The Vicar, Rev R.N. Craig, together with two remaining ringers from the old band, Harry Leggoe and Harry Painter, both of whom have now completed fifty years as ringers, recruited from the congregation a group of parishioners who showed an interest in learning the art and science of change ringing. Arrangements were made to use the bells at St. Mary's, Crich for practice and teaching during the period whilst St. Martin's bells were being repaired. This proved very successful, and so did the recruits, that in January 1971 when St. Martin's bells were again ringable there was a local team ready and able to take over. In fact they became quite competent to the extent that several of them rang in the Royal Wedding peal two years later. Time moves on and so do ringers but it needs to be recorded that one of those learners of 1971 has now given twenty five years of faithful service to the tower. Mrs Joyce Taylor not only attends regularly to ring but puts in many more hours of voluntary work about St. Martin's and as I write Harry Leggoe is still ringing at the ripe old age of 88 in addition to taking up his rota as server and at the lectern.

At the present time Alfreton, along with many towers, is experiencing difficulty in maintaining a regular band of ringers. Unfortunately the bells are

52

becoming in need of further work doing on them and it would be very appropriate if for the millennium they could be put once again in perfect order. After all, it would appear that major work has been carried out on St. Martin's bells once each century, in 1680 augmentation to three bells, in 1780 to five and in 1899 to eight. How about a complete rehanging of the eight in 1999 in readiness to ring in the Millennium and proclaim God's praise over Alfreton for another century?

As these notes are being finalised I am informed, from someone closely connected with St. Martin's belfry, as the media say, that a promise of £15,000 has been made toward the restoration of the peal. This, by any standard, is a most generous gesture and one which bell-ringers generally and the congregation of St. Martin's will be ever grateful of. An unofficial estimated figure of around £35,000 has been uttered as the possible total cost of bringing the eight bells into good working order. And of course the book does not stop there for the belfry still needs a band of ringers. As the millennium approaches can the parishioners of Alfreton once more attend to the ringing of their parish church bells as they have so reliably done at the turn of each of the past three centuries?

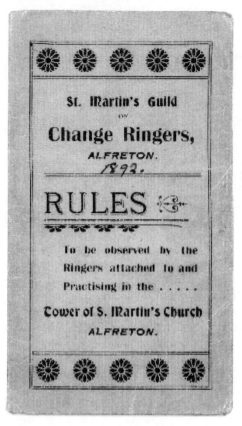

The Belfry of All Saints, Ashover

Medallion of Edward V11 & Queen Alexandra. Dumb peal for George III Coronation peal for George IV. Bells rehung for Coronation of George VI. Eighteenth century Pendal Clock. Mrs. Revel, first lady ringer, 1814.

The earliest written record of the bells ringing at All Saints Church was on the Wednesday in Whitsun week, May 20th, 1657. The occasion was the wedding of the Parish Clerk, Leonard Wheatcroft to Elizabeth Hawley of Winster. There were four bells in the tower at this time and on this particular occasion, they were rung at the express invitation of the bridegroom, by, Henry Poursgloue, Gyles Low, John Bower and Jonathan Street. The ringers, "with flying colours tied to the wrist of their hand," caused the merry bells to ring aloud. So says the note of Leonard Wheatcroft, handed down to his son Titus.

The orb finial supporting its weathercock crowns the slender spire of All Saints Church and makes a splendid centrepiece to the village. It is reputed to rise to a height of one hundred and twenty eight feet. Springing as it does from behind the embattled parapet of the western tower this elegant spire is ornamented on each cardinal face with two crocketed openings. The tower, completed by the Babingtons of Dethick after they had come into the parish in 1419, is supported by angle buttresses. The straight headed bell openings, with their fine tracery, and the three long gargoyles are worthy of note. The present clock dial, dating from last century, is situated on the south face. On the west face is a small ogee headed window, but no west door. The small door on the south is a later addition.

Inside, the tall tower arch to the nave has a profile of two double curves. Above the arch four plaques, placed side by side, have written upon them the Lord's Prayer, Nicene Creed and the Ten Commandments. In 1860 an old musicians' gallery was removed to reveal this arch and the stone plugs subsequently placed in the holes vacated by the joists are easily visible. Above is the weather line of the old roof gable. This line dates from early in the sixteenth century when the clerestory was added.

Ringing takes place almost at ground level, the ringing chamber being well appointed is divided from the nave by a fine oak screen. Two steps form the plinth on which the Norman lead font, dating from the twelfth century, stands. Behind the font, access through the oak tower arch screen, is to the ringing chamber. A carved oak plaque on the north wall of the chamber informs that to commemorate the Coronation of George VI on May 12, 1937, the bells were rehung on ball bearings at a cost of £150. The money was raised by public subscription. On the same wall a tablet records the weight and inscriptions of the old eight bells and another lists peals rung upon the bells. Above and on the wall opposite are several charity boards recording the good works of former parishioners.

At the time of writing a germ of an idea is being considered to erect a new ringing chamber at a height somewhere about the top level of the oak screen and to completely enclose the tower arch. Similar building work at other belfries has proved successful to both ringer and congregation.

The bells are reached via the spiral stone stair in the south-east corner. The tower is divided internally into four chambers. Having left the ground floor we first reach the old ringing chamber. Although no one in living memory can recall ringing taking place from this floor. Above this is the clock chamber which houses the clockworks installed in 1881 by John Smith & Sons of Derby. An earlier clock, known as a pendal clock, existed from about 1722. Above in the bell chamber hang the bells. The old eight were hung on one level and supported in the main by a metal 'H' frame over wooden beams. This frame has been dismantled and in its place a frame to hold ten bells and made of alloy has been erected.

In 1715 some twenty feet of the spire's masonry was blown down, and on looking up into the interior, the extent of this repair can be easily defined. Joseph Hodgkinson and James Milner were responsible for the rebuilding. In the latter half of the nineteenth century a few feet at the summit had to be restored and in 1932 another general overhaul of the spire was undertaken.

History has actually been made during the period whilst these words were being put to paper. Inasmuch that the peal of bells in the tower was eight in number as I started writing, but, before I finish the peal has been augmented to a peal of ten. A wonderful achievement and one which will be noted later on.

The ten bells are the work of at least four bellfounders, of whom two were in Chesterfield, two in Nottingham and one in Loughborough. The oldest bell dates from 1625 and the latest additions are dated 1997. The tenor weighs just over eighteen-hundredweight and the combined weight of the old peal of eight was three tons, twelve hundredweights and three pounds. With the addition of the two new trebles one needs to use very little imagination to realise the power of thrust created by the bells as they oscillate in peal, and in so doing, to marvel at our predecessors' building skills. That of coupling combined strength with the grace and beauty we find in a belfry such as this at All Saints Church, Ashover. The bells are inscribed:-

Treble   GIVEN IN MAY 1997 IN MEMORY OF
THE BASSETT FAMILY
OF ASHOVER AND SHEFFIELD
TO COMMEMORATE THEIR LONG ASSOCIATION
WITH ALL SAINTS CHURCH AND
ASHOVER
ALSO TO MARK THE APPROACH
OF THE NEW MILLENNIUM

On the reverse waist:-
ELISABETH AND SARA KATHERINE BASSETT
WERE RINGERS AT THIS CHURCH
BETWEEN
1927 AND 1947

2nd. TO MARK THE GOLDEN JUBILEE IN 1996
OF THE
DERBY DIOCESAN ASSOCIATION
OF CHURCH BELL RINGERS
GIVEN BY FRIENDS OF ALL SAINTS
ASHOVER

On the reverse waist:-
I RING OUT JOYFULLY FOR
ALL THE SOULS OF
ASHOVER
THE REV D TOM JOHNSON - RECTOR
ROSEMARY BLAKESLEY }
RAYMOND BROOMHEAD } CHURCHWARDENS.

On the inscription band of both bells is a border of vine leaf and grape with an elliptic medallion on the face of which in very fine Roman letters is cast, "The Millennium Commission." And, alongside, "A MILLENNIUM PROJECT. SUPPORTED BY FUNDS FROM THE NATIONAL LOTTERY." On the reverse, 1997 and a miniature medallion of John Taylor Bellfounders Ltd., Loughborough. Fine wire bands decorate the sound bow and above and below the inscription bands.

3rd. John Taylor & Co. Loughborough, Leicestershire.
Fear God Honour the King
Edward VII - June 1902
Diameter: 2ft.4inches. Weight: 5cwts.0qrs.18lbs. Note E.

It was erected to commemorate the Coronation of Edward VII. Upon the reverse waist is a medallion showing the crowned heads of Edward VII and Queen Alexandra. A fine leaf and berry border encircles the bell.

4th. To the Glory of God
This bell is given in loving memory
of Frederick Stanley Fenton, who died
April 9th, 1883. By his parents Frederick J.
Fenton and Sarah Davan Fenton.
J.B. Nodder, Rector.
J.P. Jackson,
W. Else, Churchwardens,
1890
Cast by John Taylor & Co. Loughborough, whose bell mark is upon the waist.
Diameter: 2ft.4½ins. Weight: 5cwts. 0qrs. 19lbs. Note D#.

5th.   Rev. Lawrence Short, Rector. Recast 1890
William Eaton,
Geo. Bamford Churchwardens.
The old bell rung
the fall of Bonaparte,
and broke, April 1814.
J. & E. Smith Chesterfield. B.F.
Taylors mark is upon the waist.

This bell is unique in that no other bell bears the name of Bonaparte. Napoleon I (Bonaparte), (1769 - 1821) was forced by the Allies to abdicate on April 11th, 1814 and retire to Elba. On the news of this victory reaching Ashover the bells were rung and the bell obviously broke. How, is not recorded, and there is no point in speculating but we do know that the bell was recast in Chesterfield at the Griffin Foundry of John and Ebenezer Smith. It was returned to the belfry and rehung by John Wright on May 4th, 1815 at a total cost of £28.19s.8½d. The Churchwardens delaying payment until Christmas 1816. A full account of this interesting episode and the history of this bell appears in the chapter relating to bellfounders.

It is possible that prior to 1814 this bell carried the inscription, "ANTOMUS MOVET UT CAMPANA." which was not reproduced by Smiths. Titus Wheatcroft writing in 1722 translates as "The mind moveth as the Bell."

     Diameter: 2ft.7ins. Weight: 6cwt.1qr.18lbs. Note C#.

6th.   I sweetly tolling men do call to taste on meats
that feede the soule. 1625.
Upon the crown the initials G.H.

This legend is found repeated on church bells in other towers locally. But, the real interest of this bell is in the initials G.H. to be found on the crown and almost in contact with the wooden headstock. They are plainly raised capital letters, cast straight on the crown and without being highlighted by any form of plinth or shield. The initial H has been shortened on the right by drilling of a hole through the crown to allow a bolt to be used in securing the bell to the headstock. Most probably this took place in 1890 when the bell was re-hung. The legend is typical of those used by the Oldfield foundry in Nottingham, and from this, the bell's casting could be attributed to them. Dr. Charles Cox thought the bell was cast by the Chesterfield foundry belonging to the Heathcote family whilst a third possibility emerges when studying records nearer to Ashover that the initials may stand for a local benefactor George Hodgkinson.

The above note was written prior to the augmentation to ten bells and when the initials 'GH' cast upon this bell were plainly visible. However, the re-hanging has necessitated the use of crown caps. Crown caps aid the fixing of a bell to its headstock and are in effect a circular disc of resin placed between the bell and headstock. In the case of this bell the use of the cap has hidden completely the initials 'GH' which is a great pity, but obviously is necessary from a modern bell-hanging point of view.

Returning to the initials 'GH' and the name George Hodgkinson of Overton Hall. George had an acquaintance if not a close friendship with Leonard Wheatcroft the parish clerk. When George Hodgkinson died in 1692 Leonard Wheatcroft thought fit to write:-

"He was a man that was poor man's friend
Oh, Now he's gone, who will them money lend?
Kind to the poore, a helper of the rich,
I was one once - he help'd me out o' th' ditch."

George and his wife Anne had sons, the eldest two being Sam and George. The old school, now converted into a dwelling, had the following inscription over the door in the early years of this century. "George Hodgkinson of Overton Hall and his wife Anne designed this school. It was finished by Wm. Hodgkinson his son and Eliz. his wife. Anno 1703." Leonard Wheatcroft's son, Titus, in his writings of the early part of the eighteenth century, went to great length to foster the goodwill of William (a lead merchant) and Elizabeth Hodgkinson, fabricating the casting of a bell in 1724. In his Mss of 1722 writing, "ye new Trible Bell was designed by G.H. & A. with Sam and George, their eldest sons. Done by W.H. & E. and O.H. & R. their younger children." One wonders if Titus was writing in anticipation of a gift of a fifth bell. If this was so it did not materialise for almost two decades.

The point of this aside is that it was not uncommon for a pious donor of a bell to have some mark or initials placed upon the bell in a discreet manner. And what better place than the crown of the bell, which is often above eye level. We will later come across the placing of a similar mark when looking at the seventh bell.

George Hodgkinson having died in 1692 would, one assumes, have been too young in 1625 to have been responsible for the initials upon the sixth bell, but, could they be those of his father? Solving this point still does not prove who cast the bell. Only a suggestion of who might have paid for it.

Dr. Charles Cox differed in his opinion and thought the initials to be those of Godfrey Heathcote the bellfounder of Chesterfield. Let us consider this possibility.

You will recall from the chapter outlining the Heathcotes that Godfrey Heathcote reintroduced the fylfot cross as his bellmark and that he was casting bells well into the seventeenth century. Also you will recall that he had two sons, Godfrey and Ralph by his first wife Anne who died in 1605. Son Godfrey predeceased his father but is known to have been alive in 1628. Godfrey senior was baptised in 1558 and therefore we can assume he was in the region of being seventy years of age in 1628. His will was proved in 1643 so one can also presume that he was well over eighty when he died.

A very interesting point emerges when looking at the initials 'GH' found on the crown of the sixth bell if, in fact, the bell was cast by Godfrey Heathcote senior. Why are they not placed on a simple shield as was his normal practice and why was the fylfot cross not incorporated?

The answer possibly can be found by looking closer at Godfrey the son of Godfrey. We know he was employed as a bellfounder by his father and in 1625, when the bell was cast, Godfrey would be about twenty-two years of age. Could it therefore be that he cast the bell and placed his initials discreetly upon the crown?

This bell has rung out over Ashover for almost four centuries. It has escaped the necessity of having to be recast through three augmentations. Long may it ring forth in praise and thanksgiving of its benefactor and founder, whomsoever they be.

Diameter: 2ft.10¼ins. Weight: 7cwts.1qr.14lbs. Note B.

7th.   My roaring sounde doth warning give that men cannot heare always live. 1625.

Recast by John Taylor & Co, Loughborough, 1902, whose mark is on the waist. A fine border of alternate grape and vine leaf design encircles the bell beneath the inscription band.

Diameter: 3ft.0¼ins. Weight: 8cwt.1qr.17lbs. Note A.

Leonard Wheatcroft who died in 1706 gave a note informing that, "Four bells in Ashover Church rehung 1702,"and in the Churchwardens accounts for that date, "Paid to Thomas Siddale for hanging ye bells £4.2s.2½d." A footnote states, "This was only a part payment of the total cost of £50." Also, Titus Wheatcroft in his Memorandum of 1722 states that there are four good tunable bells and a Ting Tang in the steeple. It therefore must be concluded from this that the third (Bonaparte) bell was in fact a very old bell and that Smith's when recasting it omitted to reproduce the old inscription.

The reference to Thomas Siddale is interesting for in the Churchwardens accounts for Shirland there are items dated 1730, 1740, 1743 and 1745 paid to him for work on the bells.

8th.   Abraham Redfin, C.W. 1751.
         Tho. Hedderly, Founder.
         The mark of John Taylor & Sons, Loughborough,
         Recast 1890.
         The scrollwork round this bell is beautifully finished.
         Diameter: 3ft.2½ins. Weight: 10cwt.3qrs.9lbs. Note G.

9th.   All Men that heare my mournfull sound, repent
         before you lye in ground. R.B. G.C. Wardens 1630.

Below the legend is the bell-mark of George Oldfield founder of Nottingham. On the crown are the initials 'I.B.' mounted on two plaques and positioned side by side. This bell was cast in 1630 and in that year the rector of Ashover was Immanuel Bourne. Living at Eastwood Hall he was rector from 1621 until 1669. A very troublesome period in history. Do the initials bear discreet testimony to this bell's benefactor? Incidentally, when the cope was prepared by the founder George Oldfield, in readiness for the casting of this bell, the numeral three of the inscription's date was inadvertently reversed.

Diameter: 3ft.4 ⁵/₈ ins. Weight: 10cwt.2qrs.0lbs. Note F.

In 1890 when John Taylor cast what is now the fourth bell and recast the present fifth bell and the eighth in order to augment the peal of five to six, this bell was the tenor. It is interesting to note that in their catalogue the weight attributed to the tenor in round hundred-weights is twelve. They also indicate that at this time the bells were hung in a new oak frame.

Tenor.   To the Glory of God
and in memory of
Samuel Burkitt
of Stubbing Court.
Given by his son,
1902.

John Taylor & Co., Founders Loughborough, Leicestershire is round the inscription band and beneath a decorative border similar in design to that found on the fifth bell. Diameter: 3ft.11ins. Weight: 18cwt.0qrs.10lbs. Note E.

When the octave was completed by the addition of the treble and tenor to the original peal of six bells it was necessary to recast the fifth bell. John Taylor and Co. undertook the augmentation from five to six in 1890 and twelve years later completed the octave, hanging the bells in a metal frame known as an "H" frame, over oak beams. The outcome has been for Ashover to possess a notable peal of bells for almost a century. Noted for their fine tone, in the key of E, making them a pleasure to listen to and noted by all who ring them.

The Ting-Tang bell or Sanctus bell is simply ornamented with a cable moulding, but bears no inscription or date. It hung for a period of years fixed between the mullions of one of the bell chamber openings. Then in 1890 it was housed in its bell-cot upon the east gable of the nave.

The family of Wheatcroft were entrepreneurs in Ashover through several generations. We have read of their ringing activities, and of being Parish Clerk. In addition they were the village tailor, innkeepers, gunsmiths, tinsmiths and metal founders who occupied a workshop on the east side of Prestwood House which was taken down in 1875. At one period they cast small bells and a set of handbells in the inventory of the Crispin Inn, but long since sold, were cast in this workshop. It is reputed that Nancy Wheatcroft, who lived in a cottage nearby the workshop, had an evil influence, and no bells could be cast when she was at home.

At the base of the west wall of the tower is an open stone coffin with its lid open and fastened back to the tower wall. Dating from around 1200 it was discovered in the churchyard in 1880. It contained, besides a few of the larger bones, which were re-interred, a heart-shaped piece of lead which is preserved. This lead was inscribed:- "Here was Leonard Wheatcroft buried, January III, in this stone coffin, who was clark of this Church 56 years. Aged 80. 1706. Born 1st. May, 1627, Leonard was historian of Ashover, clerk of the parish, tailor, landlord of The Hand and Shears, accomplished bell ringer and excellent singer."

Standing alongside the coffin is an old weather vane bearing the date 1854. This was replaced in 1932 by the present one. One cannot help but wonder how many other vanes have been erected and replaced during almost six centuries since the spire was built. And, oh, what must they have seen!

The present clock installed in 1881 by John Smith and Sons, of Derby, had originally a Ding-Dong Quarter Chime. Upon the augmentation of the five bells to six in 1890 the chime was altered to what has become known as the Westminster Chime on account of its use at the Palace of Westminster. This chime however was formerly the Cambridge Chime and was composed by Dr. Scrotch for the bells of Great St. Mary's Church in Cambridge.

The first record of a clock in the tower was in 1722:-
> "There is likewise a pendal clock with two hands, the one to show the congregation the time of day as they sit within ye church, and the other is on the outside ye wall to show the people what time ye day as ye pass along ye street."

From the Churchwardens accounts we find:-

1784 Paid Mr. Mason for the Clock	£10.12s.6d.
1792 New Clock coard	6s.0d.
1806 Mr. Mason mending Clock	£1.4s.0d.
1810 Wm. Wheatcroft repairing clock	7s.0d.
1837 Sam. Wheatcroft repairing clock	16s.6d.

Timothy Mason one of a numerous family of clock-makers at Gainsborough, Doncaster, Bawtry and Rotherham who commenced business at Low Pavement in Chesterfield about 1780. He supplied the Ashover clock in 1784, and died about 1822.

The following items from the Churchwardens accounts pertain to the bells and ringers:-

1773 New bell ropes and oil	£1.1s.8d.
1788 Sept 12. A set of bell ropes with Ting Tang rope 23s. putting up 18d.	£1.4s.6d.
1792 Geo Allen for ale by ringers 2 New Year's Days.	5s.0d.
1798 Paid the Ringers upon Nelson Victory. Oct.12th.	3s.6d.
1798 Nov. To the Publeck ringing	£5.2s.3d.

An item on June 17th, 1814 must refer to the "Bonaparte Bell", for we find, "to Geo. Bamford and assistants to Gett the Bell drawne up... 5 shillings." And to, "Mathew Bower for Assisting 1s.6d." These items were in respect of taking down the bell but, note that no mention is made about the cost of cartage to Smith's Foundry at Chesterfield. Next year we find, "April 16th, 1815, Ale at John Marsden at Pulling up the bell... 4s.6d."Then, on May 4th John Wright was paid £2.14.11½d for hanging the bell. The founder was kept waiting until Christmas 1816 for his dues:- "1816 Exmus. Paid Mr. Smith For repares of Bell that wass Brok when ringing Good Newes... £25.13.9d."

On February 1st, 1820 at the sad news reaching Ashover of the death of King George III, a dumb peal was rung on the bells for which the ringers received five shillings (25p). Today we would describe a dumb peal as one rung with each bell's clapper having a leather muffle strapped to each striking face thus giving a somewhat muted sound. It is more likely that an occasion calling for muffled ringing today would consist of each bell clapper only being muffled on one face. This, half-muffled ringing, produces a distinct effect of alternating open and muffled changes and creates a very moving atmosphere when the bells are clearly and well struck.

In the following year finances were improved, the ringers received £1 for ringing at King George IV's Coronation on July 19th, 1821. But, when he died in 1830 they received only ten shillings. Ten years later the payment of £1 was reinstated when William IV's Coronation was heralded upon the bells.

The Rev. John Bourne Nodder succeeded as Rector of Ashover after his father, Rev. Joseph Nodder, in 1878 and became the prime mover in the founding of the East Derbyshire Association of Change Ringers. A local man, educated at Repton and Corpus Christi College, Cambridge he was ordained in 1877 and served as Honorary Curate at Heath.

Being well versed with local village church life he, together with Rev. Jas. Oldham of Clay Cross, Rev. J.C. Massey of South Normanton set about organising the bell ringers in the area. The Association, now known as the East Derbyshire and West Nottinghamshire Association of Church Bell Ringers is still active in the area. Seven All Saints ringers became founder members:- Thos. J. Beardow, Thos. Hopkinson, J. Holmes, J.H. Beardow, W. Buxton, Geo Beardow and Walter Hopkinson. There was also a lady ringer, Mrs. Dolly Revell, who although over eighty years of age when the Association was founded, ought really to have become the first lady member. As events turned out lady ringers did not take up membership until after the Second World War in 1946.

Mrs. Revell began ringing at Ashover in the same year as the "Bonaparte" bell was broken, 1814 at the age of eight and continued to ring throughout her life. At the opening of the new peal of six on Saturday, November 8th, 1890 she was accorded the honour of ringing each of the new bells, i.e. treble and tenor, immediately after their dedication. The following tribute is to be found in C.E. Lugard's book, "The Inns and Outs of Ashover", published in 1923.

"Born at the Crispin Inn, daughter of Benjamin Wall, parish Clerk. At the age of 15, along with another sister had sole control of that house, married Edmund Revell who came to the district as apprentice to John Mellor of Littlemore, moved to the Red Lion, 1841 and to the White Lion, 1859, where she died March 1892, aged 85 years. She lived in a public house all the days of her life and never once tasted spirits, not even to sample. The police never had to complain of the conduct of her house, and her name was a household word. She had nine children, 48 grandchildren and 19 great grandchildren, her husband died in 1879. Known as a, 'wonderful old Women', she retained all her faculties up to the last. An expert bell-ringer, she could manage any of the five bells which were then in the church."

Surviving from 1683 are the "Clerk's Orders to the Ringers", and several poems relating to the ringer and the ringing at Ashover. These, as mentioned, are from the pen of Leonard Wheatcroft. Handed down by his son Titus, they give a first hand account of the importance that church bells played in rural life at this period. One will not fail to notice that ringing was somewhat detached from the ecclesiastical life of a parish, and is a direct reflection on the prevailing Puritan movement. Leonard Wheatcroft obviously kept a very tight ship with regard to the ringing of Ashover's bells, even to the extent of almost claiming them as his sole rite, and two hundred years later it was exactly this situation which the Rector, Rev. John Bourne Nodder had in mind to address when he steered the local clergy and ringers into forming an association. This facet, and the rules applied by Leonard Wheatcroft to the Ashover bell-ringers together with some of his verse are more fully researched in other chapters.

Before leaving the Wheatcrofts we find mention in 1702 of the Churchwardens instructing Samuel Wheatcroft to begin ringing the Curfew at Michaelmas and continue through to Lady Day. No indication is given as to how many years the curfew was rung or at what time nor for the exact purpose other than the general observance found in other parishes.

Another item found, says that before the clock was installed it was customary for the Dinner Bell to be rung at noon daily with the exception of Shrove Tuesday when it was rung one hour earlier at 11a.m. A bell was also rung at 8a.m. and 9a.m. on Sunday, the purpose being to enable parishioners to set their clocks and watches by. Worth thinking about, when we today use and take for granted the chime of Big Ben we are accustomed to hear over the radio or as my generation were brought up to say, wireless!

The Churchwardens laid before the Vestry meeting on May 3rd, 1854 the decayed state of the spire at its topmost quarter. they presented also a report of Mr. Brown's stating that it could not be repaired without first taking down about eight feet of masonry. The tower was also found to be taking great injury from the wet, the parapet and one buttress at the west end of it being ready to fall down with the bell chamber decaying from the same cause, the Churchwardens being instructed to have the work carried out in the best and cheapest way.

At the July meeting of the Vestry they submitted an account of the outlay for the repairs together with the requisite expenses until Easter, 1855. They proposed a Rate of two and a half pence in the pound. There was objection to the levying of a Church Rate and the meeting was adjourned.

The next meeting, on December 28th, 1854 heard how the spire had taken great injury both inside and out from rain. The weathercock had seized-up several years before and visibly rocking with every gale, threatened to crash down. Again a Church Rate of two and a half pence in the pound was proposed. But, this time an amendment for no rate to be levied was carried. The decision raised three cheers and great confusion prevailed

Thus is the simple explanation, in brief, as to how the voluntary system of depending upon subscriptions and offertories for the upkeep of the fabric of our churches came into being. In this case a collection was made in the parish, in lieu of the Church Rate, and the necessary repairs carried out.

The East Derbyshire and West Nottinghamshire Association of Church Bell Ringers has, as we have read, had a long and happy association with the ringers of All Saints, Ashover. Members have regularly visited for meetings and on the occasion of the Association's centenary in October 1987, a wonderful social evening was held in the village. A mobile exhibition, depicting the Association's history, was placed on show at the event and afterwards in church for a period. A centenary cake in the form of a bell, and suitably iced, was made and donated by Mrs Wendy Heading, a member of both the Association and of the All Saints band for many years.

In the early 1930's several of Ashover's ringers took up membership of the Midland Counties Association. Among them three members of the Hopkinson family, Edwin, Harry and Walter together with Alfred H. Bowler, Thomas Dent and John J. Revell. On Saturday, December 10th, 1938 some of them rang the following peal on the bells:-

Bob Major, 5040 Changes,
in three hours and five minutes.

Walter Hopkinson	Treble	Harry Hopkinson	5th.
V. Taylor	2nd.	J. Dent	6th.
J. Revell	3rd.	Edwin Hopkinson	7th.
H.E. Taylor	4th.	A.W.H. Bowler	Tenor.

Composed by J. Reeves. Conducted by A.W.H. Bowler.

Edwin Hopkinson rang again in the first peal to be rung on the bells after the war. That was on Saturday, May 1st, 1948. It was the first peal rung on the bells for the newly formed Derbyshire Association and is entered in the peal records as the thirty-third peal. Edwin Hopkinson became the first member of the Ashover band to join the new Association. The peal was:-

A Peal of Plain Bob Major, 5024 Changes,
in two hours and fifty minutes.

Miss Norma Howes*	Treble	Brynley A. Richards +	5th.
George H. Paulson	2nd.	Eric J. Sterland +	6th.
Miss D. Jean Dunn +	3rd.	Edwin Hopkinson	7th.
E. Glyn Holdgate +	4th.	Herbert E. Taylor	Tenor.

Composed by Amburn Wilson. Conducted by H.E. Taylor.
* First peal. + First peal of Major.

In 1946 the Derbyshire Association of Change Ringers had been founded. The first meeting at Ashover of the Association was held in 1949 and in the following year T. Dent became the second member from Ashover's band. By 1961, L.F. Miller, Miss Marjorie Cooke, Miss Brenda Slinn and Miss Joan Hinchcliffe had joined, to be followed in 1964 by James Allin and Elizabeth and William Revell. They in turn were joined later in the decade by Miss R. Miller, Miss C. Hayes, H.S. Carr, F. Swain and C.P. Miller thus forming a strong local band of Sunday service ringers in Ashover.

By the mid-1970's, ringing had fallen to a low ebb. Then Jim Heading and his wife, Wendy, took up residence in the village. After a while Jim looked in at the belfry and was fascinated by what he saw. He set about finding out all he could about Change Ringing. He also set about the task of trying to build up a band of local ringers, almost, if not entirely from scratch. Keeping one phase ahead of the team, Jim slowly, and with infinite patience brought the band's ability to one of competence. But, of course, Jim would be the first to make the point that their achievements were only possible through the combined effort of the team as a whole.

By 1981 a good resident band practised at the tower and on Saturday, January 17th, 1981, a peal was rung on the bells. No fewer than five of the ringers were ringing in their first peal in the method. A remarkable achievement at one attempt.

A Peal of Kent Treble Bob Major, 5088 Changes.

Audrey Cooper	Treble	Andrew J. Heading	5th.
Angela Beardow	2nd.	Les Cooper	6th.
Elaine Lunn	3rd.	Jeffrey P. Cooper	7th.
Jim Heading	4th.	Ronald R. Warford	Tenor.

Conducted by Ronald R. Warford.

American Independence Day, July 4th, 1981, found Father Ian Schlotterbeck, from Michigan, U.S.A. as temporary Rector. Since his arrival in Ashover, Father Ian had been fascinated by English bell-ringing and so it was decided to attempt to ring a peal on the bells and to celebrate this great American day in his honour.

The day dawned sunny and warm. This prompted the ringers to make history, by hoisting the Stars and Stripes at the top of the tower in place of the customary St. George's Cross. The ringers assembled and the following peal was rung. It took three hours and six minutes to complete.

5040 Changes of Plain Bob Major.

Andrew Heading	Treble	Jim Heading	5th.
Adrian Dempster	2nd.	David Kingman	6th.
Jane Orchard	3rd.	Simon Humphrey	7th.
Angela Beardow	4th.	Philip Ramsbottom	Tenor.

Conducted by Adrian Dempster.

Later in the year Father Ian and his family returned to America complete with many recordings of Ashover's bells being rung. As one ringer remarked at the time, "I wonder if his enthusiasm will be shared by his parishioners!"

During the intervening years several peals have been rung on the bells with the final one, before the current renovation appeal was launched, taking place on

Wednesday, May 4th, 1994. This was rung for the Derby Diocesan Association.

5184 Changes of Bristol Surprise Major.

Rosemary R.A. Ross	Treble.	Philip J.H. Hudson	5th.
Canon Frederick Ross	2nd.	Edward Martin	6th.
Rev. David Sansum	3rd.	Gordon Halls	7th.
Patricia A.M. Halls	4th.	Philip Mahew	Tenor.

Conducted by Gordon Halls.

As this article is being written the bells lay silent and in need of urgent repair. Various suggestions have been put forward regarding their future. Some are in favour of augmentation to a peal of ten. Others not. Either way, a complete overhaul of the octave is urgently needed, and it will be another great day in the history of Ashover's bells when they once again ring out over the village as they have for almost four hundred years.

We are now at the end of 1997 and as I said earlier history has been in the making at Ashover with regard to the belfry and the bells. Two fine trebles have been added. The treble as a lasting reminder of the long association the Bassett family have had with the village. The second, through the good offices of the Derby Diocesan Association of Church Bell Ringers is given simply by friends of All Saints, Ashover. They new trebles were dedicated by the Lord Bishop of Derby on Sunday, December 7, 1997.

For twenty years the Misses Elisabeth and Sara Bassett took an active part in the ringing of Ashover's bells. They worked hard for the project in 1937 to get the eight bells re-hung on ball bearings in commemoration of the Coronation of George V1. And after the Second World War helped considerably in getting a band of ringers established again in Ashover.

"I Ring out joyfully for all the souls of Ashover."
So says part of the inscription on the new second bell.
Be it God's will that all the bells may do just that.

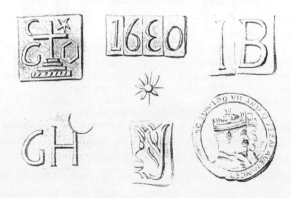

The Belfry of St. John the Baptist, Ault Hucknall

Bells, augmentation from five to eight. Thirty-five methods rung in one peal.
Four hundred year old fifth bell. Fifteenth century upper tower atop an ancient base.

The crossing tower of St. John the Baptist Church at Ault Hucknall comprises masonry work of both Norman and fifteenth century construction. As it divides the chancel from the nave the lower stages of the tower are viewed only from inside. Where, at the east end of the nave we find a fine Norman archway giving access under the tower. This archway is ornamented chiefly with bold mouldings of the beak-head and chevron pattern together with the use of other devices, including two quaint figures of men, a camel, a chalice, various human faces and a knot resembling the Stafford badge.

Passing beneath the tower into the chancel one enters through a narrow archway with a rounded top. This archway, being plain and no larger than a small doorway, is possibly of pre- Norman date, although many experts are somewhat perplexed as to its true age.

The upper storey of the tower, with its embattled parapet and crocketed pinnacles, and with square two-light bell openings was built in the fifteenth century.

Access to the ringing chamber is by an external flight of stone steps leading from the churchyard on the north side. These deliver the visitor through a small doorway into a tiny vestibule from which it is necessary to climb a short flight of wooden stairs, before emerging through a trap-door into the ringing chamber. Once inside, the ringing chamber is most comfortable and very well appointed. The bell-ropes fall in an almost perfect circle, slightly south of centre. this affords excellent rope-sight for the ringer. The bells are reached by means of a ladder directly from this chamber.

On the walls of the ringing chamber hang various painted panels. Two have written upon them The Ten Commandments, whilst another bears The Lord's Prayer and a third the Nicene Creed. A further large heraldic panel is most beautifully executed and depicts a Coat of Arms. There is a peal board and a further peal recorded in an illuminated framed panel.

The tower contains a peal of eight bells. Prior to 1976, and for the previous nine decades, a peal of five bells rang out over this very rural setting adjacent to the parkland of Hardwick Hall. One bell, the fifth, has been calling the faithful to worship at the church for over four hundred years, since it was cast in 1590, by Henry Oldfield of Nottingham. And that was the year before Bess of Hardwick began the building of her new Hall at Hardwick. Two of the others, the sixth and the tenor bell, were hung in the tower during the seventeenth century. The sixth, cast in 1615, when James VI of Scotland was in his twelfth year as King James I of England, and the tenor bell, cast in 1664, just four years after the restoration of the Monarchy, under Charles II.

Sometime in 1974 the idea was germinated of adding a new treble to the peal of five. Upon consultation with various bodies it was found that it would also be feasible to add three front bells and so put a full octave in the tower. There was certainly room in the tower but other factors such as cost, and expertise, needed to be considered seriously. An offer was eventually received that would utilise three redundant bells available from Hallam Fields, near Ilkeston. After much consideration this offer was taken up. The three bells, along with the five to be taken from the tower, would eventually have to be taken to the foundry of John Taylor & Co, Loughborough, for re-tuning. In the meantime it was agreed to provide a new steel frame and to hang the bells on ball bearings, use new hollow section cast-iron headstocks and fittings. The work of making and erecting the new frame and the re-hanging of the eight bells on their return from the bell foundry, it was agreed, would be undertaken by the local ringers with the help of friends. This was a tremendous and courageous undertaking to tackle. But, in addition, it was also necessary to raise over £2000 in order to defray the expense of materials, etcetera. So a two pronged appeal project began. By August 1975 the bells were dismantled and taken to Taylor's foundry and the fund raising well organised. Mr Frederick Pembleton, ably assisted by Mr. Leonard Edwards and friends, continued making steady progress with engineering the new frame and the removal of the old oak frame and other preparatory work in the tower. The bells were returned and hung in the new steel frame which had been erected in the tower during the early spring of 1976.

The Service of Re-Dedication was conducted by the Bishop of Derby, assisted by the vicar, Rev. Michael Brinkworth, on Sunday, June 20th, 1976. A truly wonderful achievement by any standard, and an exercise in the combined use of skill, talent and generous gifts. The bells are inscribed:-

Treble   To the Glory of God. Taylor, 1911
          Diameter 1ft.9ins. Weight.2cwt.0qrs.7lbs.

2nd.   Fear God Honour the King. Taylor, 1911.
          Diameter 1ft.10ins. Weight.2cwt.1qr.15lbs.

3rd.   John Taylor and Co., Founders, Loughborough. 1905.
          Diameter 2ft.0 $^1/_8$ ins. Weight. 2cwt.3qrs.14lbs.

4th.   John Taylor and Co., Loughborough. 1887.
          Diameter 2ft.3¼ins. Weight.4cwt.2qrs.0lbs.

5th.   Jesus be our Spede. 1590.
          Bell mark of Henry Oldfield of Nottingham.
          Diameter 2ft.2 $^{11}/_{16}$ins. Weight.3cwt.0qrs.21lbs.

6th.   God Save his Church. 1615.
          Diameter 2ft.5¼ins. Weight.4cwt.1qr.11lbs.

7th.   D Hedderly, Founder.
          Below the haunch the initials D.H.
          Diameter 2ft.9¼ins. Weight.5cwt.3qrs.23lbs.

Tenor   I.H.S. Nazarenus Rex Judaeorum. 1664.
Bell mark of George Oldfield I of Nottingham.
Diameter 2ft. 11½ins. Weight. 7cwt.2qrs.7lbs.

The first three bells are those acquired from the redundant peal at Hallam Fields. The fourth bell marks the Golden Jubilee of the reign of Queen Victoria in 1887. The fifth, as we have already mentioned, is the oldest bell, dating from the thirty second year of the Reign on Queen Elizabeth I. Henry Oldfield (I) died in 1590 and was succeeded by his son, Henry Oldfield (II), who carried on the bell-founding business in Nottingham until his death in 1620. This fifth bell could therefore have been cast by either father or son. The inscription is of no help as it was frequently used by both of them, and to compound the mystery further both had the same initials.

There is no doubt that the sixth bell was cast by Henry Oldfield II. The initials D.H. below the haunch of the seventh bell are those of Daniel Hedderly whose family had a bell foundry in Derby and Bawtry long before Thomas Hedderly took bellfounding into Nottingham in 1742. The seventh bell therefore dates from early in the eighteenth century. The tenor bell, hung just four years after the restoration of Charles II, no doubt celebrated the freedom of the Church of England from the yoke of Puritanism.

In the bell chamber, in a separate frame and hung for chiming only, hangs a small bell. For many years this bell hung in the bell-cote above the mission church of St. Andrew's, Doe Lea. It weighs approximately fifty-six pounds and carries no inscription but is thought to have been cast by Taylor's during the latter part of the nineteenth century.

In 1887 two events happened. The new treble was added to make a ring of five bells and thereby gave the ringers an opportunity to gain experience in the ringing of Doubles methods. And, secondly, the keen band that emerged obviously set about learning to ring the bells in the Change Ringing manner because they affiliated to the East Derbyshire Association of Change Ringers.

Numerous peals have been rung on the bells. On May 10th, 1930 a peal of 5040 changes of Doubles was rung by a visiting band. It comprised 960 changes of St. Simon's; 1200 changes of Plain Bob; 1200 changes of Old Doubles and 1680 changes of Grandsire. The Ringers were William Parks, treble; Arthur Smithson, 2nd; Hubert Bailey, 3rd; Wilfred Riley, 4th; and Frederick Knowles who conducted the peal ringing the tenor. It was completed in two hours and forty-two minutes.

In the year before the decision was made to augment the bells to an octave the local band rang a peal of 5040 changes, consisting of two hundred and forty changes in each of nineteen methods. This was quite an achievement, especially as three of the band, Mrs. Dorothy M. Edwards, Ron Wilson and Stephen G. Smith were also ringing in their first ever peal. But, in the following year, another peal was rung on the five bells which consisted of thirty-five methods. So noteworthy was this peal that it is recorded here for posterity.

East Derbyshire and West Nottinghamshire Association
of Church Bell Ringers.
Founded 1887.
On Saturday, March 23, 1974, in two hours, 44 minutes,
at the Church of St. John the Baptist, Ault Hucknall.
A Peal of Doubles, 5040 Changes,
being in thirty five methods as follows :-

One Extent each of :-

Reverse Quirister Bob	Ault Hucknall
Glapwell Place	Reverse Morning Star Bob
Maltby	Chevasse
Montgomeryshire Place	Callender
St Bartholomew	Reverse All saints
Reverse Minster Place	St. Sebastian
Westminster II	Blackburn Place
Dragon	St Hillary
New Bob	Huntspill
Blaisden	St. Vedast
St. Owens Place	Reverse St. Julian
Reverse Union	Reverse St. Faith
St. Simon	St. Martin
Eynesbury	St. Osmund

Two extents each of :-

St. Nicholas	Winchendon Place
Huntley	St. Remigius
Plain Bob	Reverse Canterbury Pleasure
Grandsire	

Ron Wilson	Treble	Dorothy M.Edwards	3rd.
Frank Bradley	2nd	Doreen Bradley	4th.
Frederick Pembleton+	Tenor		

Conducted by Doreen Bradley.
+ First Peal. Most methods for ringers of treble and three.
Rung by the regular Sunday Service Band.

Wednesday, March 16th, 1977 was the day when the eight bells were first rung to a peal. 5056 Changes of Plain Bob Major. It took two hours and forty-eight minutes to complete. Conducted by Frederick Pembleton, it was his first peal of Major ringing an inside bell, and also the first peal he had conducted. Since this eventful peal Fred has rung well in excess of sixty such peals. It was also the first peal attempt by Miss Alison C. Edwards, so it was quite an achievement. The ringers were:-

Alison C. Edwards	Treble	Stephen J. Smith	5th.
Herbert T. Rooke	2nd.	Peter L.R. Hayward	6th.
Doreen Bradley	3rd.	Brynley A. Richards	7th.
Frank Bradley	4th.	Frederick Pembleton	Tenor.

On October 29th, 1977 another peal was rung on the eight bells to commemorate the ninetieth anniversary of the East Derbyshire and West Nottinghamshire Association's founding, together with its fifty years of affiliation to the Central

Council of Church Bell Ringers. But the peal showing best the achievements of the local band was rung by them on Sunday, February 24th, 1980:-

A Peal of Plain Bob Minor, 5040 Changes,
being seven different extents.

Christine M. Pembleton	Treble	Dorothy M. Edwards	4th.
Alison C. Edwards	2nd.	Stephan J. Smith	5th.
Leonard Edwards	3rd.	Frederick Pembleton	Tenor.

Conducted by Frederick Pembleton.

First peal on an 'inside' bell 2nd and 3rd. First peal of Minor for ringers of 2nd, 3rd and 5th. First peal of Minor by a Sunday Service Band at this tower.

During the late 1940's and into the 1950's the tower had a band of young ringers who were led by Mr Jack Cooper. Jack was also churchwarden and served on the committee of the East Derbyshire and West Nottinghamshire Association of Change Ringers.

Enthusiasm is the key to any successful band of ringers and this was certainly the case at Ault Hucknall in the early 1970's. Two ringers experienced in method ringing, Miss Doreen Armstrong and Mr Frank Bradley, joined the team in 1972. Over the following twelve months, at their introduction, many new methods were rung on the five bells. 1973 saw rapid progression and the ringing of quarter peals prior to some of the Sunday services became normal routine. Then, in 1974 no fewer than forty-seven quarter peals were rung, again many were prior to Sunday services. By strange coincidence, they included the ringing of the same number of different methods.

Enthusiasm for method ringing was paramount, as was the desire to augment the bells from five to a peal of six in order to progress further into the field of change ringing, and the Minor methods, the extra bell would allow the ringers to practice. But, how was a small parish going to raise the inevitable cost. The skills in engineering and other crafts available among members of the ringing team could be used to help with the removal of the bulky old oak frame from the tower and the structural assembly of a new metal frame. This would considerably reduce the cost but there would still be other expense involved. So, how was money to be raised to cover the extra requirements? With equal zest the ringers not directly involved with the structural work set about raising the estimated £2000 needed by early 1976. The collecting and selling of waste paper had been lucrative, but, in 1974 the bottom fell out of this market. Jumble sales? The first raised £183, but only after endless searching, sorting, pricing and much effort by all members of the ringers, their families and friends. Over the next two years these same relatives and friends kindly undertook miles of knitting, sewing, baking and the growing of plants. Coffee mornings, bring and buys, the sale of inscribed pens, shirts, frilly nighties and the sale of scrap metal which produced more funds. Then the parish council boosted funds by donating £500, and several private gifts were received and slowly the estimated amount was raised.

Whilst the fund raising was in progress so was the work being undertaken on the frame and fittings. Earlier we read of the old frame being removed and the new one being installed. What we did not read earlier was about the effort involved. How the old frame of oak was dismantled piece by piece and manhandled from the bell-chamber, lowered to the ground and removed and disposed of. How the steel for the new frame was acquired, delivered, cut into pieces of the required size, drilled, fashioned then assembled. How the frame was actually erected in the garden of one of the ringers before being dismantled and delivered piece by piece to be hoisted into the tower and then reassembled in the bell-chamber to wait whilst delivery of the bells and fittings from Taylor's bell foundry in Loughborough was attended to. How each of the eight bells, and remember the tenor bell weighs over 7cwts, were hoisted from the delivery lorry, manhandled round the church before being hoisted into the tower to await its turn to be lifted into the new frame and for all the necessary fittings to be attached. This done, fittings such as wheels, sliders, stays, ground pulleys and rope guides were installed and when everything was in order, and only then, were the ropes attached. The ropes fall in an almost perfect circle as they enter through ceiling apertures into the ringing chamber. And last, but by no means the least, of how the ringing chamber had in the meantime been refurbished and painted.

The whole task was nothing less than a mammoth DIY job, planned, master-minded and carried out with the utmost professionalism by Mr. Frederick Pembleton, ably assisted by Mr. Leonard Edwards and members of the ringing team, their families and friends.

Over twenty years have now passed since this project was completed and DIY projects with regard to the restoration and augmentation of bells has become more commonplace. But, it must be said that what happened here during the first half of the 1970's was indeed a most remarkable and successful venture. Its ultimate success rests firmly upon the skill of one man, Frederick Pembleton, and it was he alone who had the foresight combined with the confidence and necessary engineering expertise, to undertake and see the project through to a very successful conclusion. Fred, I know, would be the first to say that he could not have achieved what was completed without the full support of his wife Christine, the St. John the Baptist team of ringers, Stephan Smith, Doreen and Frank Bradley, Len and Dorothy Edwards with Alison and Nicholas, or without the support of the vicar, Rev. Michael Brinkworth, the churchwardens and members of the P.C.C. and numerous parishioners and members of the ringing fraternity, all of whom gave, as Fred did, their services entirely voluntarily.

Elsewhere I have written a potted history of several local craftsmen who have been directly connected with the three dozen belfries under review. Of those mentioned all have been directly connected with the casting of our bells, the Heathcotes and Smiths of Chesterfield, the Mellors, Oldfields and Hedderlys of Nottingham, Midworth of Mansfield and Wheeldon of Derby. Of the bell-hangers employed at the time by these craftsmen we know almost nothing of their persons yet we still constantly meet with their skills in every one of our belfries. For, whenever we have need to be in a bell-chamber their craftsmanship surrounds us and still stands in working order for all to see. The simple fact that for several centuries our bells have rung out over village and town stands testimony to these unknown men. But what about the craftsmen working in our towers today? They, I think, deserve to have their work recorded and I am proud to be able to include this short account of a local twentieth century bell-hanger.

In the summer of 1997 television news covered the story of the re-hanging of Great Tom, the giant hour bell, weighing five tons, eight hundredweights, at Lincoln Cathedral. And, who was the bell-hanger? None other than Frederick Pembleton of Glapwell.

Since the augmentation at Ault Hucknall Fred has been called upon to carry out inspection and the overhaul of bell fittings and frames in many towers. In the early days, and as a keen ringer, he spent much time and energy helping and advising local towers on a voluntary basis. Eventually, such was the demand for his skilled engineering expertise that he launched into providing a complete and full-time bell maintenance and engineering service. This has taken him into belfries throughout England and Wales. From his workshop in Warsop, Fred now operates the most comprehensive tower, frame and bell maintenance service, where jobs, both large and small, receive his personal attention with the same enthusiasm as did his local belfry over twenty years ago. He is renowned for his skill at fashioning one-off parts, and for his approach to bell-hanging problems where stress to tower fabric is of the utmost importance. Although completely independent Fred works closely with the bell founders of today.

Finally, an amusing little incident, but not to those concerned, happened a while ago when eight ringers gathered in the tower to ring a peal on the bells. Established in the ringing chamber and with the peal well into its two and three quarter hour course some 'kind' person stealthily crept into the lower tower and secured the trap door leading directly into the ringing chamber. When the ringers finished their peal and were ready to leave they found themselves imprisoned. After thought, they removed several ropes from the bells, ascended to the roof of the tower whereupon one of the more agile and younger members of the team abseiled down the outside and freed his fellow ringers.

The logo of Bell-hanger
Frederick Pembleton

The Belfry of St. Peter, Belper

First bell cast in Mansfield. Six bells of steel. Fine pinnacles removed.
1925, complete octave cast.

Standing upon its hillside in the centre of the town, the tall slender tower of St. Peter's Church has an appearance of not being quite complete without its former pinnacles. Built in 1824 this western tower rises to a height of one hundred feet and is some twenty feet square at its base. Built of local dressed stone taken from Hunger Hill Quarry about half a mile away, it is of the Decorated style, and is supported by diagonal buttresses which by a series of set-offs terminate at the string course beneath the parapet. A decorative frieze of five stone panels lies beneath the string course and above the tall recessed two light bell openings on each face. This frieze design is repeated at a lower stage beneath the bell openings. The west door of the tower also forms the main entrance into the church which is known as a 'Waterloo Church'. Churches thus termed were built throughout the country out of the indemnity received from the Napoleonic wars.

The octagonal stumps of the former pinnacles can be seen at each angle of the tower. These were surmounted with tall piers from which crocketed spires added greatly to the tower and the fine decorative stonework panels of the castellated parapet. The whole being an imposing crown in perfect line with the architect's original plan. At sometime shortly after the Second World War, one of the pinnacles was found in danger of falling and as no money was forthcoming to rebuild it, or to restore the others, they were all removed.

As we enter the imposing tower porch, access to the ringing chamber and bells is on the left via a spiral stone stair. The first door leads onto an open gallery overlooking the tower vestibule. The compact but well appointed ringing chamber is immediately above.

A clock, costing £130, was installed by Mr Ellerby of Ashbourne in 1825 but this was replaced in 1844 by one supplied by Messrs Moore and Son, of Clerkenwell for £150. It was set going on Christmas eve. One of the four gilded dials fits snugly into a square recessed masonry panel on each face of the tower and is protected by a hoodmould.

Today, the tower possesses a good peal of eight bells which are excellently maintained. The tenor bell weighing 14cwts. 0qrs. 26lbs.

The first bell to be placed in the tower was one cast by Samuel Midworth of Mansfield in 1831. This bell was noted as being of a fine tone. It arrived in Belper on Holy Cross Day, September 14th. and when weighed locally, on Barnse machine, was found to be 19cwts. 3qtrs. 0 lbs. The total cost of £160 was raised by subscription. This was made up of £145.5s.0d. for casting the bell, delivery from

74

Mansfield and installation. No mention being made as to the cost of the frame etc. A new floor was placed in the tower at the same time by W.G. Strutt and J. Strutt at a cost of £14.1s.10½p.

Samuel Midworth had an iron foundry in Leeming Street, Mansfield and is known to have cast only a few bells. The treble bell of the old four at Warsop was cast by him in 1812 but recast by Taylor's of Loughborough in 1913, so it is quite probable that the only bells remaining that were cast by Midworth are at Skegby and at Arnold for whom he cast one in 1841.

In 1861 St Peter's discarded the Midworth bell in favour of a peal of six bells bought from Naylor Vickers of Sheffield at a cost of £334. These bells were made of steel. This was a most drastic departure from the norm and was quite an adventure at the time, for very little was known about the use of steel in bell founding. Bell-metal, which is a mixture of 78% copper with 22% of tin, was and still is the usual alloy for casting bells.

For the installation of the six steel bells Adam Ryde of Belper was employed to make the oak bell-frame.

Three years earlier Naylor Vickers had provided a ring of six bells for Eastwood in Nottinghamshire. That peal was believed to have been the first ring of steel bells to have been hung in England. Further steel bells were placed in the newly built tower at Bamford, Derbyshire at about the same period. These bells are about to be replaced as were the bells at Eastwood in 1904, (The reader will find more regarding steel bells in the chapter on bellfounders.) Sadly, almost nothing is known about the peal of steel bells here. We know not of how they handled nor of how they sounded or of why they were eventually scrapped. But scrapped they were.

The six steel bells at St. Peter's were replaced in 1925 by the present peal of eight. The complete octave was cast by John Taylor and Co., of Loughborough and tuned to the key of F#. They do credit to their founder. The bells are inscribed:

Treble	Venite.
	The gift of A.M. and E. Sanders.
2nd.	Jubilate.
	Francis J. Jackson, 1854.
	Francis F. Jackson, 1858.
	Helen F. Jackson, 1898.
3rd.	In Excelsis Gloria.
	In memoriam
	Robert Hey Vicar,
	1845 - 1885
	and Maria Jane, his wife.
4th	AD Majorem Dei Gloriam,
	From the Haynes family,
	in memory of our
	Father and Mother, J. Haynes E.A. Haynes.

5th.	Gloria in Excelsis Deo et in Terra Pax Hominibus Bonae Voluntatis.
	Vicars M. Tunstall,
	R. Hey,
	F.A. Friend,
	S.H. Clark,
	J.A. Cooper.

6th.	Deus Vobiscum.
	A.D. 1925.
	The Parish Bell.
	J.A. Cooper, Vicar.
	H. Mellor, E. Gee, Churchwardens.

7th.	Te Deum Laudamus.
	Given in memory of
	John Hunter, 1811 - 1886
	and his wife
	Margaret Hunter, 1820 - 1908
	by their six children.

Tenor	Laus Deo.
	Presented by
	George Herbert Strutt
	1925.

One can rightly assume that a keen band of ringers was in being at St. Peter's from 1861 when the six steel bells were installed but what methods were being rung remains a mystery. Obviously they were getting to grips with Change Ringing and presumably a selection of standard Minor methods was rung on the bells.

After the octave was cast and hung in the belfry in 1925 a very active team of ringers was established. Among the band were John Dyer, Ernest Fletcher, Charles Kirk, Frederick Spencer, John A. Spencer and Forester W. Walkerdine. Another keen member of the band was Percy Dudley who had rung for many years on the old steel six and who rang the sixth bell of the octave in this peal on Wednesday, December 5th, 1928. It took two hours and fifty-eight minutes to complete.

5040 Changes of Stedman Triples.

John H. Swinfield	Treble	Ernest W. Beadsmore	5th.
Charles Draper	2nd.	Percy Dudley	6th.
Maurice Swinfield	3rd.	James S. Hutchby	7th.
John P. Tarlton	4th.	Henry Fletcher	Tenor.

Brook's Variation of Thurstan's Four-part.
Conducted by Maurice Swinfield.

Many such peals have been rung on the bells but never as many as in the last few years since the installation of adjustable soundproof shuttering to the bell openings. The brainchild of tower captain, Arnold Morley, Arnold designed and experimented with numerous systems before he successfully devised the one now in use at St. Peter's. Its efficiency is best defined by the fact that a peal of over 5000 changes is rung on the bells almost every week without complaint. And this, in spite of private houses, bungalows and businesses being situated within a stone's throw of the belfry. Then, when the bells are required for church service ringing, weddings etc. the soundproofing is rolled back and the public hear the fine peal of bells as normal. Arnold often rings the fifth bell to many of these peals and at a recent count was fast approaching the ringing of his five-hundredth peal.

King George VI died on February 6th, 1952 and his funeral took place at Windsor on February 15th. On Saturday, February 9th a band of ringers assembled in St. Peter's belfry to ring a peal in memoriam. With the eight bells fully muffled they rang them at a relatively slow pace in keeping with the sad occasion, taking three hours and fourteen minutes to complete the peal:-

A Peal of 5184 Changes of Double Norwich Court Bob Major.

Alan Taylor	Treble	Albert E. Thompson	5th.
Jack Bailey	2nd.	Harold Taylor	6th.
William H.T. King	3rd.	Mark J. Barker	7th.
Francis R. Lowe	4th.	Philip H. Whitaker	Tenor.

Composed by J.W. Washbrook. Conducted by Jack Bailey.

As with many towers, bands of ringers become established for a period of time and then ebb again as life unfolds and this has been apparent at St. Peter's over the years. During the late fifties and early in the sixties a strong team was in residence. Among them, Jack Dark, Anthony Nicholson, Keith Yates, Harold Hunt, Richard Fox, Peter Taylor, John Morley, Peter Davies and Paul Melbourne. Arnold Morley was already tower secretary at this period and is still holding the office as I write. During the 1980's we find George Pickwell, Gill and Graeme Hughes, Philip Hughes and John Booth joining the band. A further injection of young learners came in the early 1990's with Barbara Pickwell taking up the challenge of bell-handling and change ringing in order that she and George could enjoy a common interest together. During this later period Gill and Graeme Hughes have undertaken the very difficult and exacting task of organising the training of learners at St Peter's and it is great to see the results of their labours as numerous of their learners make a successful attempt at ringing in their first quarter peal.

An interesting Staffordshire Ware jug depicting hunting scenes is on display in the ringing chamber. It is thought to date from about 1860 but as for what purpose and function it had with the ringers has been lost in time.

The Belfry of St. Werburgh, Blackwell

One of oldest church foundations in Diocese. 1824: Order insists on total demolition.
Architect begs pinnacles be put on new tower.
1945: Victory in Far East celebrated by Peal. Festival of Britain marked by Peal.

Looking at the rebuilt tower of St. Werburgh's Church today, it is difficult to imagine that on this ancient site is most probably one of the oldest church foundations to be found in the Diocese.

There are few churches dedicated to St.Werburgh, Princess of Mercia and Abbess of the Convent of Ely who died in 699A.D. She was buried first at Hanbury, in Staffordshire. Then, on the approach of the Danes to Repton two centuries later, her body was removed to Chester and placed in a little Saxon church for safekeeping. This church became known as St. Werburgh's and today is of course the beautiful cathedral, the shrine of St. Werburgh being situated within the Lady Chapel.

It is believed that the Normans severely suppressed any respect that was found in the locality for the Saxon saint, to the extent of destroying buildings and replacing them with their own.

By the end of the first quarter of the nineteenth century the church was very much in need of repair. We find recorded the contents of a letter written from Shrewsbury on August 4th, 1823, by Archdeacon Butler, complaining of the very dangerous state of the church. Then, on June 5th, 1824, after much correspondence, his final order was written insisting the building be taken down bodily and rebuilt. Almost two centuries later one just wonders if demolition was in the best interests of the parish. But, the fact remains that we now have a tower built in 1828 on one of the oldest consecrated sites in the Diocese.

The embattled tower, built without the support of external buttresses, was for many years uncrowned by pinnacles. This caused the architect, Daniel Hodkin some concern. For, when nearing completion he wrote the churchwardens pointing out that in his opinion the tower would look unfinished without them, and begging them: "I hope you and the parishioners will think with me that the tower will remain in an unfinished state if the four pinnacles are not put on, and you will always wish they had been done when you see the effect so much different. The situation of the church will cause them to be showed at so grate a distance. I cannot take leave without begging you to raise your spirits and say with one voice we will have them done and look as respectful as any of our neighbours." But the tower remained uncrowned of pinnacles for many years after it was rebuilt in 1828.

Of the old tower we find only one note. Bassano visited Blackwell about 1700 and noted the keys of St. Peter cut on a large square stone above the belfry window on the north side of the tower. Dr Cox writing around 1875 and after asking about the neighbourhood was of the opinion that the old tower and much of the body of the church had been of Norman design.

It is probable that at the time of Bassano's visit three bells hung in the tower. One bell, which by 1875 was known to be very severely cracked and therefore in need of re-casting. It carried an inscription that was only partly legible, "UBI EST SONUS." A second bell, bearing the mark of the Nottingham founder, Henry Oldfield with the legend, "Jesus be our Spede, 1587,"and a third bell was inscribed, "God save his Church, 1611."

In 1901 two treble bells were added. These were cast by John Taylor at the Loughborough foundry and commemorated the reign of Queen Victoria. In 1945 the same foundry cast another treble to augment the peal to six. Of the original three bells the cracked bell was recast in 1901, the Oldfield bell became the fifth and the tenor was recast. This bell weighs 7cwts.2qrs.0lbs.and has a diameter of 34½ inches and is tuned to note A.

The first peal, consisting of 5040 Changes, to be rung on the bells took place on Wednesday, July 25th, 1928. It took two hours forty five minutes to complete. As there were only five bells the peal was of Doubles and consisted of 720 changes each of Stedman and St. Simon's Bob; 1440 changes of Plain Bob and 2160 changes of Grandsire. The ringers were :-

Thomas W. Hopson	Treble	John W. England	4th.
Fred. W. Knowles	2nd.	Herbert G. Fretwell	Tenor.
William Swain	3rd.	(Conductor)	

Over thirty peals have been rung on the bells for the East Derbyshire and West Nottinghamshire Association. Two ringers, Arthur Smithson and Wilfred Riley both rang their first peal together on the bells in 1928 and commemorated fifty years of service as bellringers by ringing together in another peal on the bells.

On Wednesday, August 15th, 1945, the bells rang out in celebration of the end of hostilities in The Second World War. On the very day, the local ringers climbed the belfry steps and proclaimed victory. It was one of only a handful of peals of 5040 Changes that was rung in the country actually on V.J. Day. It was also one of the last peals to be rung on the five bells.

On Wednesday, August 15, 1945, in two hours 48 minutes,
A Peal of Doubles, 5040 Changes,
being 2400 changes of Grandsire and 2640 of Plain Bob.

Willis Bramley +	Treble	William Steele x	3rd.
Arthur Smithson	2nd.	Frederick Boam +	4th.
Albert Wheeler +	Tenor		

Conducted by Arthur Smithson.
Rung to celebrate Victory in the Far East that day.
+ First Peal. x First peal on 'inside' bell.

79

Three years after the augmentation to six the local band rang the first peal of Minor upon the bells.

On Sunday, October 24th, 1948, in two hours fifty minutes,
A peal of Minor, 5040 Changes,
being two extents each of Oxford and Kent Treble Bob,
and three extents of Plain Bob.

William Steele	Treble	Willis Bramley	4th.
Leonard Fisher	2nd.	Arthur Smithson	5th.
Frederick Boam	3rd.	Albert Wheeler	Tenor.

Conducted by Arthur Smithson.
First peal on bells since augmentation to a ring of six.
Rung in memorium to Rev. T.S. Hudson, Vicar for thirty seven years.

The bells, again rung by the Sunday Service Band, rang out in peal to mark the Festival of Britain on May 7th, 1951, and at the homecoming of H.M. Queen Elizabeth II in 1954. The peal rung to commemorate the Festival of Britain in 1951 consisted of:-

A Peal of Minor, 5040 Changes,
being two extents each of Oxford Treble Bob and Kent Treble Bob
and three extents of Plain Bob.

Fred. Boam	Treble	Mrs. F.D.A. Boam	4th.
Alfred Tomlinson	2nd.	Frank Bradley	5th.
Arthur Smithson	3rd.	Albert Wheeler	Tenor.

Conducted by Frank Bradley.

Preserved in the ringing chamber, and in excellent condition, is a framed copy of the Rules and Objects of the East Derbyshire Association of Change Ringers, founded in 1887. The ringers of Blackwell affiliated in 1903, shortly after the peal of five bells were hung in the tower and from that date have taken a leading roll in the Association's affairs. Arthur Smithson having held the office of President, and Wilfred Riley, the office of Ringing Master.

In October 1977 Wilfred Riley and Arthur Smithson completed fifty years of ringing together. As teenagers they both began ringing at St Werburgh's Church. Arthur suffered a wartime accident in which he lost his right hand. This might have threatened his ringing career but for his determination and courage to master afresh the art of bell-handling. With an appliance fitted to the stump of his right arm he mastered anew the controlling of a bell and went on to ring in numerous peals. Arthur was elected as Tower Captain in 1931 and continued to maintain the tower, bells and clock for upwards of fifty-five years. Wilf, whilst always faithful to St. Werburgh's belfry was the prime mover in training a group of young ringers at Tibshelf over many years. It is to his credit that this young band rang numerous quarter peals as a regular feature of their Sunday Service ringing. It was also due to Wilf's dedication to this young band that Elizabeth Hill, at the age of twelve rang the treble to a peal of Plain Bob Minor in 1977 and in the following year her sister Sarah, aged fourteen, repeated the performance.

To commemorate fifty years as ringers, Arthur and Wilf rang in the following peal on the bells of St. Werburgh's. It was brought home in two hours and forty-seven minutes on Tuesday, October 25, 1977.

East Derbyshire and West Nottinghamshire Association.
A peal of Minor, 5040 Changes.
Being one extent each of Cambridge Surprise, Oxford Treble Bob,
St. Clements College Bob, Kent Treble Bob, Single Oxford Bob
and two extents of Plain Bob.

Arthur Smithson	Treble	Frederick Pembleton	4th.
David C. Lester	2nd.	Eric J. Sterland	5th.
Wilfred Riley	3rd.	Adrian Dempster	Tenor.

Conducted by Adrian Dempster.

Arthur rang some three dozen peals and when, after fifty years of ringing, he was asked by a local newspaper reporter how he had managed to overcome the difficulty of handling a bell after losing his right hand, he, in his usual unassuming way, replied, "It was a bit of a problem, he admitted, but gradually I got used to it, although I still can't work the heaviest bells."

The Belfry of St. Mary and St.Laurance, Bolsover

A fine broach spire. Handbells presented. Quick repair of stay, at wedding.

First recorded peal for Association.

"The flames attacked the tower, and as the wooden framework was consumed, the bells fell one by one."

This sad and quite frightening item of news was taken from a contemporary account of the serious fire which ravaged the church early on Sunday, January 24th, 1897. The fire started in the vestry at about three o'clock in the morning and quickly spread, severely damaging the interior of the church, the clock, and soon reaching the four bells hanging in the thirteenth century tower.

The tower, built of light grey stone during the early English period of the thirteenth century is supported by broad buttresses covering the angles. One, at the south-west corner, is enlarged to accommodate the spiral stair giving internal access to the ringing chamber. A low broad shouldered octagonal broach spire springs straight from the walls of the tower. The spire has two tiers of wooden louvred dormers on each cardinal face, one tier is high in the spire whilst the lower tier lies between the huge broaches. The tower has two light louvred bell openings and on the west a lancet window and a door, with the double chamfered arch running into small columns. The spire is considered to be of a later date than the tower although it is thought to form part of the original design. A further fire in 1960 damaged the church but fortunately the tower, clock and bells escaped.

Situated between the bell chamber opening and the lower dormer, on the west and north face of the tower, is a lozenge panel wrought in metal. Within the filigree of each lozenge is accommodated the clock's dial. The Roman numerals, minute points and clock hands being highlighted in gilt. The clock was last overhauled in 1994 and its mechanism drive converted from a hand operation to the use of electricity at the bequest of a former churchwarden, Jim Wright. A tablet of brass, placed to the south of the tower arch within the nave, records the event.

Restoration after the first fire was completed by the following year, and on September 21st, 1898, the church re-opened. The tower containing a peal of six new bells and a new clock. The church had also been furnished with new pews and a new organ. Today, the organ pipes are accommodated on a gallery that completely fills the lower middle section of the tower and projects on piers that extend out into the nave. When viewed from the chancel step the organ pipes take in the full width of the nave and together with the painted timber roof members hide the tower arch completely from view. The base of the tower is used as a vestry and a fine oak screen, with sadly, its top section masked by the heavy organ gallery, is worth noting. Another brass tablet informs us:- This screen was erected by the Parishioners

82

to the Glory of God and in memory of Joseph Revill. For many years warden of this church, who died January 13th, 1911, and his wife, Anne Revill who died January 9th, 1914.

The old peal of four bells carried the inscriptions :-

1. Hic Campana Sacra Fiat Trinitate Beatae.
   The founder's mark, in the form of a shield, of Richard Mellour of Nottingham between the initials N.D.

2. All Glori, Honor, and prayse be given to God, 1585.
   The founder's mark of Henry Oldfield of Nottingham.

3. Te Deum Laudamus/ A.D.1585.
   The founder's mark of Henry Oldfield of Nottingham.

4. Henry Ba low. 1616 God save his church.
   The bell mark of George Oldfield.

The old inscriptions extracted from Rev. Charles Cox's book, Churches of Derbyshire, published in 1875, do not necessarily place them in order and there is some doubt as to the fourth bell being cast by George Oldfield as he did not succeed his father, Henry, in the business until 1620. Henry Oldfield had a bellfoundry in Nottingham in 1539 and was succeeded by his son and grandson both named Henry. They carried on as founders until George Oldfield took over in 1620. Earlier, Richard Mellours had a bellfoundry in Nottingham from 1488 until 1508 and was Mayor in 1499 and 1506. A brief history of the Nottingham founders is the subject of a separate chapter.

In 1898 the six new bells were cast by John Taylor and Co., Loughborough. The tenor weighing 14cwts. 3qrs. 1lb. in the key of G. They are inscribed :-

Treble	Jesus be our speed.
	F.J.Turner, Chairman.
2nd.	Soli Deo Gloria in Excelsis.
3rd.	Hic Campana Sacra Fiat Trinitate Beata.
4th.	Hoc Aedificium Igne Deletur Adix Kal, Feb.MDCCCXCVII.
5th.	Deus Fac Salvam Eclesiam.
	J.R.Simken B.T.N. Tatlow, Ch.Wardens.
Tenor	Te Deum Laudamus.
	Thomas Charles Hill, Vicar.

Four years later two trebles were added to complete the octave. These were cast by Taylor's at Loughborough and are inscribed :-

Treble	Adeste Fidelis.
	A.V.Colston, Vicar. 1902.
2nd	Vivat Edvardvs Vii
	Rex et Imperator
	August 9 1902.
	T.N. Tatlow, J.Revill, Churchwardens.

The dedication of these two trebles took place on Saturday, December 27th. 1902.

Early in the day ringers began to assemble from various places, and the six were kept ringing to different methods ranging from London Surprise to Oxford Treble Bob. As service time drew near it was found that ringers were present from Chesterfield, Eckington, Norton, Staveley, Sheffield, Killamarsh, Treeton, North Wingfield, Ripley and the local band.

At 5p.m. all were present in church for the service which was to have been taken by the Lord Bishop of Derby, but owing to the death of the Archbishop of Canterbury he was unable to be present, so the Rev. Canon Hacking, Vicar of Chesterfield, kindly consented to preach and was assisted by the Revs. A.V. Colston (Vicar) and F Brodhurst. A shortened form of evensong was used.

As the congregation was leaving the bells were rung by C.H. Hattersley, W. Burger, W. Lomas, J. Holman, G.W. Bemrose, A Knights, G. Holmes and G. Goodwin to a touch of 312 changes of Stedman Triples conducted by C.H. Hattersley.

One of the prime movers in getting method ringing off the ground at Bolsover was Thomas Bettison. Thomas had moved to Bolsover in 1901 and joined the band at the time when the augmentation from six to eight bells was being put in hand. Such was his enthusiasm of change ringing that within a short period of joining the band the quality and improvement of ringing was most marked. However, his time in Bolsover was short and on Saturday, July 7th, 1906, on the occasion of him leaving the parish, we find the ringers presenting him with a pocket set of handbells. These were cast by Messrs Shaw, of Bradford, and accommodated in a leather bag, suitably inscribed to show a token of the ringers gratitude.

The local band at this time were again keen on showing their appreciation by giving another small sets of handbells. A report in Bell News on July 25th, 1908 informs us:- "On Tuesday, June 50th, a very interesting ceremony took place in the belfry, when Mr. F.E. Parsons, on behalf of the whole company, in a few appropriate words, asked Mr G.W. Moss to accept a small set of handbells which had been subscribed for by his brother ringers, to mark the occasion of his marriage with Miss L. Morris, which interesting event took place at Harwich on Whit-Monday. The bells which are a very nice set, were supplied by Messrs. Shaw, of Bradford, and reflects great credit on them for their tone and finish. The tenor bears the following: 'Presented to Mr. G.W. Moss, by the Bolsover band, on the occasion of his marriage, June 8th, 1898'." The dates are quoted as reported, also the tener! Mr. Moss in thanking the ringers expressed the hope that they would be able to score many peals on the handbells.

The Bellringer, another weekly journal, dated June 1st, 1907, gives an account of the unveiling and dedication of a marble tablet recording a peal of Bob Major rung by the local company prior to the induction by the Bishop of Southwell of the Rev. B.S. Batty to the living of Bolsover. The cost of the tablet and other improvements consisting of match-boarding the ringing chamber walls to a height of six feet, providing a cupboard, substituting chairs for the plank forms, relighting the belfry and covering the floor with cork linoleum was £22. The tablet being the work of Mr. D. Brearley, of Deepcar, a ringer. In addition the church clock having been out of repair for a period of some four or five months was thoroughly cleaned and repaired by Messrs. Smith & Sons, Derby. The other improvements being done by the ringers and local tradesmen.

Moving on by sixty seven years and to a report in the <u>Ringing World</u>, today's bellringers' weekly journal, on May 17th, 1974, we find another instance of DIY in Bolsover. It was penned by Mr. Denis Cooper a member of the band for many years.

"We often read reports in the Ringing World of records being set with regard to long lengths, number of methods to a peal, etc., but can anybody beat what I think must be a record in another aspect of our Exercise. I refer to the fitting of a Hastings stay.

More than twenty years ago we were ringing for a wedding and had come into rounds, when a somewhat inexperienced ringer arrived. The ringer of the seventh offered him his rope and during the transfer the stay was broken. Our tower-keeper and a ringer who is also a joiner nipped up the staircase, took down the broken stay and the section from the socket and went across the road to the local undertaker, who gave permission to use his tools. They made the new stay, brought it back, fitted it and the bell was ready for ringing as the happy couple left the church. Time about twenty-five minutes.

The bridegroom was and still is a ringer, also a joiner, so he appreciated what had been done. The stay is still in use."

Two years later another item appeared in the same weekly:-

"A story from Bolsover.. It was the pre-war custom to ring a passing bell when a local inhabitant died. As soon as this was heard, a local taxi proprietor used to dash to church to find out who had passed away with a view to obtaining a bit of business.

On one occasion Stanley Slaney was ringing the bell when in dashed the taxi proprietor. - Conversation: Taxi man: 'Who's dead?' Stan: 'Nobody living in this parish'."

The first recorded peal to be rung for the East Derbyshire Association of Change Ringers was rung on the six bells on Saturday, January 26th, 1901. The bells were rung deeply muffled as a token of respect to her late Majesty Queen Victoria. The Peal of 5040 changes of Plain Bob Minor was rung in three hours and three minutes by S. Coupe, treble; C. Coupe, 2; J Goodwin, 3; F. Wagstaffe, 4; J. Severn, 5 and J. Flint ringing the tenor. A brass tablet unveiled on May 4th, 1901, by Mr. J. Bingley records the event. The peal was conducted by John Flint.

Some six weeks later, on Saturday, March 9, 1901, another Peal of 5040 Changes of Minor was rung on the bells to commemorate the erection of a new stained glass window at the east end of the church in memory of the late Baroness Bolsover by her children. The dedication of the window being held over to a later date on account of Lady Bentinck being away from home in Germany. The Peal, again conducted by John Flint, consisted of four extents of Plain Bob Minor and three of Canterbury Pleasure. It was rung in two hours and fifty minutes by F. Wagstaff, treble; W. Butler, 2nd; J. Goodwin, 3rd; J.T. Butler, 4th; J. Severn, 5th; J. Flint, tenor.

November 9th, 1902 saw the ringing of the last peal upon the six bells before their augmentation to eight by the addition of two new trebles. This was the first peal of Treble Bob Minor undertaken by the local band and quite an accomplishment for it consisted of six methods, City Delight, College Pleasure, Killamarsh, Duke of York, Kent and Oxford Treble Bob. It was rung by Silvester Coupe, treble; William Lambert, 2nd; Frank Godber, 3rd; Frank Wagstaff, 4th; Thomas Bettison, conducting from the 5th. and John Flint ringing the tenor. The peal was rung in honour of the birthday of His Majesty King Edward VII.

Seventy-five years on from the first peal an anniversary peal was rung on the bells. This was of 5040 changes of Plain Bob Major and was brought home in two hours and forty-four minutes. The ringers being:- Treble, Kenneth Hemm, 2nd; A. Robert Mewes, 3rd; Elizabeth I Lounds, 4th; Wilfred Riley, 5th; Herbert T. Rooke, 6th; E. Glyn Holdgate, 7th; Eric J. Sterland, Tenor; Brynley A. Richards. Conducted by B.A. Richards.

In 1952 John Taylor and Company were again engaged to re-hang the bells. This time they were placed on ball bearings and all the fittings were overhauled.

Two tablets fixed to the lower tower wall, on the north face, record the life of two former bellringers. Thomas Riley, 1880-1954, who was a ringer at Bolsover for forty years. Joseph Paxton, 1912-1969, who was also a regular member of the Bolsover team for many years and became a founder member of the Derby Diocesan Association of Church Bellringers when it was founded in 1946. During his membership he rang thirty-nine peals for the Association.

The Belfry of St. Mary and All Saints, Chesterfield

30,714 Changes rung in two days. Bells ring out for opening of railway.
George Stevenson centenary peal. The silent years.
This stupendous machine. Pancake Bell and Ringers' Jug.

Whichever way you turn your eye,
It always seems to be awry;
Pray, can you tell the reason why ?-
The only reason known of weight,
Is that the thing was never straight:
Nor know the people where to go,
To find the man to make it so;
Since non can furnish such a plan,
Except a perfect upright man :-
So that the spire, 'tis very plain,
For ages crooked must remain;
And while it stands, must ever be
An emblem of deformity.

The tower and spire of St. Mary and All Saints Church, Chesterfield needs little introduction. With its crooked spire rising to a height of about two hundred and twenty eight feet it is a landmark from many miles around.

Rising from the central tower the spire springs from behind a plain parapet and four octagonal pinnacles, all of which date from the fourteenth century. A "crows nest" door situated high up in the apex of the spire, on the north-east face, affords an unforgettable view in that direction. The maze of woodwork within is, in its way, sheer beauty. The warping of the spire, which some consider to be of a later occurrence, is due to each stage of its wooden frame having turned a few degrees upon the section beneath, but more about this later. The lead plates covering it are laid in an herring bone pattern which give a channelled appearance to each of the octagonal faces, when in fact, each face is quite flat.

The central tower rests on four very tall pointed arches springing from clustered pillars and all resting on the foundation of a Norman building. Externally it is supported above the intersection of the nave, chancel and transepts by shallow buttresses of three courses. The lower stage below the top of the buttresses is divided externally by two horizontal lines of receding moulding. Between these mouldings, on each face, are two single light windows of the clock chamber. The double windows of the bell-openings are of fine proportion with good tracery. The parapet is unpierced and not divided into battlements but is adorned with a band of moulding similar in character to that on the towers at Crich and Denby. To each face above the bell-opening is fixed a clock dial. Access is gained from the north transept and joined above by direct access from the churchyard by way of a flight of stone steps.

Internally, the only awareness of what rises above are the four clustered pillars at the crossing of the choir, nave and transepts, together with the tiny window over the nave arch, which gives a bird's eye view of the nave from the ringing chamber.

An interesting observation appeared in an article by Mr. H. Ryde and published in the Derbyshire Archaeological Society Journal for 1921. "Standing at the west doorway and looking to the High Alter one is surprised to what extent the choir is 'orientated' towards the north east. In fact the tower is proportionately as distorted to the north-east, as is the spire to the south-west, for no angle of the tower is rectangular. The tower arch likewise appears to lean somewhat to the north side. Whether it is really an ancient symbolical representation of the Redeemer's head so hanging on Calvary's Cross - whether the inclination is accidental, or whether a correction of the line of orientation, is another of the queries of the ancient building" At St Leonard's Church Shirland, a similar inclination occurs when viewing the chancel from the archway of the western tower. Quite independently, the author had put to him by the Rector, Rev. Chismon, when working on the redecoration of the interior of Shirland Church, the same symbolical representation as above described, for that chancel not being square with and in line to the nave.

Many views have been put forward as to why the spire is crooked, and several legends also. The lines at the beginning, from the pen of John Munnings, probably express the true feeling of most people seeing it for the first time. Most legends attribute the deflection to his Satanic Majesty. One legend goes that Lucifer, who was flying from Nottingham to Sheffield, alighted for a moment on the apex of the spire. At that moment a waft of incense from below so irritated his unholy nostrils that he gave a violent sneeze so great that he twisted the whole structure of the spire. Various opinions, and innumerable arguments, have been advanced for and against the spire being in a perpendicular direction. It appears to lean different ways according to the sides on which you approach it. When the spire was erected is not known exactly. No documents can be found referring to the subject and it is quite probable that any that may have existed were lost at the time of the Commonwealth. Various opinions have been handed down concerning the mode of its first building. Some affirming that it was and others that it was not intended to be straight. In 1698 Celia Fiennes visited Chesterfield as did Daniel Defoe in 1723 and neither of them mention any abnormality when writing of their respective visit.

In 1817 things were different and the spire became the subject of concern, great scrutiny and examination after being declared in no uncertain terms dangerous. One expert declared, "It is the most ill-designed and ill-constructed mass of confusion I ever surveyed." But there was no hint of surprise that such a faulty structure should have been built on so strong a tower and there was no enquiry as to whether or not it had become twisted within living memory. In January 1818 measurements were taken and the ball on which the weathercock is fixed was found to lean six feet from the perpendicular of its base toward the south, and four feet four inches from the perpendicular toward the west. By comparison a more recent survey gives the lean to the south at 8ft 6ins; 3ft 9ins to the west and 9ft 8ins to the south west.

At a meeting of the Vestry early in January 1818 the opposition to its recommended demolition was so strong that a further opinion was sought. Later that same month Mr. James Ward of Sheffield reported that with slight repairs, it might stand almost indefinitely:- "The foundation or basis of the carpenters' work was firm and good, which rendered it impossible that it should ever fall, until the base itself gave way". This report was confirmed by three practising carpenters and the adjourned Vestry came out in favour of the steeple remaining. An in depth account of these deliberations can be found in several publications including a History of Chesterfield published by the George Hall in 1822.

At a cost of between £400 and £500 a peal of ten bells was hung in the tower in 1820 and it is known that a peal of six bells was in being prior to 1700. From the year 1700 until 1718 the tower contained the odd number of seven bells, a situation very uncommon amongst peals of bells and yet as recently as 1985 St Helen's, Selston became similarly placed. This seventh bell at Chesterfield was donated by the will of Paul Webster and hung as a new treble to the existing six. A further treble was added in 1718, from money raised by public subscription, to complete the octave. In 1774 the eight bells were rehung and the sixth bell recast by Thomas Hilton at his foundry at Wath on Dearne, Yorkshire. This peal of eight rang out over the town for the next half-century until in 1820 Thomas Mears of Whitechapel, London cast the new peal of ten bells. These bells were considered a very excellent and musical peal, and reflected the highest credit on Mr. Mears, the founder, and Mr. Hanson the bell-hanger. The weight of the tenor being 24cwts.2qrs.

The opening took place on Monday, May 22nd, 1820 and continued through Tuesday when thirty thousand seven hundred and fourteen changes were rung in six different peals by visiting bands of ringers. Each band completed their peal at the first attempt which was an achievement never before performed in the annals of change ringing. Each band performed as follows :-

1st. The Society from Oldham, Lancashire, rang a peal of 5147 Changes of Grandsire Caters.

2nd. The Society at the Parish Church, Sheffield, rang a peal of 5003 Changes of Grandsire Caters.

3rd. A miscellaneous band from the Societies of Leeds, Wakefield, Sheffield Independents, and others a peal of 5180 Changes of New Treble Bob Royal.

This completed the ringing on Monday. Then on Tuesday morning ringing began with :-

4th. The Ashton-under-Lyme Company rang 5000 Changes and upwards of Grandsire Caters.

5th. The Nottingham Society of Sherwood Youths rang 5364 Changes of Grandsire Caters.

6th. The Society from Mottram, in Cheshire rang 5000 changes and upwards of Grandsire Caters.

At least nine hours of almost continuous ringing on each of the two days. One wonders what today's noise abatement followers would make of that? But oh! how proud the parishioners of Chesterfield must have been of their new peal of ten bells.

The inscriptions found on the old peal of eight when they were removed from the tower to make way for the ten bells was:-

Treble   Multi numerantur amici.
              Geo. Swift, P. Wildebore, Churchwardens, 1718.

2nd.   Haec campana est ex dona Pauli Webster.
              Geo. Swift, P.W. C.W.
              Laus domini nostra mobilitate viget. 1700.

3rd.   Sweetly tolling, men to call,
              To taste on meats that feed the soul.

This inscription is also found upon the sixth bell at Ashover which was possibly cast in 1625 at Chesterfield by Godfrey Heathcote. The seventh bell at St. Peter's, Mansfield and the fourth bell at St Clement's, Horsley, also bear the same inscription but they were cast in 1615 and 1620 at Nottingham, by the Oldfields, whose mark they carry. This inscription, like that on the next two bells, was popular at this period. As the third, fourth and fifth bells were all cast in 1612, could it possibly be that they were cast in Chesterfield by Godfrey Heathcote who at this same period had a thriving business in town, "that butts the water of Rodder", presumably the river Rother, says the will of Ralph in 1502. Ralph being the great grandfather of Godfrey above and whose grandfather George had cast the tenor in the previous century. Several generations of the family taking a leading roll in the town's affairs.

4th.   Jesus be our speed. 1612.

5th.   God save his Church. 1612.

6th·   John Wood, Vicar: H.Withers,R.Marsden,Churchwardens.
              Thomas Hilton of Wath, Founder. 1774.

7th.   George Shaw, Peter Dowker, friends of this bell.
              Anthony Legat, Wil. Holland, Wardens. 1661.

Tenor   I.H.S. Haec Campana sacra fiat Trinitate beatae.

The founders' mark a shield with a cross in the centre lying between the initials 'G.H.' Below the initial 'G' a fylfot cross, and below the initial 'H' a section of a bell showing the clapper exposed.

Without doubt this tenor was cast within a short distance of the church by George Heathcote between 1525 and 1558. This establishes that a peal of at least four bells hung in the tower from 1612 until 1661 when a fifth was added by George Shaw and Peter Dowker. The interesting fact here is that the Heathcote foundry had ceased trading in 1647 so this bell was cast by another founder. Who? The

Heathcote foundry, which existed in Chesterfield from about 1502 until 1647 is the subject of a separate chapter.

Of the sixth bell there must be some doubt as to it only having been newly cast in 1774 because of its position in the octave. The two trebles may or may not have been new at the dates inscribed but the sixth by reason of its intermediate position in the octave must have been recast by Thomas Hilton at Wath on Dearne in 1774. By coincidence, the Hilton foundry was in existence until 1809 but the earliest record of them casting bells is in 1774 when this bell was cast and the eight re-hung. If it was recast by Hilton, what a pity it is that the old legend was not reproduced on the bell.

An interesting aside: found in one of the old registers is an entry of 1774 telling of the curious way in which the first organist's salary was raised. The Schnetzler built organ was first used in October, 1756 and the organist was paid partly by the pew rents of the west gallery, and partly from the extra fee of two shillings charged to those who required the great bell tolling on the occasion of a funeral. Those not wanting to pay for the tolling of the tenor, and "paupers", had to be content with the tolling of the fourth or fifth bell. However, in 1788 an order was made that henceforth the great bell should be rung for all persons.

Thomas Mears provided the peal of ten bells from his foundry at Whitechapel, London in 1820. We have already mentioned the esteem by which they were judged, the cost and the extensive ringing at their opening. What is interesting is that this foundry at Whitechapel is still casting bells and that they were engaged in 1881 to overhaul the peal and again in 1947 to re-cast them.

During the intervening one hundred and twenty seven years the old ten bells rang out on numerous, royal, civic and ecclesiastical occasions. They have heralded royal visits and proclaimed victories. They rang out to mark the news reaching Chesterfield, in 1836, and after a very precarious passage through Parliament, of the North Midland Railway Bill for the building of the railway from Derby to Leeds having received consent. On this particular occasion the bells rang throughout the afternoon and a subscription for the benefit of the bell-ringers was liberally contributed to.

One hundred and ten years later, on Friday, August 13th, 1948, the George Stevenson Centenary celebration was marked by a peal of 5040 Changes of Plain Bob Royal on the one-year-old bells. The ringers were Herbert O. Chaddock, Herbert T. Rooke, Cyril Wright, Pamela J. Leaning, Sam Scattergood, Walter Allwood, Frederick A. Adams, Harold Kent, Joseph Saxton and the Conductor, G. Gordon Graham.

It was the customary practice for the ringers to ring a peal at the start of the Chesterfield Race Meeting during the early part of the nineteenth century. Then in 1829, the Vicar, Rev. Thomas Hill, forbade the ringers to ring for the commencement of the Race meeting on the grounds that the races constituted, "one of the greatest moral evils that can affect the parish." There was a great outcry from the parishioners who argued that the bells were owned, and the ringers paid, by them. The argument raged into the following year. In September, 1830, the Mayor, William Battison, Esq. was petitioned to call a public meeting in order to try and secure the ringing of the bells at that year's approaching races. This meeting resulted in lengthy letters being exchanged with the Vicar. These were read at the adjourned meeting in the following week when Mr. Baxter of Doncaster addressed the meeting on behalf of the Vicar, stating that he conceived the law to be quite explicit on the subject, "It is laid down in one of the Canons of the Church, that the bells are not to be used, except upon occasions to be allowed of by the Vicar and Churchwardens".

After Mr. Baxter had withdrawn, Mr Thomas, the Chairman said he was glad the course recommended by himself, of giving patient hearing to that gentleman had been adopted. Mr. Baxter had very fairly stated the only authority which was to be found on the subject, and that was one of the Canons of our Church. Mr. Prince then addressed the meeting. He censured in strong terms the conduct of the Vicar, in refusing the use of the church bells to his parishioners, who had paid for them, and concluded by moving a resolution for calling an early vestry meeting, to take into consideration the propriety of reducing the ringers' salaries and other expenses now illegally paid out of church assessment.

Mr. Hopkinson seconded the motion, and after it had undergone certain alterations and amendments, at the suggestion of Mr. Waller, and Mr. John Gillett, it was passed upon a show of hands.

In consequence of the passing of this resolution, the Vicar wrote to the Churchwardens outlining the motion that was passed at the meeting accepting that the outcome had been occasioned by an act exclusively his own and expressing his desire that the impasse would not extend beyond his incumbency.

The Vicar continued to remain firm to his original resolution and the bells never again rang for the opening of the race meeting in spite of the races being continued to be run at Whittington Common for almost a further century.

In 1986 a disagreement arose between the ringers and the Vicar and as a result the bells were not rung for a short period. The popular press and Yorkshire Television focused the story and as a result of the publicity the non-ringer became aware of the situation and formed an opinion which was at the time widely bantered about town. But, irrespective of which opinion was taken it must be remembered by all that bells are committed to the custody of the incumbent, to be used only with his consent, and subject to the control of the Bishop of the Diocese.

A good number of peals of over 5000 Changes have been rung on the bells through the years. The earliest complete peal noted was on June 2nd, 1800 when in three hours and twenty minutes 5040 of Grandsire Trebles was rung by W. Rollinson, treble; Edward Dean, 2; John Pickard, Conductor, 3; Joseph Fogg, 4;

Isaac Siddall, 5; John Hearnshaw, 6; Samuel Tetley, 7; and Peter Maden, tenor. For well over a century the annual reports of the Midland Counties Association, the Yorkshire Association and the Sheffield Society of Change Ringers have note of more peals being rung in this tower than any other in this district. Especially during the time the late Arthur Knight was in his prime did peals of all standard and some Surprise methods follow one another in rapid succession. The favourite method was Stedman and Grandsire Caters, Plain Bob and Treble Bob Royal of which most were compositions rung for the first time.

Arthur Knight joined the band in 1880 after removing from the village of Brome, near Eye, Suffolk. For many years he was tower captain until the condition of the tower was deemed unsafe and all change-ringing ceased, the bells being simply chimed for services. It was one of his great disappointments that his efforts to secure restoration was not fulfilled within his lifetime. He died on March 1st, 1939 at the age of 79 years. About four hundred and thirty original peals of Treble Bob Major and over three hundred of Treble Bob Royal stand to his memory and there has been nearly one thousand two hundred of his compositions rung. He rang his first peal at Chesterfield on July 15th, 1882 and of the six hundred or so peals he rang he conducted well over two hundred of them.

One of the peals he composed and conducted is commemorated on an old Ringers Jug. This peal of 5004 Changes of Canterbury Pleasure Caters, was rung on Saturday, March 23rd, 1895 by:- Arthur Craven, Arthur Knights, George Toplis, William E. Tydeman, Arthur Worthington, George Davies, Albert E. Thompson, John W. Thompson, John Goodwin and George Mee. Just four days before Christmas, December 21st, 1961, fire broke out in the north transept of the church and immediately threatened the tower and spire. Very prompt and astute action by the Chesterfield Firemen saved them from severe damage and the belfry and bells escaped. During the fire the old Ringers' Jug was lost but eventually to be rediscovered in a public house nearby and returned to the belfry.

It was a fitting tribute that on Monday, August 4th, 1947 the first peal to be rung on the new bells was, "In Grateful memory of the composer and his long and distinguished connection with this tower". It happened also to be the eleventh peal rung for and recorded by the Derbyshire Association of Change Ringers. This Association had been founded in the previous year and was afforded Diocesan status a few years later.

A Peal of Stedman Caters, 5067 Changes,
in 3 hours 22 minutes.

T. Groombridge, jun.	Treble	J. Fredk. Milner	6
Sidney Briggs	2	David Vincent	7
Harold Pailing	3	T. Vernon Jennison	8
Clement Glen	4	Frederick A. Salter	9
Joseph A. Fenton	5	Walter Nichols	Tenor

Composed by A. Knights.   Conducted by Clement Glen.

Let us now take a brief look at the Church Clock. In 1836 the existing clock was exceedingly old and worn out. It produced universal complaint and the new Town Council agreed that it was necessary to establish a correct standard of time. So, at their meeting on February 9th, they passed the following resolution:-

"That the Church Clock, Being in so decayed a state as to be useless to the inhabitants of the town and neighbourhood, a recommendation be made from this meeting to the Churchwardens, to attempt the establishment of a new clock at the church; and that they convene a meeting of the inhabitants in vestry, to consider the expediency of granting a church-rate to defray the expenses of a new clock, also the propriety of lighting the same with gas."

The churchwardens duly called a meeting of ratepayers in the vestry. Discussion took place and some concern was shown regarding the lighting of the clock by gas on the grounds of safety. An estimate was given by Mr. Whitehurst of Derby who advised against an illuminated dial. It was agreed to defray the expense of a new clock by an assessment on all property liable to a church-rate of four and a half pence in the pound.

A Chesterfield clockmaker, Mr. J. Robinson wrote to Mr. Paine , the horologist, of London who in due course came and examined the tower. Mr. Paine was of the opinion that one dial could be illuminated without concern and duly sent in an estimate. "For the best description of works, with three dials to face north, south and west, (the last to be illuminated), and quarter jacks to strike upon four bells, £319; mason's and joiner's work, £33; total £352. To be completed by August." The committee agreed. The gas and water company offered to supply requirements and on the night of October 25th, 1836 the clock was complete and with the west dial lit for the first time. Following is the description of this beautiful piece of mechanism.

"This stupendous machine stands on a most substantial foundation, and the whole work has such a precise uniformity in appearance, as to strike with pleasure every spectator. The frame that contains the work is very massive, with a stout cast-iron Tuscan pillar at each corner, and weighs nearly seven cwt. It is well put together with brass lion's-head nuts, highly finished and lacquered. The three trains of wheels for the going, hour-striking, and quarters, are firmly attached to the frame with brass nuts and iron screws; between each of these is its corresponding detent bar. At the top of the centre bar is a raised tablet with the Royal Arms of England, cast in the metal and picked out in gold, with "Paine, London, fecit," also in raised letters, gilt. Below this there is a handsome brass engraved and silvered dial, with the maker's name in the centre, over which a delicate blue steel hand makes the revolution of the dial in two minutes, and beats once in two seconds. About a foot below this, to the right, is the minute dial, with blue hand also, which revolves exactly once in the hour. Connected with this dial are the rods of communication attached to bevel wheels and universal joints, to the minute hands on the outside of the tower, so that by altering the hands of this dial, a corresponding effect takes place with the external hands, although at a distance of more than fifty feet from the machine below. On this dial, which is also of brass silvered, is inscribed:- "This Clock was erected by Rate expressly for the purpose. Gilbert Crompton, Esq., Mayor; Rev. Thomas Hill, B.D., Vicar; Mr. Edward Heane, and Mr. Henry Claughton, Churchwardens, 1836. Committee - Edmund Gilling Maynard, Esq.; Rev. Robert Wallace, Mr. John Sayer, Mr. R. Tennison." Exactly uniform, on the left, is an hour dial, over which a hand revolves every twelve hours. On this dial is finely engraved:- "For improvements in Public Horology, the maker of this Clock was awarded the large Silver Medal of the Society of Arts." Then follows further detail. The pendulum rod being of African teak and measures thirteen feet and eight tenths of an inch in length and that the ball weighs 150lbs. The large clock-hammer weighs fifty pounds with the four quarter hammers in proportion. The hour is struck on the tenor bell, and the quarters on the treble, second, third and sixth bells, very musically, and in delightful contrast, from the fall of an octave between the quarter and the hour bell. The three dials are each nine feet in diameter with the numerals eighteen inches long, the minute pointer four feet ten inches and the hour hand two feet six inches in length. The centre plate of glass is four feet five inches in diameter, and three eighths of an inch in thickness. By a simple but effective plan, the clock itself lights and extinguishes the gas, which consists of five bat's-wing burners."

A fantastic piece of machinery by any standard. In fact a whole book could be written about local church clocks and alas space does not allow more than but the briefest glimpse at what is another of the tower-keepers proud acquisitions and constantly in need of his loving care. Fifty years ago the clock in Chesterfield was lovingly cared for by Sam Scattergood whom the author remembers very well, seeing him make minor timekeeping adjustments by either adding or removing a small coin of the realm to a moving part of the mechanism.

Another small bell used to hang in the belfry, it was about one foot, six inches tall and some fifteen and a half inches in diameter. This bell, known as the Pancake Bell, was rung regularly until about 1900 for fifteen minutes starting at 10.45a.m. on Shrove Tuesday.

Originally it was rung to call parishioners to their annual duty as Shrove Tide implies. The time when it was imperative on everyone to confess to his parish priest, and by him be shriven. During this period it was known as the Shriving Bell and it was only later when the custom of shriving had lapsed that it became known as the Pancake Bell.

As Pancake Bell its ringing was a timely reminder that Lent was to begin on the morrow. Lent being a strict period for fasting meant that all additional luxuries to the basic diet ought to be used-up and one way of doing this was by making the delicacy known as pancakes. As it was considered necessary for this mixture to stand before being cooked the ringing of the Pancake Bell indicated the appropriate time to commence preparation of the mixture.

At one period this bell was also known as the Curfew Bell. This was at the time of the war with France, when between 1804 and 1814 about two hundred French prisoners of war were stationed in Chesterfield. Being allowed out into the town on parole of honour, the Curfew was rung to inform them to return to their quarters at nightfall.

In February 1980 the bell was stolen from the belfry. The Vicar, Rev Harry Puntis, estimated this shriving bell to be over four hundred years old and weighing almost an hundredweight. It was either manoeuvred down eighty feet of narrow staircase or lowered on a rope down the outside of the tower. Police Superintendent Wendy Stocks told the press the thieves probably got in with keys stolen from a workmen's' hut the previous November. She added, "The police would like anyone with information to give them a ring. Or better still, give them a bell".

On Tuesday, June 24, 1997 a new Sanctus bell was blessed. This small bell, roughly the size of its predecessor, was cast at the Whitechapel Foundry in London and brought into church for the service of blessing. Later in that week it was installed in the bell-chamber and fixed to a tall metal gantry. This was designed in order that it could be raised above the level of the louvred openings, and in so doing allow its sweet chime to be distinctly heard from the streets below. The bell is fitted with a modern electronic device that allows it to be chimed, by the simple pressing of a button, from within the chancel, at the elevation of the host, and at other appropriate times during liturgy. The same device can also be used to chime the bell prior to services. Thus, a modern innovation comes to the aid of the age old custom-that of reminding parishioners that prayers are being said within this ancient building. For many centuries past, the daily office has been read within, and it is great news that once again those who hear the chime of this Sanctus bell are reminded that they too can, for a few moments, join in prayer.

The Sanctus Bell is inscribed simply, Harold, and is cast to the memory of Harold Franklin. It is a fitting tribute to a man who died whilst in office as churchwarden of the Church of Our Lady and All Saints here in Chesterfield.

Born on October 2, 1930, Harold spent his early years in the village of Morton before moving to Chesterfield upon his marriage to Enid. As a young man, one of Harold's many interests was that of bell-ringer. Having become a regular member of Morton Holy Cross Church, Sunday Service team of bell-ringers in his early teens, Harold was able to ring in his first peal, consisting of 5040 Changes of Treble Bob Minor, on the bells in honour of the wedding of H.R.H. Princess Elizabeth and the Duke of Edinburgh on Thursday, November 20, 1947. He went on to ring over a dozen peals, mostly on the six bells at Morton. Sadly, Harold died on February 25, 1995. On Sunday, August 3, 1997, in the presence of his family, fellow bellringers and congregation, the Sanctus Bell was dedicated by the vicar, Rev. Michael Knight.

Belfries of
St. Mary, Denby. *(top left)*
St. Mary, Crich. *(top right)*
St. Mary and All Saints,
                    Chesterfield. *(left)*

The recessed spires at Chesterfield, Crich and Denby spring from behind plain moulded parapets which have a frieze of pierced pointed trefoils. This suggests that the same, early 14c, mason built the three towers. Crich and Denby spires are built of stone but at Chesterfield it is of timber, sheathed in lead. The lead panels are placed upon the timbers in a herring-bone pattern giving the illusion each of the eight faces is chanelled.

i

Belfries of
St. John the Baptist,
Ault Hucknall. *(top left)*
St. Matthew, Pentrich.
(top right)
St. Werburgh, Blackwell.
(left)

Both the central belfry at Ault
Hucknall and the western tower at
Pentrich have much Norman masonry
in their lower portions. At Blackwell
the 19c tower replaced a much older
edifice that stood on an ancient
foundation.

Belfries of St. Bartholomew, Clay Cross. *(top l)* All Saints, Heath. *(top rt)* of St. Wilfred, Kirkby in Ashfield. *(bottm l)* St. Andrew, Swanwick. *(bottm rt)*

Which of these belfries was built in the 20th century? Kirkby was built in 1860 to the original 13c design. Clay Cross and Heath were built between 1851 and 1853 with the spire at Clay Cross being added in 1857 and the tower at Swanwick was built in 1902.

Belfries of
St. Lawrence, North Wingfield.
(top left)
St. Michael & All Angels,
South Normanton. *(top right)*
All Saints, South Wingfield. *(left)*

Three belfries of the Perpendicular period. North Wingfield, with its frieze of alternating portcullis and uncharged shields, rises to over 100 feet. South Normanton and South Wingfield, built about 1440, are the work of the same mason.

Belfres of St. Mary & St. Laurance, Bolsover. *(top l)*
S.S. Peter & Paul, Old Brampton. *(top rt)* St. Mary, Edwinstowe. *(bottm l)*
St. Edmund, Mansfield Woodhouse. *(bottm rt)*
A varied group of 14th and 15th century broach spires that spring directly off the walls of older towers.

Belfries of St. Giles, Matlock. *(top l)* Holy Cross, Morton. *(top rt)*
St. Michael, Pleasley. *(bottm l)* St. Leonard, Shirland. *(bottm rt)*

Four embattled towers with crocketed pinnacles, large gargoyles, high bell-chamber
openings and diagonal buttresses represent the skill of 15th century masons.

Belfries of St. Martin, Alfreton. *(top l)* St. Peter, Belper. *(top rt)*
St. Lawrence, Heanor. *(bottm l)* All Saints, Ripley. *(bottm rt)*

These four town belfries, each with a peal of eight bells, are linked today by the civil administrative area of Amber Valley Borough Council.

The Belfries of S.S. Peter & Paul, Mansfield, *(top l)* Mary Magdelene, Sutton in Ashfield, *(top rt)* St. Leonard, Scarcliffe, *(bottm l)* S.S. Peter & Paul, Warsop. *(bottm rt)* Magnesium limestone spires. Sutton in Ashfield 600 years old, the 1669 steeple at Mansfield replaced a wooden structure covered with lead. The 1848 tower at Scarcliffe replaced a 13c one with a broach spire. Warsop is chiefly Norman with a 14c top storey.

The Belfries of St. Helen, Pinxton. *(top l)*, St. Helen, Selston. *(top rt)*, St. John the Baptist, Tibshelf, *(bottm l)*, St. Katherine, Teversal, *(bottm rt)*

The unique 'brick on end' belfry at Pinxton contrasts with the embattled towers of Selston, Teversal and Tibshelf. Between them they house twenty seven bells cast between 1551 and the present decade.

Belfries of
All Saints, Wingerworth.
(top left)
All Saints, Ashover.
(bottom left)
St. Helen, South Darley.
(below)

Built in 1419 the spire at Ashover rises to a height of 128 feet. The 15c belfry at Darley was damaged by storm in 1703. Repairs lasted until 1902 when further major work was carried out. In 1770, at Wingerworth, a sun dial was fixed to the south face of the 15c belfry

Fine gargoyles, especially on the west, depicting a muzzled bear and an ape are of note.

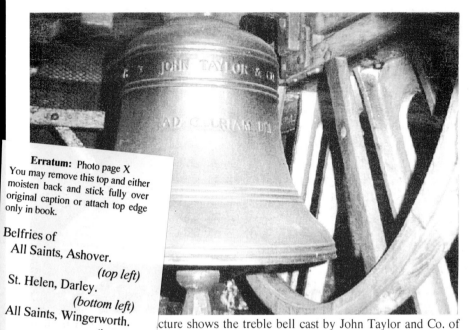

Belfries of
 All Saints, Ashover.
                    (top left)
St. Helen, Darley.
                (bottom left)
All Saints, Wingerworth.
             (below)

cture shows the treble bell cast by John Taylor and Co. of
ind in 1971. The other is a much older bell in the tower at
Crich. This bell was renung by Taylor's when the five bells were augmented to eight
in 1928.

The Bell Chamber. Note the compact way in which bells and frame are installed. Here we show an oak frame. Today, metal frames are used which save on space. These bells are in the 'rung up' or inverted position and are ready for ringing in changes. Bells in this position can be very dangerous if the ropes are handled by the inexperienced.

The lie of the clapper. A bell 'rung up' and showing its position at the end of the handstroke change. Held momentarily in this position by the ringer the bell is then projected by a pull on the rope through 360 degrees to take up a similar position on the opposite stroke, known as Backstroke. The clapper remains lying upon the bell at the point of contact until passing through the bottom of the arc. This is the critical moment when the bell strikes and a moment the ringer must anticipate with great accuracy.

Bells are rested in the inverted position using a stay and a slider. Below the conventional stay and slider are seen low in the pit of the bell's frame. Above is the Hasting's system. A stay is made from ash which is supple in use allowing it to snap if the rope is overpulled by the ringer and so avoids damage to the bell's fittings. The clock hammer is positioned without the swing of the bell during ringing. At other times it is released onto the bell so that it can strike when activated by the clock's mechanism. Bell ropes are attached to the wheel as shown.

Ting Tang Bell. Ting Tang, Parson's Bell, Sermon Bell, Sanctus Bell, Curfew Bell, Angelus or Noon Day Bell are but a few names by which small bells are known.

A royal injunction of 1547 ordered that a bell be tolled before the sermon and another ancient use is the chiming of a bell at the elevation of the host in the Eucharist.

Illustrated is the small bell at St Mary's Crich.

The Tower Clock. Clocks form an important part of many belfries. In the past much labour was put in by a tower keeper in an effort to maintain a clock's accuracy.

Today, with electrical winding gear in use, the number of hours needed is reduced but regular attention to the mechanism is still very demanding.

Illustrated is the clock's works at Tibshelf. So typical of many being maintained in pristine condition locally.

Mr Frederick Pembleton surveying empty bell-pits during
a rehanging and restoration contract.

Mr Eric Sterland undertaking routine maintenance work on the heavy six at St. Andrew's,
Swanwick.

"Though I speak with the tongues of men and
of angels, and have not charity, I am become
as sounding brass, or a tinkling cymbal."

1 Cor. X111 v 1.

As previously mentioned, Thomas Mears cast the original ten bells and they were placed in the tower in 1820. These bells all carried the same inscription, "T. Mears, of London, Fecit 1819."and on the tenor: "Rev. George Bossley, Vicar, Richard Dixon, John Wright, Churchwardens."

The same firm completely overhauled them in 1881.

For several years prior to the last war the tower was considered to be unsafe for the bells to be rung. But in 1947 it was decided to have the full peal of ten bells recast and hung at a lower level within the tower. Once again the work was entrusted to the Whitechapel Bell Foundry, London.

Upon the new cast bells returning to Chesterfield, they were placed in the south transept to await 'Baptism'. This 'service for the dedication of the Bells' took place on Saturday, April 12th, 1947. It was conducted by the Vicar, Ven. T. Dilworth - Harrison, with the sermon being preached and the bells dedicated by the Right Revd. Bishop O'Ferrall, D.D., Assistant Bishop of the Diocese. This was a most moving service based upon the Order for Evening Prayer.

At the appropriate moment in the service the choir and clergy followed by representatives of various belfries processed to the south transept for the "Baptism" of the Bells. On reaching the bells the priest said :-

Reverend Father in God, we request you to dedicate these bells to the glory of God, to the service of His Church, and in honour of His blessed saints and of the mysteries of our Salvation.

The Bishop replied:-

We are ready so to do. Let us pray.

Almighty God, we humbly pray 'that Thou wilt accept this offering at our hands. Bless + sanctify and hallow these bells, and grant that for generations to come they may resound to Thy Glory, Who livest and reignest, One God, blessed for ever. Amen.

The Bishop sprinkled the bells, after which he named them in due order, beginning with the tenor to the treble, saying:-

In the Faith of Jesus Christ our Saviour, we dedicate these bells
to the Glory of God; and thus we designate them for all time:-

Tenor:	DOMINA:	in honour of the Mother of our Lord.
9th.	ALL ANGELS:	Do thou ring to the Heavens the glorious praise of God.
8th.	ALL SAINTS:	Sing praise of them to whom they first did consecrate this Church.
7th.	ALL SOULS:	On whose behalf thou mayest echo all our prayers.

6th.	THE HOLY CROSS:	Do thou sound forth the praise of Him Who died and rose again.
5th.	SAINT PETER:	Speak for him whose Faith and grief bring men to Christ.
4th.	SAINT CATHERINE:	As thou resoundest to the skies, tell out the Martyr's praise.
3rd.	SAINT OSWALD:	We name thee Patron Royal of men; call them to serve their King.
2nd.	SAINT CHAD:	Praise for the father of our Church, the Apostle of our Shire.
Treble:	THE HOLY SPIRIT:	The highest honour thine to sound, that Still Small Voice of Calm.

The Bishop then censed the bells, after which he said:-

Grant, O Lord, we beseech thee; that these bells may ring out with gladness to summon multitudes to the King's Feast; make them to cheer the bed-ridden who fain would enter Thy House; may they utter thanksgiving for the abundance of Thy mercies; may they, tolling for the departed, call forth their fellows' prayers. Finally, we ask Thy blessing upon all who ring, that they may render this service unto Thee, O Father, Who with the Son and Holy Spirit livest and reignest one God, world without end. Amen.

The service included the singing of Psalms 122 and 150 and five hymns:-

When morning gilds the skies
Christ is our corner-stone
Pleasant are Thy courts above
The Church's one foundation
Thy Hand, O God, has guided

In due course the bells were hung aloft in their new frame and as already mentioned the first peal of over 5000 changes was rung on them on August 4th, 1947.

Nearly thirty years later it was deemed necessary to have the bells overhauled. In a cost cutting exercise it was considered wise to attend to such items as rebuilding wheels, renewing pulleys and sliders. Whilst these items were not strictly necessary at the time it was prudent to do so and the ringers themselves provided much of the voluntary labour required of their own free time over many weeks, thus saving the Churchwardens considerable expense. In fact, Mrs Marjorie Phipps and husband Malcolm put in a tremendous amount of work raising extra cash to offset the cost as well as assisting within the tower. They and the other ringers also undertook the painting of the bell-frame. Two new balanced clappers were provided for the ninth and tenor bells and John Taylor and Co. of Lough-borough, who co-ordinated the project, completed the overhaul.

A century ago, The Bell News and Ringers' Record, on Saturday, October 17th, 1896, (Vol.XV.No.758.) carried a front-page article about Chesterfield Parish Church. The following few lines about the spire are taken from the article:-

"It creaks sometimes, when the wind savagely assails it and makes the door of the crow-hole clatter; it quivers when the bells make gleesome riot; but the steeple is in no immediate danger of collapse. It will most likely stand for years yet; but, when it does decide to vacate its lofty position - may it fall gently!"

It remains only for the inscriptions found upon the ten bells and the detail of their size and weight to be recorded.

Treble.	VENI SANCTISSIMA SPIRITUS VOX PARVA QUIETIS
2nd.	ORA PRO HAC ECCLESIA SANCTA CEDDEA
3rd.	DA NOBIS DOMINI ROBUR BEATI OSWALD REGIS
4th.	CATHERINA VIRGO PURISSIMA MEMENTO NOS
5th.	O CRUX AVE SPES UNICA
6th.	SANCTE PETRE CONFIRMA FRATRAS TUOS

In addition, each of the six bells above bear upon the waist:

	M & S LONDON 1947 (AAH)
7th.	ANIME OMNIUM FIDELIUM REQUIESCANT IN PACE
8th.	OMNES SANCTE ORATE PRO NOBIS
9th.	OMNES ANGELI "GLORIA IN EXCELSIS "CLAMANT

In addition bells seven, eight and nine bear the founder's mark 'AAH' upon the waist.

Tenor.   DOMINA SANCTA MARIA ORA PRO NOBIS
ALL CAST 1819, T.M. RECAST 1947 MEARS & STAINBANK 'AAH'

Bell:	Diameter:	Weight:			Bell;	Diameter:	Weight:		
	Inches.	Cwt.	QRS.	Lbs.		Inches.	Cwt.	Qrs.	Lbs.
1.	28	5.	1.	27	6.	36	8.	3.	10
2.	28¾	5.	1.	18	7.	39½	10.	2.	8
3.	30⁷⁄₈	6.	1.	9	8.	41	12.	0.	25
4.	31¼	6.	2.	9	9.	45½	17.	2.	2
5.	34	7.	3.	3	10.	52³⁄₈	25.	1.	5

The Belfry of St. Bartholomew, Clay Cross.

Weathercock adjusted for 40 pence Home to an Association.
Bells rung dumb during the war. Victory Peal, won and lost.
First lady Ringing Master.

Clay Cross is the home of the East Derbyshire and West Nottinghamshire Association of Church Bell Ringers. The Association under the title of the East Derbyshire Association of Change Ringers was founded here in 1887. Just thirty eight years after the laying of the foundation stone of the church, some thirty five years after Clay Cross became an ecclesiastical parish, and only thirteen years after the fine peal of six bells was placed in the tower.

When the Lord Bishop of Lichfield consecrated the Church to St. Bartholomew on January 25th, 1851, the western tower stood uncrowned of its spire. This was built some six years later, in 1857, of stone hewn from Bole Hill at Wingerworth. It cost £366.9s.0d. to complete and is octagonal in plan, with half pyramid broaches. The broaches set off the two light dormer openings that are placed between them on each cardinal face. The spire springs immediately from behind the plainly moulded string course parapet of the tower walls. The whole being to the design of H.I. Stevens.

An interesting item in the church accounts two years after the building of the spire reads: 'David Brown.. for inspecting and adjusting the weather cock, ... 8s.0d.' One wonders what, if anything; forty pence could buy in the way of building work today? Just think of the cost and the effort involved in reaching the weathercock! Incidentally, repairs to the weathercock and spire were again undertaken in 1938 but the cost is not recorded.

The tall tower is supported by angle buttresses that rise to bell-chamber level on the south and west. The north east buttress is replaced by a turret staircase. The louvred bell-openings are of three single lights set distinctly beneath a high frieze and within a recessed panel. On the south face, and in line with the top of the buttresses, is the clock dial. Powered by electricity it was installed in 1946, and given in grateful and loving remembrance of Mr. and Mrs. J. Steen by their niece Evelyn Martin. Mr Steen having formerly served as churchwarden, and was for many years Secretary of The Clay Cross Company.

The tower contains a peal of six bells. Originally cast by John Warner and Son at Cripplegate, London, in 1874 and subsequently recast by John Taylor & Co. at Loughborough in 1937 to commemorate the Coronation of George VI. The cost of recasting the bells was gifted by Gertrude Parkins whilst the cost of re-hanging was met by public subscription. How funds for the original bells was raised appears to be unrecorded and the inscriptions upon the bells shed no information.

The six bells are inscribed :-

The treble, second and third bell each bear the same inscription, viz:

Cast 1874.
Taylor Loughborough.
Recast 1937.

4th. Cast 1874.
The medallion of John Taylor.
Recast 1937.

5th. As fourth and on the reverse waist :
"Come and Pray"
These bells were recast by the gift of
Gertrude Parkins in memory of her son
Leslie who died, 16th December, 1919,
Aged 21 years.

Tenor. As fourth and on reverse waist :
Think and Thank
These bells were rehung
by public subscription
to commemorate the Coronation
of King George VI
12th. May, 1937.
H.C. Snape, Vicar.
J. Spriggs, H.E. Marshall, Churchwardens.

The tenor weighs 8cwts. 2qrs. 16lbs. has a diameter of thirty six inches and is note A.

The foundries of John Warner & Sons (established 1763) were two, at 27 Jewin Crescent, Cripplegate, London E.C. and at Spitalfields, London E. Prior to 1850 all their bells were cast in sand and this method limited the size of each bell to a diameter of less than eighteen inches, but in that year they commenced using loam which allowed them to cast larger bells. Their catalogue, published in 1895, lists many peals of bells including Clay Cross and a six at Eckington and at Glossop. For their trademark they used a bell within a crescent. No doubt adopted from the locality of their foundry which stood on ground said to have been occupied by the Jews, and given - upon their banishment in the twelfth century - to the Dean of St. Paul's - hence the name Jewin St. and Jewin Crescent. One of Warner's features was a very handsome decorative band encircling their bells and the use of fine Gothic letters. They were also noted for their chiming apparatus but unfortunately none was installed at Clay Cross or at Glossop, only at Eckington.

Fifty one years earlier the Vicar, Rev Joseph Oldham and seven of St Bartholomew's ringers, became founder members of the East Derbyshire Association of Change Ringers. In fact the Vicar had been one of the prime movers in forming the Association and throughout its history one or other of the Clay Cross band have taken leading rolls, the seven founder members being: Thomas Walters, Jas. Green, Thomas Clough, Ger. Brown, Wm. Brown, J.J. Cook and Jos.

Wilbraham. James Green was the Association's first secretary, an office which was echoed after the Second World War by the election of John W. Price as secretary for a number of years and then followed by his daughter Mrs. Florence Davis. At the same period Miss Mary Hudson became the first lady to be elected as Ringing 'Master'. And, as I write, this office is held by Miss Karen Jeffrey with the office of President being held by her father Terrence A. Jeffrey.

Many peals have been rung on the bells for the Association. The first on May 14th, 1904 and the second on October 5th, 1905 were both of 5040 changes of Plain Bob Minor.

By the fifth year of the Second World War a young band had been formed and was actively training at Clay Cross in what little spare moments they could muster. They began by using handbells to gain experience in ringing changes. They then moved on to using the tower bells made silent by the removal or blocking of the clappers. The silencing of the bells was accomplished by either removing the clapper or more usually by fashioning wooden blocks which when fitted stopped the clapper from striking the soundbow of the bell. This simple but effective device conformed to the Government's war time ban on the ringing of church bells, except in the event of the enemy's invasion, but it also enabled this new band at St. Bartholomew's to be fully trained in the Art and Science of Change Ringing by the time the ban was lifted in 1943. So good were they as a team under the expert tuition of Mr. John (Jack) W. Price, the tower captain, and William Swain of Morton, that on Saturday, November 25th, 1944, they rang a Peal of 5040 Changes of Plain Bob Minor, consisting of seven different extents, in two hours and fifty minutes. The ringers being, Miss F.M. Price, treble; Miss Mary Hudson, 2nd; Mrs M. Hatton, 3rd; John W. Price, 4th; D. Birkinshaw, 5th; William Swain, ringing the tenor and conducting.

This same band again rang the bells on Tuesday, May 8th, 1945, to celebrate Victory in Europe that day. This time the peal consisted of 5040 Changes of Minor, being three extents each of Kent and Oxford Treble Bob and two of Plain Bob. Although many belfries throughout the land had their bells rung to mark the cessation of hostilities in Europe this day most of the ringing was of touches and quarter peals and it so transpired that this peal at St Bartholomew's was one of only a handful of full peals consisting of over five thousand changes to be rung at belfries throughout the country on the actual day of victory.

Following on from the Victory Peal came the Royal Wedding Peal on Thursday, November 20th, 1947 in honour of the wedding that day of H.R.H. Princess Elizabeth and H.R.H. The Duke of Edinburgh. A further peal was rung on the bells to commemorate the Coronation of H.M. Queen Elizabeth on June 3rd, 1953, the day after the crowning in Westminster Abbey.

At the time of the Queen's Coronation the tower was undergoing several changes internally. The organ was being removed into the tower together with the choir seating. This meant that the ringing chamber was being moved up the tower by one storey. Work was in full progress at the time the Coronation Peal was rung and the ringers arrived to find a drop of several feet immediately under the rope of the second bell due to the new staircase not being in situ. After some deliberation a nine inch wide builder's plank was located, placed across the opening and the author remembers standing on the plank to ring the second bell in the peal which was brought home in two hours and forty six minutes.

On April 7th, 1956, a peal was rung in memory of Frederick Marshall who had been a ringer here for over sixty years. Fred had combined his ringing activities with that of tower captain and steeple keeper.

On the occasion of the Golden Wedding Anniversary of Mr and Mrs. William Swain a peal was rung in their honour on Wednesday, April 6th, 1968.

On December 31st, 1973, the Sheffield Morning Telegraph ran the headline, "Churches Plan to Harmonise on Sundays" and stated:-

"Sunday evening singers at Clay Cross Methodist Church face competition - Their first hymn always clashed with a resounding peal of bells. The 6.15 service had barely begun when bells from the parish church opposite pealed for 6.30 evensong. But harmony has now been restored. The parish church service will in future start at 6.15 p.m. so the bells can summon worshippers to both churches."

At the invitation of the Vicar, six members of the East Derbyshire and West Nottinghamshire Association of Church Bell Ringers assembled in the belfry on Wednesday, July 29th, 1981 and rang a Peal of 5040 Changes of Minor in two hours and 29 minutes on the occasion of the Royal Wedding that day, at the Cathedral Church of St. Paul's, London, of H.R.H. The Prince of Wales to Lady Diana Spencer. The peal consisted of one extent (720 changes) each of Cambridge Surprise; Norwich Surprise; Kent Treble Bob; Oxford Treble Bob; Oxford Bob; St. Clement's and Plain Bob. The ringers were, Treble, Wilfred Riley; 2nd. E. Glyn Holdgate; 3rd. R. John Sterland; 4th. Christopher B. Richards; 5th. Eric J. Sterland; Tenor, Brynley A. Richards who conducted the peal.

A less successful attempt to ring a peal took place on the bells on 8th. May 1995, when on reaching the last but one change of the first extent the rope of the second bell broke and fell at the feet of the amazed ringer. The second bell was being handled with such finesse by the lady ringer that the bell set. As the very next change brought the extent into rounds, the conductor, ever alert, called "stand" this everyone did, and so the extent was rung minus just one blow of the second bell missing. After re-splicing the rope the ringers took hold again and rang a well struck quarter peal. But the real sadness of this occasion was that the church was in use later in the day and there wasn't time for the ringers to attempt a second ringing of the intended peal. This was a double blow as the peal had been specially organised to commemorate the fiftieth anniversary of V.E Day and the celebrated victory peal which had been so proudly and well rung on the bells by St. Bartholomew's band in 1945.

The Belfry of St.Mary, Crich

*Ancient Sermon Bell. Ringer of bells in 1280 provided ropes! Spire pointed in
white lime mortar. Oldest original cast bell 1910? Generous gift in 1928.*

The steeple of St. Mary's Church stands prominently upon one of the
southernmost ridges of the Pennine range of hills, and is, together with its near
neighbour, the Memorial Tower of the Sherwood Foresters' Regiment, a landmark
over many miles.

The Perpendicular or late English Gothic style western tower is supported by
recessed angled buttresses and adorned by a handsome moulded parapet. This
consists of a finely carved and effective band of wavy lines and trefoils instead of
the more usual order of battlements. The recessed octagonal spire has two tiers of
dormer windows. One tier placed near the base on each cardinal face and four
smaller openings toward the apex. There is no west door, in its place a window
admits light into the ground floor ringing chamber. Inside, over this window, can be
seen in the masonry, traces of a former archway. It is thought from this that a west
doorway did exist at a very early date but was removed to make way for the large
well-moulded ogee-headed niche we now find as a feature on the exterior wall.
There is no figure within the niche but there was a belief in the late nineteenth
century that the figure of the Blessed Virgin once resided there and was removed to
St. Mary's Church at Nottingham. Dr. Charles Cox, when compiling his notes,
mentions the story and goes on to say that this tradition first reached him through a
letter in the Derbyshire Times, dated August 8th, 1871, and signed by W.H. of Crich
Carr. Remarking on there generally being some basis for every tradition, he goes on
to suggest a possible connection arising from the exchange of benefices, between
the vicars of Crich and Nottingham, in the fourteenth century. Above the niche is
fixed the clock dial, and in the upper storey, two light louvred bell-openings, placed
on each face, mark the level at which the two tier bell-frame is positioned within.

Today, Dr. Cox would be very pleased to see that the pointing of the spire,
which he so vehemently criticised for being rendered with white lime mortar, has
now mellowed. Writing in 1879 he went to the trouble of inserting a footnote,
warning how the visual effect of the spire had recently been spoiled by its use,
having given it a patchy and semi-new appearance. Adding, "The simple and
costless expedient of mixing a little wood-ash or other colouring ingredient with the
lime should always be adopted in re-pointing old stone work." It is also interesting
to find among his account a further line informing that "The steeple and spire had
been previously pointed in 1769."

Within the tower, the clock and bells are reached via a stone spiral stairway in
the north west corner. This terminates at the base of the bell chamber. The doorway
to this stair is well above the level of the present ringing chamber floor and a

protruding stone is used as a step. This, together with the indications found upon the masonry of the lower tower walls, suggests that the belfry floor was at some period much higher than at present.

The bell chamber is entered through a small aperture immediately beneath the girders supporting the frame of the fifth bell. A splendid and uninterrupted view of the interior of the spire is obtained from this point.

The first floor of the tower accommodates the clock's works. These are housed in a large wooden case so made as to allow the movement of two bellropes to pass unhindered within. The clock dates from 1820 and was supplied by Whitehurst & Son who later became John Smith & Sons and who today are renowned as Smith of Derby. The pendulum, with its timber arm, is housed in the suspended case central to the bell-ropes in the ringing chamber below, whilst the case on the south wall encompasses the clock's two weights.

In addition to the eight bells there is a small bell hanging within a frame affixed to the north wall and above the top tier of bells. It is slightly chipped on the lip and bears no inscription or date. It is possible it could once have been the Sanctus bell and hung in the bell-cot situated upon the east gable of the nave. Or, it was probably known as the Parson's Bell or Sermon Bell. After a lapse of about seventy years, on account of the bell being without its clapper, the ringing of the sermon bell was reintroduced in 1769. The ringing of the Sermon Bell arose from a Royal Injunction of 1547 ordering a bell to be tolled before the sermon. The method, apparently, being to ring the Sermon Bell first, then chime all the bells, and finally to ring the small bell called the Ting Tang. Two ropes pass down the tower wall to the ringing chamber. These allow for independent chiming to take place. One rope is directly to the Sanctus bell and the second activates the hammer which in turn strikes the Tenor bell. A simple form for tolling and very convenient for use at weekday services and at funerals.

Today, eight bells hang in two tiers in the bell chamber. On the lower level are bells two, three, five, seven and tenor, and placed centrally above, are, from the south wall, treble, fourth and sixth.

During the reign of Edward VI (1547-1553) we know that four bells hung in the steeple and that a further handbell was in being. One cannot but wonder if this small bell could possibly be the same Sanctus or Sermon bell alluded to.

But, the earliest mention of bells at Crich dates from 1280 when Archbishop Peckham appears to have visited Crich and was called upon to settle a dispute between the parishioners and the Abbot of Darley, as Rector. The Archbishop appointed two Canons of Lichfield as his commissioners in the dispute and their decision was that the Abbot should find some one whose duty it should be to ring the parish bells and that he should provide ropes for the bells. To have had more than one bell over seven hundred years ago is of great interest and must surely and rightly imply that the church here at Crich carried great importance locally.

The present bells bear the following inscriptions :-

Treble   A gift of Francis E.S. May. In memory of her father
           and mother, Benjamin and Ann Taylor and family 1928.

The inscription is in half-inch Roman capitals and the inscription band is decorated with an alternating ball and stud design. Cast By John Taylor & Co., Loughborough.

2nd.   The gift of Frederick Alton, 1928. In memory of
           Winfield Alton, Ambergate, Died 11 Dec. 1924. Also
           of Millicent Smith Alton, Ambergate, Died 12th. Oct. 1894.

Also cast by Taylor's in 1928 and bearing beneath the decorated inscription band of entwined leaf and flower design is an embossed rectangle inscribed Taylor, Loughborough.

3rd.   John Taylor & Co., Loughborough. 1910.

The inscription band is beautifully decorated with leaves and fruit. This bell was not recast in 1928.

4th.   John Dod, John Feepound, C.Wardens MDCCXXI.
           Recast 1928 in memory of Capt. W.E. Else, 17th.
           Notts. and Derby. Killed in action, Paschendale,
           Jan. 3rd. 1918.

The inscription of the 1721 casting is faithfully reproduced around the inscription band whilst on the waist is added the 1928 memorial. This bell was treble to the peal of five.

5th.   Feare God honor the King 1671.
           Recast 1928 by the parishioners.

This bell was originally cast in Nottingham by George Oldfield and his founder's mark is faithfully reproduced beneath the old inscription. Recast 1928 by John Taylor & Co.

6th.   L Saxton, C Silvester Churchwardens,
           I Goddard Minister 1771
           Taylor's medallion
           In memory of Harriet Poyser Died 1897.

This bell formerly carried the inscription "Jesus Be our Spede, R.R.B.W." and the founder's mark of Henry Oldfield of Nottingham, with the date 1583 circumscribed within a small circle. However, as this old bell was later found to be broken, it was sent by the churchwardens, L. Saxton and C. Silvester, on Saturday, March 30th, 1771, to Rotherham to be recast, but I am unable to establish by whom. It was again recast by Taylor's in 1928. Note that in the inscription I. Goddard is referred too as Minister, not Vicar?

7th.   Hec Campana Sacra Fiat Trinitate Beata 1616.
           Recast 1928 by the Church Work Party.

The old inscription in Lombardic capitals was highly decorated. This bell was first cast in Nottingham and bears the same inscription as one of the old bells that once hung in the tower at Bolsover. That bell also carried the founder's mark of

Richard Mellour. However, the date 1616 is interesting, as this places it firmly at the time of Henry Oldfield who was casting bells in Nottingham. Further, Robert Quarnby had succeeded to the Mellor business and married Francis, the daughter of Henry Dand who was in partnership with Henry Oldfield, so we have here a bell possibly cast at either of the Nottingham foundries. For more of their history turn to the chapter, 'Bellfounders of Nottingham'.

Tenor   All men that heare my mournful sound
Repent before you lye in ground 1626.
Recast 1928. R.O. Wilson Vicar.
H.J. Rankin, J.H. Smith Churchwardens.
Weight 12cwt. 1qr. 9lbs in the key of F#.

A contemporary report in the Ringing World on October 19th, 1928, describes the dedication.

"Saturday last was indeed a 'red letter' day in the history of the old Derbyshire village of Crich, when the population was more than doubled by the influx of visitors to attend the dedication of the peal of eight bells.

It would be difficult to visualise a more ideal place in which to place a peal of bells than Crich Church, for it stands on the top of a hill 'neath the shadow of the famous war memorial stand, known to thousands who have visited the Peak District.

The dedication ceremony was performed by the Lord Bishop of Derby assisted by the Vicar of Crich (the Rev. R.O. Wilson), many other clergy also being present from neighbouring parishes. The quaint old village was a 'Mecca' of nearly a hundred ringers, such old stalwarts of the Exercise turning up as Messrs. John Flint, Tom Bettison, John Holman, Alf. Wright, Jos. Lord, James Paget, S. Dawson, Jesse Moss, H. Robins, Ed. Gobey, John Brothwell, James Hutchby and 'Jack' Tarlton, and many others from within a radius of fifty miles, including Messrs. John Oldham, Colin Harrison, John Fiddler, David Collins and several other employees of Messrs. Taylor and Co., who have carried out the scheme of restoration.

The original proposal was to recast the old peal of six bells, with the exception of the treble, which was added in 1910 by the Loughborough Foundry. The old five bells, were of exceedingly poor tonal quality, but even then some of the parishioners were loath to part with them, and efforts were made, through the medium of the local press, to retain them from an archaeological point of view. The correspondence on this matter brought about an article from a North Wingfield reader, who suggested that not only should the bells be recast and made worthy of the church, but that they should be augmented to a peal of eight. This letter caught the eye of Mrs. F.E.S. May, of Chesterfield, who, with a relative, spontaneously offered to defray the cost of the proposed two new treble bells. The scheme, which few believed would ever mature, is now an accomplished fact, and even those who objected to the recasting of the old bells must surely realise what a glorious peal they have in place of the old 'pots'.

The peal is tuned on Taylor's 'true harmonic' system, with an even balance of tone from treble to tenor, and the effect, as one stands and listens to them in the valley below, is truly enchanting.

The opening touch was rung by Messrs. W. Piggin, S. Greenhaigh, G. Ashman, W.E. Drake, A. Allwood, H. Allwood, F. Roberts and E. Ashman, after which ringing was arranged by bands in order that everyone present could have chance of a pull.

Tea was arranged in the village schools, two sittings being necessary.

The Vicar spoke in eulogistic terms of the way in which subscriptions, both large and small, had been raised, Mrs May being specially thanked for her generosity. He also referred to the fine way in which Messrs. Taylor and Co. had carried out their work, and the splendid spirit in which they had met them over various matters. - Mr. Oldham responded on behalf of Mrs May, who was too modest to reply herself, and on behalf of the Loughborough firm.

That the 'go' of the bells is all that can be desired, may be judged from the fact that practically all the touches attempted were brought round, the touches ranging from standard methods to Superlative Surprise. As the evening drew on, ringers made their way to the Black Swan Hotel, where a convivial hour was spent with handbells and friendly talk among old friends, who had come specially to hear the transformed effect which they knew could be expected from the 'treatment' the old bells would receive from the famous firm of Messrs Taylor and Co. at Loughborough."

Adorning the walls of the ground floor ringing chamber are several peal boards and an old weathercock. It would be interesting to know if in fact this happens to be the old weathercock purchased from Bird's of Mansfield by the churchwardens John Beardah Senr. and Thomas Booner in 1692 at a cost of forty shillings. Itemised in the accounts as being twenty-eight shillings for the vane, and twelve shillings to have it gilded. David Woodhouse and George Bacon Jnr, who were churchwardens in 1769, had it taken down and re-gilded.

The tower screen was erected in 1966 and together with the galleried pipes of the 1914 organ above fill this fine narrow arch to the nave. Hidden from general view behind the mass of organ pipes is the remains of the weather line of a former gabled roof to the nave.

A marble tablet records another occasion when work was done on the bells. To commemorate the Coronation of Edward VII.

"This tablet was placed here by the ringers of this church in recognition of the work of Mr. J.T.Lee, Parish Churchwarden, in connection with the rehanging of these bells by his energy the sum of £170 was obtained. Ringers: W. Piggin, G. Holmes, H. Allwood, G. Brown, J. Piggin, S. Piggin, Coronation Day, June 26, 1902."

Four of the ringers, G. Holmes, G. Brown, J. Piggin and S. Piggin being founder members of the East Derbyshire Association of Change Ringers when it was formed in 1887.

For a time in the late 1960's and now sadly missing was a hand written ode to Frank Ashman. Written by an unknown author for Christmas 1968 it so moved Frank that he reluctantly allowed it to be copied. You will find it quoted in full in the chapter of belfry jingles, rhyme, verse and hymn.

The first peal of 5040 changes to be rung on the bells took place in 1911 after the addition of the new treble in the previous year. It was of Minor and comprised five extents (720 Changes) of Kent Treble Bob and two of plain Bob. It was rung on January 28th, 1911 by George Pipes, Henry George, Thomas Stimpson, John Flower, Herbert Fretwell and F. Watkinson who conducted the peal.

The first peal to be rung on the octave took place three months after they were hung. On Saturday, January 26th, 1929, a peal of Grandsire Triples, 5040 Changes, being Thurston's Five Part, was rung in two hours and fifty nine minutes by, Geoffrey Ashman, Wilfred H. Buxton, Frank F. Hill, William A. Parsons, William E. Drake, Joseph Lord, Herbert G. Fretwell and Edgar Ashman. It was conducted by Joseph Lord.

Triples is of any method using seven bells in changes. The tenor bell covering or coming in last at each change. Major however, is the term used when all eight bells are involved in the changes and the first peal of Major to be rung on the bells took place on Saturday, July 6th, 1929, when a Peal of Plain Bob Major, 5120 changes composed by F. Hopgood was conducted by Joseph Lord. The ringers on this occasion were, Geoffrey Ashman, George E. Allin, Thomas Bettison, Wilson Allin Snr., William Swain, Ernest A. Wilson, John W. England and Joseph Lord.

The Belfry of St. Helen, Darley

Tenor: In memoriam Victoria Reginae. Severe storm damage to tower, 1703.
Two ringers serve over sixty years. 'Eccentric in some detail' the tower.

There is nothing left standing of the church which stood here in Saxon times and which was extant when the Domesday survey was compiled. Nor is there much evidence of the Norman work, for the church appears to have undergone a thorough renovation when the Early English style was in vogue about the end of the 12th century. To the Decorated period of the 14th century belong the arches that separate the nave from the side aisles. Those on the south are of octagon construction and of later date than the circular pillars supporting those on the north. But the two narrow pointed arches next to the tower are older than the rest. They spring from corbels which are ornamented with nail-head moulding and seem to belong to the Early English period.

The tower, built in the 15th century, is rather eccentric in some of its detail, the buttresses being unusually shallow for the style. The archway into the tower is open and reveals the large west window. Beneath this window stood a wide entrance until about 1820 when it was converted into a window on the direction of the Rev. S.C. Saxton, the apex of this converted doorway being carved into an animal shape. In the inner north-east angle of the tower a corbel in the shape of an ugly monster serves for the projection of the turret staircase. The summit of the tower is embattled with crocketed pinnacles adorning the angles. The nave roof is not at the same elevation as the one covering it when the tower was first built as can be seen from the weather mouldings. It also cuts off a small section from the apex of the tower arch. To the left of the old tower doorway are to be found on a stone two animals of rather nondescript form. These are probably Norman and may have formed part of the tympanum over the Norman doorway and were considered of sufficient interest to be built into the tower when it was reconstructed.

On the night of November 27, 1703, a terrific storm swept through England causing great devastation. At St Helen's the battlements and pinnacles of the tower were severely damaged necessitating their renewal in the following year. This repair lasted two hundred years before being again rebuilt, in 1902, together with the lower part of the west wall of the tower, and the roof re-leaded. As much of the old masonry as possible was used.

Prior to 1876 the tower contained five bells with a sixth being added that year. In 1902 these were augmented to a peal of eight and represent four different bell founders. They are inscribed :-

| Treble | John Taylor & Co. Founders. Loughborough. |
| | In Memory James & Sarah Smith. |

2nd.	James Barwell Founder. Birmingham. 1876.
3rd.	God save this Church. I. Hoyden, A. Vickers, Ch. Wardens 1704.
4th.	James Barwell Founder. Birmingham, 1876.
5th.	+ God save the church 1628. Recast 1902.
6th.	Mears & Stainbank Founders, London. 1876.
7th.	Sacra Clango Gavdia Pango Funera Plango 1710. Tenor Laus Deo. In memoriam Victoria Reginae Reverendissimam in Christo Obdormit, 22 Jan. 1901.

Dedicated to the memory of Queen Victoria this tenor bell, weighing 15cwts. 2qrs. 2lbs, was hung in the tower along with the new treble in 1902. At the same time the fifth bell was recast in order to produce an octave in the key of F. The tower was restored and greatly strengthened with a new iron frame for the bells being installed. The total cost amounting to £1241.

In 1876 James Barwell cast two bells for the tower. The new treble and a replacement for a bell cast by Henry Oldfield in 1618 which was badly cracked and on which the inscription, "God save the church, 1618", and the mark of Henry Oldfield appeared.

The sixth bell cast by Mears & Stainbank, also in 1876, was probably a recasting or a replacement for another bell that hung in the tower and simply inscribed, "R.B. M.P. 1628". According to Rev. Charles Cox this bell had an ornamented border incorporating Fleur-de-lis, the initials were probably those of the churchwardens, and it was cast during the reign of Charles II. An interesting mixed peal.

On Wednesday, July 16th, 1986 a large congregation attended the funeral of the beloved ringer and nonagenarian George Paulson. George, aged 95 years, had been a ringer at St. Helen's for well over sixty years.

The service was conducted by the Vicar and the Rev St. John Smith, a former incumbent of St. Helen's from 1963 until his retirement. St. John Smith himself a very able and keen ringer, spoke with affection of George saying how he had welcomed him as a visiting bellringer to the tower some fifty years ago and long before he became Vicar. George was captain of the ringers and tower keeper. He also took an active part in the church's life, serving on the P.C.C. and in several other capacities. After the service and burial in the churchyard the bells were rung half-muffled by the local band and visiting ringers as a mark of respect for a grand old gentleman ringer.

On October 28th, 1984, the local band had rung a quarter peal of 1260 changes of Plain Bob Triples in honour of George's 94th birthday. The ringers were, Richard Taylor (aged 12) Treble; J.H. Percy, 2nd; I. Duff, 3rd; H.E. Taylor, 4th; Pauline A.

111

Percy, 5th; J.E. Dakin, 6th; S. Humphrey, Conductor, 7th; E. Paulson, Tenor

For many years the parishioners of Darley have been proud of their church bell-ringers but never more so than in 1981 when members of the band won the Derby Diocesan Association Six-Bell Striking Contest, Horsley Cup, in competition with ten other teams. The ringers on this occasion were, Herbert E. Taylor, J. Howard Percy, Pauline A Beaumont, David Kingman, Peter D, Taylor and Simon Humphrey, scoring 225 points out of a possible 240 ringing the bells at Horsley.

Long service as bellringers at St. Helen's is quite the norm. Herbert Taylor has completed over sixty years and several other members of the band including Peter Taylor are fast approaching this goal.

After the first World War and through into the late twenties and early thirties a strong band of change ringers was firmly established at St. Helen's. William Taylor, Alfred Wright, John Siddall, Edwin Blackwell, Bernard Allsop, George Paulson, George Hughes, Alfred Smith, William Blagshaw, Robert Allsop, Herbert Taylor, John Taylor, Ronald Allsop, Hugh Gregory and Denis Scott. Practice night was then, as it is now, on a Wednesday evening and peal ringing was very much the order of the day. Most were rung and recorded for the Midland Counties Association of Change Ringers of which the following is typical.

On Wednesday, October 21, 1931, in 2 hours and 59 minutes,
5040, GRANDSIRE TRIPLES.

John Taylor	Treble	Herbert Taylor	5th.
George H. Paulson	2nd.	John H. Paulson	6th.
William Blagshaw	3rd.	Bernard Allsop	7th.
Edwin Blackwell	4th.	Robert Allsop	Tenor

Conducted by George H. Paulson to Holt's Ten-part plan.

The ancient yew that stands in St. Helen's churchyard is well known. Such is its fame that much has been written about it. Nothing better than the poem written by a former Rector, and Canon of Southwell, who came to Darley in 1881, the Rev. Frederic Atkinson, in his "To the Darley Yew" which he published in the Parish Magazine. Of the twenty six verses that touch on many aspects of our national history, just two of them make mention of the bells of Darley:-

> "And anglers loitering late by Derwent's side
> Heard Darley bells ring in the happier times;
> And up from Matlock, as the cadence died,
> And down from Winster came responsive chimes;
>
> Right gladly rang they; for that day unmatched
> Restored our king, and healed our nation's sores:
> And dim with joy was many an eye that watched
> Its last light die behind the Stanton Moors."

The Belfry of St. Mary the Virgin, Denby.

Three bells in tower by 1553. Chesterfield and Nottingham Founders.
Bellframe removed after 300 years. English oak used throughout belfry.

The western tower, supported by angle buttresses, is surmounted by a broach-spire that rises from behind the plain parapet. Built of coarse-grained sandstone it forms a fair example of Decorated work and judging from the west window, is early in that style and dating from about 1300. Note the large ogee-shaped moulded niche higher up the west elevation, and the absence of a west door. One wonders if the figure of Our Lady once occupied this niche. Note also, the handsome frieze of pierced pointed trefoils ornamenting the parapet. These correspond to those found upon the Decorated towers of Chesterfield and Crich and are most probably the work of the same mason. The octagonal spire has two tiers of dormer openings on each cardinal face. At the bell chamber level are four, two light, louvred openings and the spire is crowned with a fine weathercock rising from an orb finial.

Inside, the former ground floor ringing chamber is separated from the nave by the tower arch. At little over eleven feet square this old ringing chamber has been refurbished admirably.

In the summer of 1993 it was decided to relocate the bellringers to a new elevated chamber. A new floor was built within the tower on level with the spring of the tower arch to the nave and just above the height of the oak screen. The upper arch was glazed in order to conserve heat. The new work is well constructed and fine oak banisters independently positioned across both the arch and the west window take nothing away from either. In fact the effect is most pleasant as it allows the ringers to be closeted and yet at the same time to be on view from the nave. This creates, in a very symbolic satisfactory manner, the fact that bellringers do belong too, and are active serving officers of the church.

The ceiling of the ringing chamber is of English oak as is the one above, beneath the bells. Access to the top of the tower is by a spiral stairway in the north-west corner. The three doors giving access to and from the stair are also of English oak and together with all the iron door furniture were made by local craftsmen. The iron hinges, latches and the escutcheons being wrought from the old bell hangings. It was somewhat fitting that in building the new ringing chamber English oak was again used and that local craftsmen were employed. The ringers and other members of the congregation gave considerable assistance and John Marshall undertook much of the joinery work

The tower contains a ring of six bells. Three bells rang out over the parish prior to 1604 when a tenor bell was added. These four bells rang out for a further three centuries until in 1907 two treble bells were added to make a ring of six. A new metal frame was erected with accommodation for eight bells at this time by John

Taylor & Co., of Loughborough and the old oak frame was dismantled. A fragment of this old oak frame and showing clearly the date of 1604 is preserved. Of the three ancient bells it is very probable that the present fourth bell was placed in the tower soon after it was built but more of that later.

Details of the six bells are:-

Treble   Weight, 3cwts. 2qrs, 0lbs. in Note E.
       "Glory to God and:
       In Loving memory of
       William Drury Nathaniel Drury-Lowe
       of Locko Park
       Born July 13th 1828.
       Died August 31st 1906.
       Given by his widow and children.
       Thy Will be Done 1907."

Second   Weight, 4cwts. 0qrs. 20lbs. in Note D.
       Inscribed as treble.

Third   Weight, 3cwts. 0qrs. 26lbs. in Note C.
       "God save his Church."

The bell mark of Richard Mellour flanked by the initials 'H.D.' in Lombardic capital letters.

Richard Mellour of Nottingham cast bells from about 1488 until his death in 1508. His son Robert carried on the business until he died in 1525.

The initials 'H.D.' however most probably refers to bellfounder Henry Dand who was reputed to have been in partnership with the Nottingham bellfounder, Henry Oldfield in the latter half of the sixteenth century. Dand's daughter, Frances, married Robert Quarnby on 26th January, 1567/8. Quarnby was the son of Elizabeth Mellour the daughter of Robert. This raises the question. Was this ancient Mellour bell recast by Henry Dand toward the end of the sixteenth century? Dand was known to be still casting bells in 1591 and alive in 1597.

Fourth   Weight, 4cwts. 3qrs. 12lbs. in Note B.
       "I.H.C. Nazarenus Rex Judeorum."
       There is no founders mark on this bell.

This omission is quite common with pre-Reformation bells. Mark Fryer in his book "Some chapters in the history of Denby" published in 1934 puts this as the oldest bell in the tower and has this to say:- "The initial cross and stop are the same as on bells made by Johannes de Stafford, a bell-founder who lived about the middle or latter half of the fourteenth century. The date of the tower is fourteenth century, and this bell is without doubt one of the original bells placed in the tower. A John de Stafford was Mayor of Leicester in 1366 and again in 1370, and was in all probability the same individual as the bell-founder."

Mark Fryer also gives an alternative reading of the inscription "I.H.S. Jesus Hominum Salvator." with the note "Some old forms of 's' were like 'C'" Cox however uses the one ascribed.

Fifth	Weight, 6cwts. 1qr. 23lbs. in Note A.

"I.H.C. Gloria in excelsis Deo. 1604."

The founders mark is a fylfot cross in a shield surmounted by the letters G.H.

This is the mark of Godfrey Heathcote, of Chesterfield who cast bells there from 1578 until 1643.

Tenor	Weight, 9cwts. 3qrs. 20lbs. in Note G.

"Patrick Lowe Esquire, Anno Do. 1604."

The mark is a cross of Calvary between the initials 'H' and 'O' with a crescent and a star above.

This bell-founder's mark is that of Henry Oldfield of Nottingham and is richly ornamented. In 1907 it was found to be broken but was faithfully recast by John Taylor. In the ornamentation appear the figures of an owl, a squirrel and a monkey, signifying wisdom, industry and wit.

In the Church Goods Commissioners report in 1553 under Edward V1. we find, "iij in the steple - j little bell called a saunce bell - j sacrying bell and j hande bell."This would suggest that two of the three bells in the "steple"were recast in 1604 which in turn becomes interesting when we read above of two bell-founders, Heathcote and Oldfield, doing work here in the same year?

A bronze plate in the ringing chamber reads :-

"To the Glory of God
and in memory of
William Drury Nathaniel Drury-Lowe of Locko
The Tower and Spire of this Church were restored and the
ancient bells were rehung by his son
William Drury Drury-Lowe
and
Two new bells were added by
his widow and younger children
A.D. 1907."

On Saturday, January 29th, 1927, a Peal of Grandsire Doubles, 5040 Changes, was rung on the bells, in three hours and three minutes, as a last token of respect to the late Mr. Francis Weston, who for 54 years had been a bellringer at this church. The bells were rung half-muffled by: Percy Weston, Treble; Thomas Cresswell, 2nd; George Wilson, 3rd; Benjamin Walvin, 4th; Herbert G. Fretwell, 5th; Frank F Hill, Tenor. No mention is made of who conducted the peal.

An extended peal of 5760 changes of Minor was rung on the bells on Saturday, April 2nd, 1921. This took three hours and 24 minutes to complete. It consisted of three extents (720 changes) each of Oxford and Kent Treble Bob, and two extents of Single Oxford. It is the longest peal to be rung on the bells. The author had the pleasure of ringing in a Peal of Minor, 5040 Changes, in six methods, on the bells on Saturday, July 20th, 1974. The first peal to a five bell method, known as Doubles, was rung on the bells on Saturday, November 3, 1923 when 5040 Changes of Grandsire was rung by Benjamin Walvin, treble; Thomas Cresswell, 2; Charles Walvin, 3; Walter Briggs, 4; Herbert G. Fretwell, 5, and Percy Weston covering on the tenor bell. The peal was conducted by Herbert Fretwell and was the first peal by local ringers Thomas Cresswell and Walter Briggs and the first of Doubles by Percy Weston. It was also the first peal by the treble ringer who together with ringers of bells four and five hailed from Swanwick.

In August, 1908 St. Mary's ringers joined the East Derbyshire Association of Change Ringers. This was within a year of the bells being augmented to a peal of six and they became the twenty-third tower to affiliate.

EAST DERBYSHIRE ASSOCIATION OF CHANGE RINGERS

BALANCE SHEET for Year ending December 31st, 1915.

INCOME.	£	s.	d.	EXPENDITURE.	£	s.	d.
Balance in hand of Treasurer, Dec. 31, 1914 ...	3	15	0	Printing Account (Jos. Spriggs, Clay Cross) ...	2	12	0
Invested in P.O. Savings Bank	7	15	10	Ringing Scheme Certificates (J. Ainsley) ...	3	0	0
Honorary Members Subscriptions	2	7	6	Frames for Certificates (Boots)	1	1	0
Ringing Members Subscriptions	2	6	6	Secretary's Remuneration	1	10	0
23 Entrances	1	3	0	Auditor's Remuneration...	0	6	0
				Postage and Incidental Expenses	1	7	5
				Invested in P.O. Savings' Bank	5	15	10
				Balance in Treasurer's hands, Dec. 31st, 1915 ...	1	15	7
	£17	7	10		£17	7	10

Life Member	1		HAROLD SMITH, Treasurer.	
Hon. Members	14	2 now deceased	T. ALLIBONE, Secretary.	
Ringing Members ...	173	Increase 2	Audited and found correct, Feb. 9th, 1916,	
Towers in Union	21	Lapsed 2	FRED WATKINSON, ⎫ Auditors.	
Ringing Members		Lapsed 21	HARRY B. WALTERS, ⎭	

The Belfry of St. Mary, Edwinstowe

Early Christian site. Steeple rebuilt after storm damage.
'Decayed oak' unfit for ship timber used. Irregular polygon spire.

"Those who believe in Robin Hood, believe that he married Maid Marian in the 12th- to 13th- century church at Edwinstowe.....?"

The ancient church, dedicated to Our Lady, is situated in the Sherwood Forest countryside of Nottinghamshire, and has origins going back to Saxon times. The name "Edwinstowe" means the holy place of Edwin, who was the first Christian King of Northumbria. Tradition has it that Edwin's body rested here awhile, probably in a little church built of wood, after being killed at the Battle of Heathfield, in 633 A.D. by Cadwallon.

Edwin had been baptized on Easter Eve, 627 A.D., at York, also in a wooden church that had been specially erected. Two years earlier, in 625 A.D., an Italian monk called Paulinus, who had arrived in England about four years after S. Augustine, and who had worked in the south of England, was consecrated Bishop in order that he could accompany a Kentish princess by the name of Ethelburga on her way north to marry Edwin, King of Northumbria.

On arriving at York, Paulinus found himself in very similar circumstance to that of Augustine when he had first arrived in Canterbury. Paulinus had a strong supporter in the queen, and a heathen king, who at least showed some slight interest in the faith of Christians. Paulinus began at once to preach the Gospel to the king and his nobles, and, like Augustine, was soon rewarded for his labours.

Paulinus worked indefatigably in Northumbria as Bishop of York. He travelled over much of Yorkshire, Nottinghamshire and north Lincolnshire preaching the Gospel in the villages and baptizing people in the clear waters of their brooks and rivers. So great was his success that in the year 634 he was made archbishop and the pallium was sent to him from Rome. However, before the white vestment reached him the whole situation in the north had changed dramatically: Edwin was dead, Paulinus had fled south, and the newly established Christian Church had practically disappeared.

The mission had obviously been undertaken much too quickly and in consequence only superficial. Be this as it may, there did remain one faithful soul who was known as James the Deacon, and who lived near Catterick. In imminent danger of death, James quietly ministered to the needs of the faithful few. Then, with exception to the heroic work being carried out by James the Deacon, the Christian Church in the north of England collapsed altogether. For a year there was chaos, and it seemed if all the good work done by Paulinus would be destroyed. But in 634 the remaining Christians began to take heart again for far away in Iona was a young man called Oswald who had been sent there on the death of his father in 617. Oswald had been brought up on Iona and educated by the monks. Shortly after the death of Edwin, he succeeded to the combined kingdoms of Deira and Bernicia, and immediately raised an army to drive out the heathen usurpers. The forces met at Rowley Burn, south of Hexham, in 635; Oswald set up a wooden cross and called his soldiers to prayer before the battle. Cadwallon was defeated, and Oswald became undisputed King of Northumbria.

He immediately set himself the task to restore damage which had been done to the cause of the Christian faith in the "disastrous year", and sent to Iona for a bishop to evangelize his people and help restore faith to the waste places. The first who came fled in despair; "The people are hopeless", he said. But the second was Aidan, one of the most saintly and gifted of the monks of Iona, and it was he who restored Christianity in the north.

We, of course, must return to our story and the fabric of a later church building here at Edwinstowe but for anyone wishing to follow on Aidan's success you will find "A History of the Church in England" by Dr. J.R.H. Moorman a marvellous compendium of information.

The actual date of the present Church is not known, but there are clues which lead us to place it about 1175A.D. Take a look at the architecture of the tower. It is in transitional Norman style - thick walls, and a wide splay in the interior opening of the windows, with rounded tops, but with a lancet top and narrow opening on the outside.

The steeple is a conspicuous landmark for miles around. At first sight the spire appears to be contemporary with the tower, but on closer inspection it will be seen that the spire is at least three centuries later and possibly added in the 15th century when the north aisle was re-constructed. In building a good polygonal spire, the tower top from which it springs should be four square, but in this case the spire is built on a tower where the width from east to west is greater than the breadth from north to south and in consequence the spire is an irregular polygon.

The original spire didn't last long. probably until 1672 when it was brought down by a storm. In 1679 we learn that the parishioners sent a petition to King Charles II asking for "£200 or two hundred decayed oaks which are unfit for ship timber", from the royal forest of Sherwood towards the cost (£300) of repairing", the body of the church", which was "extremely shaken and in a very ruinous condition", occasioned by the fall of the steeple, which about seven years ago "was beaten down by thunder".

The kings of England hunted in Sherwood Forest, and would know Edwinstowe well and it is thought that King Henry II. took an interest in the building of the stone church. The carved head of S. Thomas of Canterbury on top of one of the pillars of the north arcade point to this. Thomas was martyred in 1170, and Henry II built churches and monasteries as acts of reparation for the murder.

Again, sometime in the 1870's the steeple was once more the victim of storm and was struck by lightning, causing the top portion to be rebuilt in matching magnesian limestone. The dormer lights on each cardinal face of the spire may well be mistaken for Early English work when seen from below, but scrutiny at close quarters reveals them to be of a much later date. They correspond with the square pinnacles set upon the broaches and all are set at the springing of the spire. The plain spire above is pierced on each cardinal face and surmounted by a weathercock.

We now take a look at the massive tower with walls all of three feet thick, and affording an internal measurement of nineteen by eighteen feet at the base. It is lighted on the south and west by graceful lancets. The one on the west face being unique, tall and narrow and treated in an unusual manner by the introduction of a transom. This window, with its wide internal splays, forms a very effective feature when seen from the east end enclosed within the lines of the spacious pointed arch of the tower. Two extraordinary heads, one with great staring eyes and the other with open mouth look down from this arch.

The oak beams of the old tower roof are still in position and a structure spanning the corners of the tower at the base of the spire, known as squinches, consist of two concentric pointed arches in two orders with the addition of corbel stone and lintel.

Introduced, probably in the 13th century, are the double light, louvred openings of the bell chamber. These replaced the openings to be seen in the upper stage, and built up with stone to form blind arcades of three obtusely pointed bays within a semi-arch. That upon the east face being obliterated from view by the dial of the clock. On the south-west corner a broad, flat staircase projection gives access to the bells and clock.

The Chantry was dissolved by Henry VIII, but earlier in this century the medieval stone altar, with two crosses, was found set into the floor of the belfry. It was recovered, and put into use again to form a war memorial.

Whether St. Mary's tower contained any bells prior to 1662 is not recorded. We do know however that a bell of this date carried the inscription, "God save His Church" and was believed to weigh five hundredweights and eighteen pounds. We also know that a century later there were two more bells, both inscribed "1752 Thomas Hedderly Founder, Roger Oldham C.W."

It is interesting that with a history stretching almost from the birth of Christianity in the north of England, a massive tower dating from the twelfth or very early in the thirteenth century and which incorporates what amount to be two tiers of bell-openings (the higher openings being then filled up at the time when the original steeple was added in the late fifteenth century) yet we find the earliest mention of bells being hung in the tower only takes us back in history just over three hundred years. Could it possibly be that an ancient peal of smaller bells existed and were positioned in the top stage of the tower?

After all, bells filled a more important place in the lives of our ancestors than they do in ours. From the time Britain became Christian until the Reformation, there was scarcely an event in public or private history into which bells did not enter. Then, in 1552, we find in the last paragraph of the Preface of the Second Prayer Book of Edward VI instruction to:-

"The Curate that ministreth in every Parish Churche or Chapell, beying at home, and not beyng otherwise reasonably letted, shall say the same (Mornyng and Euenyng prayer)in the Parishe Churche or Chapell where he ministreth, and shall tolle a belle thereto, a convenient tyme before he begyn, that suche as be disposed maye come to heare Goddes worde, and to praie with hym."

In 1889 Mears and Stainbank of Whitechapel, London, recast the three old bells and absorbed them into a new peal of six. On the treble and four middle bells the only inscription is that of the founder's name. The tenor bell inscription however records the event:-

"These six bells were erected by public
subscription A.D. 1889.
Rev. Henry Telford Hayman, Vicar.
John Thomas Bullivant, Edgar Gibbons,
Churchwardens.
My sound it is all men to call
To serve the Lord, both great and small."

The weight and diameter of the bells is:-

	cwts.	qrs.	lbs.	ft.	ins.
Treble	3	0	17	2	0
2nd.	3	2	23	2	$1^1/_8$
3rd.	4	1	14	2	3
4th.	4	2	18	2	$3^7/_8$
5th.	5	1	1	2	6
Tenor	6	1	12	2	8½

On Saturday, October 31, 1931, in two hours and forty five minutes a Peal of 5040 Changes of Minor was rung on the bells being two extents (720 changes)each of Oxford and Kent Treble Bob and three extents of Plain Bob. The ringers were: Wilfred Riley, Treble; Thomas E. Mallender, 2; Bernard Bailey, 3; Arthur Smithson, 4; Hubert Bailey, 5; Fred. W. Knowles, Conductor, Tenor. This was the first peal to be rung on the bells for the East Derbyshire and Nottinghamshire Association of Change Ringers.

The Belfry of St. Lawrence, Heanor

Tower sees nave rebuilt twice. Oldest surviving bell dates from 1634.
Four bells in tower in 1548. New bell-frame erected in 1902.

For over five hundred years the tower of the Church of St. Lawrence, Heanor, has taken command of this eastern ridge of Derbyshire. Standing over four hundred feet above sea level, its embattled tower stands in fine prospect to the north-east corner of the market square.

Built about 1454 it is supported by angle buttresses and has on each face two large, two-light bell openings with transoms which were altered, possibly in 1868, when much of the church was rebuilt. This rebuilt nave was again demolished and rebuilt in the 1980's as the old gabled weather course to be seen on the eastern face of the tower will reveal. The tower has modern pinnacles and the west door forms the main entrance with a fine west window above. There is a clock with four illuminated dials.

So, here we have a unique situation of a belfry having twice witnessed the major rebuilding of its adjacent nave, and within the space of 120 years.

The 1868 restoration was recorded upon a board in the base of the tower:- "This Church was restored 1868, Frederick Corfield, Vicar. George B. Gregory, Fletcher Draper, Churchwardens. Date of tower 1454. Probable date of old Church 12th. century. Wm. Cowlishaw, Clerk." The precise date of the tower being built is questioned by some who think it more probable that the tower would have been rebuilt about twenty years later, in 1473/4.

The earliest record relating to the church having bells is to be found in the first year of the reign of Edward V1 in 1547/8 when the Church Goods Commissioners report states:- "iiij bells in the steeple. ij hande bells. j sakering bell." It is also of interest to note that during the sixteenth century the church was dedicated to St. Michael and the tower is the only remaining part of that church. In 1902 there were five bells in the tower dating from the seventeenth and eighteenth centuries. In that year the five were augmented into an octave and dedicated on the evening of Monday, 8th December. They are inscribed :-

Treble	A.M.D.G.
	This bell was given A.D. 1902 by John Holbrook, Churchwarden, in loving memory of his dear Son-in-Law who died December, 17 1900. Aged 27 years.
2nd.	God save the King + 1902.
	C.E.L. Corfield + M.A. + Rector.
	Thos. Mayfield J.P. Jno. Holbrook, Wardens.
	Guild of St. Lawrence.

3rd.	The Churches praise I sound always. 1781. Thos. Hedderly of Nottingham Fecit.
4th.	+ GOD SAVE HIS CHVRCH 1634.
5th.	H.C. LAUS DEO. This bell was recast A.D. 1902 when increasing the peal from 5 to 8.
6th.	Gloria in excelsis Deo. This bell was recast in memory of Florence Astle. 1972.
7th.	I TOLE THE TVNE THAT DVLFVL IS TO SVCHE AS LIVD AMISSE BVT SWEETE MY SOWND SEEMES VNTO THEM WHO HOPE FOR IOIFVL BLISS DEO WESTWOOD 1686. Recast 1972 Taylor, Loughborough.
Tenor	John Taylor & Co. Founders, Loughborough. This bell together with new frame work and chimes was erected by public subscription to the glory of God. A.D. 1902. John Andrews, Chairman. H.J. Windle, Secretary. Weight: 15cwt. 2qrs. 4lbs. Diameter; 45 inches.

Of the five old bells hanging in the tower prior to the Taylor augmentation to the octave in 1902 only two of them, the third and the fourth, remain as cast by the original founder. The fifth was recast by Taylor's of Loughborough in the 1902 augmentation and the sixth and seventh bells recast by them seventy years later when further work was undertaken in 1972.

Of the two original bells the third cast in 1781 by Thomas Hedderly was hung as the treble. Today it measures $29^3/_8$ inches in diameter and weighs 4 cwt. 2 qrs. 21 lbs. In addition to the inscription given, the bell carries a band of pattern, a feature of Hedderly's casting. In the registers for 1781 is an interesting memorandum, "Little bell recast at the cost of £14.14s.0d. Old bell cast £1.8s.0d per hundred, metal added at 1s.2d per pound."

It would therefore appear that two older bells existed in the tower and that these two bells were recast with the addition of more metal. In the Cole MSS he refers to six bells being in the tower in 1765. Could it be that two bells, ie. "Little" and "Old", plus extra metal at 1s.2d per pound went into Hedderly's new treble in 1781? To do this would provide the tower with a tuneful five, instead of possibly an odd sounding peal of six.

The 1634 bell, now the fourth, is the oldest surviving bell. Probably cast at Nottingham by George Oldfield. A note in an article on the Rectors and Vicars of Heanor written in 1898 states: "In 1634, bell number two was placed in the church tower, it bears the following inscription, God save His Church, 1634." This leaves the question. Which bell was already hung in the belfry? We have two possibilities, the fifth and the sixth.

The sixth, cast in Chesterfield by Godfrey Heathcote was most probably the third bell to have been hung.

However, the fifth's original inscription was a stamp bearing IHS, two cross stamps and a founder's mark of three small bells in a shield and over the shield a crown which Rev. C. Cox in 1878 noted, and remarked that he had not seen any such mark upon any other Derbyshire bell. Richard Brasyer of Norwich, who died in 1513, cast a bell for Repton bearing his mark, a shield bearing three bells but with a crown between them. In the 14c, an ancestor of Richard Brasyer learned his trade at a Nottingham foundry prior to removing to Norwich. Although interesting, and, I am sure, Cox would know about the Repton bell, this is an inference and the bell has of course been recast.

So, we will move on for a look at the seventh bell cast in 1686 by William Noone of Nottingham, who at the age of 91 years died on August 13th 1732, his life bridging the period when two very important local bell founders, the Oldfield's and the Hedderly's were operating in Nottingham.

"I tole the tune that dismal is to such as lived amiss, but sweet my sound seems unto them who hope for joyful bliss." This amended inscription to be found on the seventh bell is, when compared with the original quoted earlier, interesting for two reasons. When Rev Cox wrote of this bell he says:- "This lettering is in Roman capitals close together, without any break between the words, in two lines round the haunch, except "oiful blisse" and the two following words, which are in a third line. The words "Deo Westwood" are in Lombardic lettering. The initial 'D' must have been wrongly affixed to this bell, by a careless workman, instead of 'G'; it being evidently intended for the name of George Westwood, vicar of Heanor, in 1669. The couplet is also evidently confused. From a somewhat similar couplet found in Hedderly's pocket book it seems that "dul evil" should read "dismal". It is interesting that Cox should couple this inscription with Hedderly and make no mention of Noone. We know that the Hedderlys began their business in Bawtry and Derby before Thomas took to casting bells at Nottingham from 1742. So the mystery remains as to why in Hedderly's pocket book should be found an amendment of this inscription.

Of George Westwood, whose name appears on the seventh bell as Vicar of Heanor in 1686, we know he was, "the son of Edward and Ellen Westwood of Heynor and was baptised August 11th, 1647. He was authorised to officiate ye cure in ye parish church of Heynor February 27th, 1669." In the Horsley parish registers is the following:- "Georguis Westwood Clericus de Heynor et Maria Baker de Allestry widua nupt: Cum licentia septimo dio mensis Augusti Anno Dom 1677."He died whilst "Minister of this parish and buried May 21st. 1698."

To have access to a complete history of the bells of Heanor, as with most of our other belfries, would be shear delight. But, alas, we are left with only fragments. For instance, within the parish of Heanor stood Codnor Castle, home to the Greys since the time of King John. The old church had much stained glass and monuments to that family and it is just probable that the tower and the bells may have reflected their influence and patronage in earlier years. After all, there were four bells in the belfry at the time of Edward VI and the manor of Heanor was a parcel of that at Codnor at the time of the Domesday Survey.

The ringers of Heanor joined the East Derbyshire and Nottinghamshire Association of Change Ringers in 1930 and for a period of over twenty years took an active part in its affairs. On Saturday, November 26, 1927 a peal of 5040 changes of Grandsire Triples was rung on the bells. The ringers being, Treble, F. Cook; 2nd. W. Poyser; 3rd. C.J. Jennings; 4th. W.H. Buxton; 5th. J. Lord; 6th, W.A. Parsons; 7th. W. Lancaster; Tenor, J Walters ringing his first peal which was conducted by W.A. Parsons.

One point of general interest noted from a report of the 1902 dedication of the octave by the Right Rev. Bishop Hamilton Baynes reads:-

The Bishop receiving the ropes said, "By virtue of our sacred office, do we solemnly set apart and separate from all profane and unallowed uses these bells, now dedicated to the Glory of God, for the benefit of His Holy Church." He then delivered the ropes to the Rector, asking him to receive those bells as a sacred trust, and then, turning to the Churchwardens and Ringers, he said, "Take notice that these bells are committed to the custody of the Rector of this Parish, to be used only with his consent, and subject to the control of the Bishop of the Diocese."

An old photograph taken in 1886, and now carefully preserved by the Heanor and District Local History Society, depicts the ringers of St. Lawrence ringing handbells. They are photographed at some venue other than by the church, and although they have handbells poised as though they were actually ringing, with a handbell in each hand, they had obviously broken circle in order that the photograph could be taken. Between the seven ringers we can see fourteen handbells which suggests that tune ringing was the order of the day. The same men, G. Bryan, E. Berrisford, J. Bennistone, William Bryan, Walter Bryan, W. Newton and R. Lomax rang the five bells hanging in the tower of St. Lawrence at that time.

In 1971 advice was sought on problems arising from proposals to recast the sixth and seventh bells. Both bells being of archaeological interest they were however of a poor tone. The Central Council of Church Bell Ringers, Care of Churches Committee deliberated this fact and ruled that it was permissible to recast them. This work was carried out in 1972 and completed in 1973. The work was undertaken by the foundry of John Taylor and Co, Loughborough who placed their mark upon each of the recast bells. Twelve years later, in 1985, Mr. Fredrick Pembleton from Ault Hucknall carried out re-bushing and ancillary work to all the bell clappers.

The Belfry of All Saints, Heath

Original bell cast in Chesterfield. Tower - built - rebuilt - demolished.
Three bells removed to new tower. Ellacombe chiming fitted.

The five bells of All Saints Church were hung in the tower four years before the founding of the East Derbyshire Association of Church Bell Ringers. At the time, 1883, restoration work was in progress on the spire. The tower and spire, like the nave and chancel are not old. They had been erected just thirty years previously in 1852-3, to supersede the old church that stood in isolation a quarter of a mile east of the present village. The area around the old church being known as Lowne or Lund, and it was not until cultivation of the moorland at the top of the hill began, and the parishioners built homes there, that the village became known as Heath.

It would appear that the tower of the old church at Lowne had been rebuilt some half century before the church, with the exception of the porch, was demolished and relocated in the village of Heath. The tower of the old church was at the west end and adorned with pinnacles. However, the Rev. J. Hunter, who visited the church early in the nineteenth century noted that:-

> "The upper part of the steeple is made of wood, and has a leaded spire like Chesterfield, but not very high. It appears very ancient."

In the old tower were three bells bearing the following inscriptions:-

I.   "Anno Domini, 1847. God save His Church."

II.   "Ihc. Gloria in excelsis Deo", Round the haunch in Lombardic capitals. Beneath the 'Ihc' is the founder's mark - G.H. with fylfot cross below.

III   "God save His Church. 1704."in Roman capitals round the haunch.

These three bells were removed into similar positions in the new tower. About thirty years later, they were again removed and with the addition of more metal used to augment the new peal of five bells.

The casting of this peal of five bells was undertaken during 1882. The old inscriptions being omitted and replaced by:- "J. Taylor & Co. Founders, Loughborough, 1882."on the treble second and third whilst the fourth and fifth carry, "Bellfounders "in place of "Founders ". The tenor bell has a diameter of 3ft. 7½ inches; and weighs, 14cwt. 2qrs. 26lbs. and is tuned in F#.

Looking at the present tower we find a low embattled structure built of rock faced stone in the Decorated style with the short octagonal spire rising from behind the parapet. On three sides of the tower are two-light, louvred bell openings, but on the east, and because of the high pitch of the roof of the nave, no bell opening exists. Toward the base of the spire on each cardinal face are small dormers with a single louvred light. The single dial of the clock is accommodated within the arched brace of the south facing bell opening. The bells are reached by way of a spiral stone stairway within the south-west buttress which on reaching the roof terminates in line with the battlements with a low pitched roof. The spire is crowned with a fine orb finial. The ringing chamber, open to the nave, is reached internally via a wooden stairway and a trap door.

Of the old bells, number one above, but not necessarily the treble, points to there being much activity and interest at the old church tower at Lowne. For we find that just five years prior to the tower being demolished this bell was cast, in 1847. Of its history or by whom we know not, nor do we know if it was an older bell recast. Part of its inscription, God save His Church, was identical with that on bell number three above which was cast in Nottingham in 1704 but by 1847 neither Oldfield nor Hedderly were still in business.

Bell number two above was cast in the locality, just down the road at Chesterfield. This is without doubt a Heathcote bell and with one exception the inscription compares exactly with the sixth bell at Alfreton. The difference being on the bellfounder's mark. At Alfreton we find only the initial 'H' placed upon the shield whilst here we find 'G.H.'. This refers to Godfrey Heathcote who was baptised in 1558/9 and whose will was proved in 1643. There were however two sons, Godfrey and Ralph, both becoming bellfounders. Godfrey died before his father and from this we deduce that this bell was cast sometime at the end of the sixteenth or during the early seventeenth century. The identical inscription is to be found on the fifth bell at Denby and bearing the date 1604. A more detailed account of this foundry is the subject of a separate chapter.

The third bell above may have been originally cast in Nottingham by George Oldfield. From 1672 and following the death of George's father, Hugh Oldfield, we find that Hugh's wife carried on the business in the name of and on behalf of their infant son George. This George Oldfield lived until 1741 when his son, also George, continued the business until his death in 1747/8. At this time the foundry passed into the hands of the Hedderlys. "God save His Church", was a favourite inscription of the Oldfield foundry.

So, three very interesting bells were unfortunately abandoned in the name of progress over a century ago.

The bell-ringers of Heath affiliated to the East Derbyshire Association of Change Ringers before the first recorded meeting was held at Easter 1889. Of the early members, the vicar, Rev. F. Brodhurst was elected President in 1900. On Saturday, June 3rd 1905 members of the Association joined the Heath ringers for their quarterly meeting. Touches of many methods were rung, including Stedman Doubles, to everyone's enjoyment. On June 12th, 1909, forty-nine Association members again visited Heath to ring and were entertained to tea in the "beautiful

Vicarage garden," by the Rev. F. Brodhurst. A keen historian, the Rev. Brodhurst who was also vicar of Ault Hucknall at this period, was the author of a comprehensive handbook to Hardwick Hall in which he describes the tapestry, principal portraits, and chief objects of interest. In 1910 three members of the Houldsworth family were ringing at All Saints Church together with Frank Smith, James Evans and Arthur Godfrey.

On December 15th, 1917, a meeting of Association Bell Ringers fixed at Heath had to be cancelled in order to comply with the Government's restriction on lighting. Whilst toward the end of the Second World War, Heath ringers became active immediately the Government ban upon bells being rung was lifted. A well-attended meeting was held at the belfry on September 21st, 1946 when Tom Jennings and his fellow bell ringers made every visitor most welcome. Further visits were made on October 20th, 1951 and in September 1953 when at the Ringers' Service was included a solo, "The Blind Ploughman", sung by a visitor at the invitation of the organist. At this meeting a collection toward a Roll of Honour of Church Bell Ringers who had served in the Second World War, and to be placed in St Paul's Cathedral, London, was subscribed to.

An Ellacombe Chiming Apparatus was supplied and fixed by Taylor's of Loughborough at the same time as the two additional bells were installed. Sometimes it is desired that one person should be able to sound the bells. In such a case the best arrangement is the installation of hammers striking the side of each bell with operating cords extending down to a console. These are usually known by the name of their originator, the Rev. Canon H.T. Ellacombe, as "Ellacombe" hammers. Like clock hammers it is essential that they are lowered clear of the bells before change ringing takes place, and for this purpose it is best that the console be situated within the ringing chamber.

During 1985, Mr. Frederick Pembleton rehung the five bells on new ball races and at the same time provided new pulleys and refurbished and re-bushed the clappers.

The Belfry of St. Wilfrid, Kirkby in Ashfield

Tower rebuilt to 13th century design. Metal of clock and Sanctus bells recast.
Caretaker saves concert in Miner's strike. Augmented to a peal of five in 1927.
Three bells since 1552.

The one thing in common with each of our belfries is that at sometime in the past there has been an urge within to augment the existing peal of bells. During the late sixteenth and seventeenth centuries this urge was in the main for villages to strive for a peal of five bells. Later this became six and then eight. Now ten is not uncommon, but on a personal note I do feel that for a village to press for a peal of ten bells is somewhat irrational if for no other reason than to man this number of bells week in week out, just for the prime duty of providing a full peal of bells ringing for the services of the church, is almost an impossibility from the bell-ringers available in any one village. Sunday service ringing is a very time-consuming exercise and must rank as one of the church's offices that demands the utmost dedication from its ringers. And, any parish today that is blessed with a full complement of bells being rung regularly for its church services should be justly proud of the achievement and of its team of bell-ringers.

Somewhat typical of many belfries is the 1973 augmentation here at St. Wilfrid's when the peal of five bells was increased to a peal of six by the addition of a new treble. In October that year the following article appeared in "The Ringing World", the official weekly journal of the Central Council of Church Bell Ringers. It was written by the tower Ringing Master, Ernest J. Sollis, and illustrates fully what can be achieved by just a few like-minded parishioners.

> "Up to 1927, St. Wilfrid's Parish Church had three bells, one dated 1618 and another 1803. Two bells were added that year to complete a ring of five, since which time much has been said about adding a sixth but nothing done.
>
> Our story starts at Easter, 1970. One of my first jobs as Secretary of the East Derbyshire and West Nottinghamshire Association was to arrange an evening meeting at Kirkby, and I suggested (half jokingly) that it would be nice to have six bells at Kirkby, if we could find a cheap bell, perhaps a redundant bell, and hang in the tower ourselves.
>
> Herbert Rooke, captain at Warsop, told me that they had been offered a redundant clock bell by the then Mansfield Co-op Society. I contacted the Secretary and arranged to purchase the 3cwt. bell and put it in church as the centrepiece of an appeal. It rested on two blocks of wood to avoid damage to the floor and a box was made and fastened to the top of the bell to help raise money. The next step was to talk to John Taylor and Co., of Loughborough, and discuss costs and a method of installing the bell in the tower. Paul Taylor and Tony Clayton came up with what they called "an ingenious idea but a tight fit" and would cost in the region of £350, including the cost of the frame

which was to be made by local engineers. The bell-ringers (whose age at this time averaged 14) decided to try and raise the full amount.

Mrs. C.B. Ellis (mother of one of our young ringers) opened her house to 80 or 90 folk and persuaded them all to drink coffee, bring and buy and purchase raffle tickets. At about this time another bell-ringer's mother set us all off selling bookmarks, pens and pencils and the like, all bearing the legend "St. Wilfrid's Belfry Fund". Another competition was to guess the weight of the bell we had bought. A film show was arranged, but due to the postal strike the films only turned up about five minutes before the show!

The next event was a sponsored walk, but this had to be cancelled as several people had been killed on these walks and the adverse publicity was of no help. To offset this the vicar and ringers of Rawmarsh (Yorks) gave us a scrap sanctus bell weighing about sixty pounds, which would add to the metal of the new bell.

A dance was arranged in the parish hall and a buffet was put on by parents of the bell-ringers.

Perhaps our biggest venture was arranging for Jacqui and Bridie, two Liverpool folk singers, to give a concert. The first took place in January 1972, and was very nearly a disaster because the school was unheated due to the miners' strike. The head caretaker and his staff made a superb job of locking in Friday's heat in the theatre and the temperature was a comfortable 68 degrees.

A return concert was arranged in the new Library Theatre at Sutton later in the year and this was also very well attended.

A saying of my newsagent was: "There is no such thing as bad publicity". I made it my job to have a mention in the local papers as often as possible. It was a report in a local paper which prompted someone to present us with £238 early in 1972, and we were able to place the order for the frame and bells. We took the Rawmarsh bell to the foundry and the church handbells for restoration at the same time.

A year after, the bells were delivered to Loughborough, the frame was made and installed and the work of lifting the bells began soon after. By the end of July the bells were installed in the tower ready for ringing. The majority of the work involved in hanging the bells was carried out by my father and myself, though the work could not have been completed without Frank Smith (and his lifting tackle) and Stanley Harpham.

The final chapter in the story was written on September 9, when the Rt. Rev. Denis Wakeling (Bishop of Southwell) received the bell from Mr. A. Clayton, representing John Taylor & Co., and, having blessed it, passed the rope to the rector, Rev. C.J. Young. Rounds were rung on the bells during the service by Albert Sollis, Helen Overfield, David Barratt, Angela Barratt, Stanley Harpham and Ernest Sollis."

Following the devastating fire on January 16, 1907, the tower and spire of St. Wilfrid's is now the oldest surviving part of the church. It had been rebuilt about forty years earlier with very few variations from that of the thirteenth century tower it replaced. Shortly before midnight on the fateful night a signalman coming off duty from the Bentinck Station signal box on the recently opened Great Central Railway, noticed clouds of smoke billowing from the church. Fire had broken out in the organ chamber, and before the flames could be extinguished, nearly all trace of the old church had disappeared. Every foot of glass had gone, and not a vestige of the organ, altar or pulpit remained. Mural tablets lay smashed among the debris. Only the tower and the spire were relatively undamaged.

The broach spire springs from the tower without the intervention of parapet or pinacles and quickly assumes an octagonal form, the oblique faces being formed of a plain splay above the squinches. Lucarnes or spire lights are positioned high on each cardinal face of the spire which culminates in an orb and finial. The short angled buttresses climb to half way on the western corners of the tower. Immediately above the bell chamber string course are well proportioned two light louvred bell openings and centrally to the north face is the clock dial and beneath the small ringing chamber window. A further ringing chamber light is situated on the south face.

Inside, the thirteenth century tower arch is richly moulded with two half columns. A door in the south-west corner leads onto a spiral stone stairway giving access to the ringing chamber and bells. The former being somewhat heavily beamed with wooden framing in support of the clock works and housing, the rope of the tenor bell being threaded through one of the beams.

In 1552 the old tower contained three bells but by 1740 Brown Willis in his survey lists the church as having four. However in the Stretton MSS we read there were three bells and frames for two others. In 1927 the three bells were recast and two bells added with the inscriptions of the original three being faithfully reproduced. The six are inscribed:-

Treble   Given by the Bellringers and an Anonymous Benefactor in memory of his wife.
E.J. Sollis, Ringing Master.
Charles J. Young, Rector.
Ralph Harrison, John E. Pickering, Churchwardens.

2nd.   The Working Party. 1927.
Taylor's medallion on waist.

3rd.   I.H.S. Maria (Q) (K) (H.O. Mark)
Recast 1927. Taylor's medallion on waist.

This bell bore the Royal Heads of Edward III. and Queen Phillipa and the letters ascribed to William Rufford, who was a London Bell-founder in 1380. The right to use these Royal Heads was probably granted to John Rufford, who had been appointed a Royal Bell-founder in 1367. In the 15th century they were found on bells cast at Worcester before eventually finding their way to Nottingham, where, together with the letters, they were used by the Oldfields when casting some of their bells. The bell-founder's mark was an unusual one belonging to Henry Oldfield and one he used less frequently.

4th.   + IHESVS BE OVR SPEED 1618. (H.O. Mark)
            Recast 1927. Taylor's medallion on waist.
This bell bore plain capital letters between a cable patterned border and the mark of Henry Oldfield (1582 - 1620).

5th.   Thomas Wheeldon, Fecit 1803.
This bell is one of only two known to have been cast by this founder in Derby and very little is known about him. His second bell, cast fifteen years later, hangs in the tower at Meerbrook, Staffordshire.

Tenor   J.W. Smith, Rector.
            J. Taylor and J. Kershaw, Wardens, 1927.
            This inscription is in two lines round the waist.

The introduction of five bells in 1927 brought an interest among the bell-ringers to enter the realms of change ringing and within three years they had affiliated to the East Derbyshire and Nottinghamshire Association of Church Bell Ringers. On Saturday, February 11, 1928 the first peal was rung upon the bells. It consisted of 5040 Changes of Grandsire Doubles. The ringers being, Cornelious J. Partridge, treble; George Wilson, 2nd; Herbert G. Fretwell, 3rd; Samual Hurdle, 4th; John Bleby (ringing in his first peal), Tenor; the peal was conducted by Herbert G. Fretwell and took two hours and fifty minutes to complete.

Two further peals were rung in September that year. On the 25th, another peal of Grandsire being 42 six-scores in ten different callings conducted by Edwin Lee. The ringers were G.H. Galland, treble; W.W. Gardner, 2nd; Edwin Lee, 3rd; T.E Cope, 4th; A Smitheringale, tenor. It was the first peal by all the band. Two days later a Peal of 5040 Changes of Bob Doubles, being 42 six-scores was rung by the same band.

After the augmentation to six in 1973 the first peal of Minor was not recorded until Saturday, September 12, 1981. when a Peal of 5040 Changes of Plain Bob, conducted by Eric J. Sterland was rung to welcome the Rev. I.G. Collins as Rector. The ringers on this occasion being, Ernest J. Sollis, Treble; Wilfred Riley, 2nd; George L. Hall, 3rd; David Barratt, 4th; Eric J. Sterland, 5th; E. Glyn Holdgate, tenor.

It was fitting that Ernest Sollis should ring the treble, the bell which he had done so much to procure, and yet at the same period holding office as Secretary to the East Derbyshire and West Nottinghamshire Association of Church Bell Ringers.

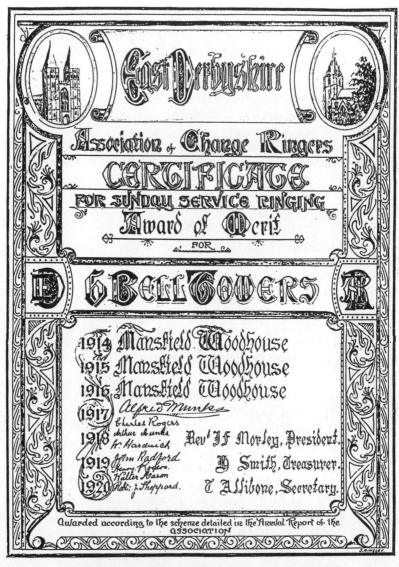

Certificate awarded for Sunday Service ringing. Mansfield Woodhouse ringers being awarded the six bell certificate in 1914, 1915 and 1916

The Belfry of S.S. Peter and Paul, Mansfield

The third year of the Atomic Age   A day of doubt -
Men's hearts failing them for fear   Still we ring out
That all the voice of God may hear.

This inscription, added to the tenor bell when it was recast in 1948, brings our ancient art straight into the twentieth century. No doubt these words are just as dynamic to our own generation as the original inscription was to our ancestor's, when the bell was first cast almost four centuries ago, in 1610.

"Tow summons by this bel we have
One to the church, one to the grave."

Standing but a few feet away from a busy thoroughfare, almost in the centre of town, the un-buttressed tower of SS Peter and Paul has foundations dating back almost a thousand years. The top stage of the tower dates from the fourteenth century and the short spire, with its pediment dormers and crowned by orb and weathercock was built of magnesian limestone in 1669. There seems to have been an earlier wooden spire covered with lead, for the repair of which the steward of the manor gave eight trees in the reign of Elizabeth I.

The tall two light, louvred bell openings of the tower, with nook-shafts, are of the Decorated period. And, worthy of note, are the off-centre gargoyles, the west door and window above.

Inside, we find the tower arch with window above and surmounted by the line of a former roof, all of the Norman period. The ringing chamber, clock chamber and bells are served by a spiral stone stairway rising in the north west angle. The immaculate ringing chamber is tastefully decorated. Hanging upon the walls are numerous modern boards recording some of the peals that have been rung on the bells. An oak bench, in loving memory of John Robinson, a ringer here for over fifty years, and who died April 11, 1979, sits in a window recess and serves his friends admirably between touches.

An inventory of church goods taken in the reign of Edward VI lists the tower as having three bells. During the reign of Charles I, the Churchwardens Inventory of 1634 gives five bells, a clock and chimes. Sometime after 1634 a treble was added to make a peal of six, for we know that in 1762 this bell was recast when the peal was again augmented to eight, by the addition of a further two treble bells. In 1897 the bells were again rehung and the spire restored as the brass tablet affixed to the lower tower wall records. In 1948 all the bells were recast, the old inscriptions being faithfully recorded, together with additional inscription being added to the seventh and tenor bells. Finally, in 1979 a major overhaul was again undertaken. The bells bear the following inscriptions:-

Treble	The gift of Robt. Watson.
	Carpenter and Ch.warden..
	Lester & Pack of London. Fecit 1762.

Robert Watson lived in a house in Church street which later became an inn, The Eight Bells. Samuel Brunt, in memory of whom the bells are, was a former owner, and it was he who had been largely responsible in augmenting the peal of six to eight. The inn, apparently a very curious building, was demolished and a new building erected in 1925.

2nd.	At proper times my Voice I'll raise
	And sound to my subscriber's praise.
	Lester and Pack of London. fecit.

The cost of this bell was raised by subscription.

3rd.	Robt. Watson and Ralph Brocksopp.
	Churchwardens 1762.
	Lester and Pack of London. Fecit.

This bell was the treble of the old ring of six bells. It had been added sometime after 1634 and it would appear that any inscription there might have been on the bell was lost in the recasting of 1762.

4th.	Mathy Walker and Thom Brelsforde.
	Churchwardens 1611.

Dating from 1611 this bell was cast at Henry Oldfield's foundry in Nottingham. The initials 'G' and 'L', in Gothic letters placed on either side of a maltese cross are the initials of George Lees a travelling foreman of the firm. In 1590, George married Ellen Oldfield. He became manager of a branch foundry at Congleton, Cheshire. It is very likely that he also managed the Nottingham foundry at this time on behalf of Henry Oldfield, Senior, who died in 1619 and who had survived his son Henry by about twenty years.

5th.	When thes bels ringe
	Their friendli gifts are sounded
	1610 Hy Oldfield mark.

The inscription is in small plain capitals and on the waist the initials T.D. and the founder's mark. The initials refer to one Thomas Dand who was born in 1568 and who became a Governor of the Grammar School. In 1622 he held seventy acres of land.

6th.	Thomas Dand and Francis Wass
	Churchwardens 1603
	Hy Oldfield mark.

This bell could possibly have been recast to celebrate the accession of James 1. (1603 - 1625) An entry in the Registers states that on March 31st, 1603, "James ye first, Kinge of Scotts, was solemnly at the Market Crosse in Mansfield proclaimed King of England by Sir John Byron, Knight; Mr. Ayscough, high sherife; Mr Griffithe Markham, Mr Henry Chaworth, esquire; Mr John Byron, Esq. Mr Gabriel Armstrong, and Mr George Chaworth and divers other gent, and caused ye belles for joy to be rung, and gave ye ringers two shillings and sixpence."

7th.   I sweetly toling men do call
              To taste on meats that feed the soule.
              1615. Hy Oldfield mark.
              Recast 1948 in memory of
              Alderman William Benjamin Spencer.

A popular inscription used with regularity by the Oldfield Foundry whose mark appears upon the waist of the bell.

This bell is known also as the Shroving Bell due to it having been rung over many years at 11a.m. on Shrove Tuesday to warn parishioners to prepare themselves as this is the last day before the commencement of Lent. Its secondary but more popular name being the Pancake Bell, the ringing of which was interpreted by the housewife as a reminder to use up any luxury food she may still have in store in preparation for the family's Lenten fast.

Tenor   Tow summons by this bell we have
              One to the church, one to the grave.
              Francis Dand. 1610.
              Recast 1948
              The third year of the Atomic Age
              A day of doubt -
              Men's hearts failing them for fear
              Still we ring out
              That all the voice of God may hear.
              S.C. Bulley. M.A. Vicar.
              N.M. Lane, S. Richardson, Churchwardens.

The old inscription was in Gothic capitals and are the words found on Funeral Bells. No doubt one of the main functions of this bell has been to be tolled upon the death of numerous parishioners since it was first cast in 1610.

In addition to bearing the date 1610 were the initials I.R. which was an abbreviation for James Rex (1603 - 1625). A second mark, a shield charged with three crescents and the letters G and L to the respective sides of the shield. If these initials are of George Lees as seen on the fourth bell then it is of interest to ask, why place a charged shield between instead of a cross?

Francis Dand was churchwarden at the time this bell was cast which weighed 14 cwts.

In 1948, when the bell was recast, the vicar, Rev S.C. Bulley and the churchwardens must be commended for their foresight in having recorded upon this bell the world's most scientific development, the birth of the Atomic Age just three years earlier.

The recast tenor weighs 16cwts. 0qrs. 11 lbs.

A mechanical tune-playing apparatus was placed in the tower in 1762 possibly through the efforts of the churchwardens, Robert Watson and Ralph Brocksopp. This was at the same period as the augmentation from six to eight bells.

The clock, dated 1802, is by Benjamin Downs and whether this clock replaced an older one I cannot establish. Likewise, whether the chiming apparatus was independent of any clock there might have been before 1802 I don't know. What we do know is that the two were connected sometime about 1802. There are records of it being repaired in 1796 and again in 1839. The tunes changed daily and could be heard at 9, 12 and 4 each day and night. The tune being:-

Sunday	Hanover.
Monday	Life let us cherish.
Tuesday	Ring of Bells.
Wednesday	Blue Bells of Scotland.
Thursday	King and Miller of Mansfield.
Friday	The Harp that once through Tara's Halls.
Saturday	Old Metrical Psalm.

In 1880 four unknown gentlemen worked diligently at repairs. But, in 1891 the chimes stopped and were silent for thirty years until efforts of the Old Mansfield Society restored them. This would have been a major job for when the bells had been rehung in 1897, during the "silent" period the old chiming hammers had been removed.

For over four centuries the bells have rung to celebrate many events and in the wake of many customs. We have touched upon the proclamation of James I. The churchwardens' accounts mention the Coronation of William III and Mary II together with ringing on Gunpowder Treason Day, Christmas and New Year's Day. Then we have the passing bell, 3x3 for a man, 2x2 for a woman, and the funeral bell. The Shroving bell or Pancake bell are but a few occasions additional to the normal Sunday Service ringing which has taken place down the centuries and for which Mansfield bell-ringers have a record second to none.

On New Year's Eve during the last century it was customary for large crowds to gather outside the church to listen to the bells. The ringers rang out the old year with the bell clappers half muffled. The landlord of the nearby Ram Inn, no doubt in gratitude to the ringers for creating good casual trade, used to provide them with two buckets of hot elderberry wine and a basket of mince pies which were brought upstairs to the ringing chamber. This coupled with the remuneration from the churchwardens, as many old accounts itemise, provided the ringers well for their labours.

A curfew bell used to be rung every night at eight-o-clock. William Gosling, a bell-ringer of nearly eighty years association with the belfry rang it regularly for a period before he took up change ringing in 1839. He died at the age of 92 years in 1919 and could remember a board which gave details of a peal rung on the six bells in 1732, conducted by someone of the name of Gent.

Although full details of this peal are lost, another peal, this time on the eight bells, was rung on September 26, 1774 by a band from Nottingham. It consisted of 5280 changes of Oxford Treble Bob Major and took three hours and thirty five minutes to complete, the ringers being: Richard Peat, Treble; James Wilkinson, 2; Robert Metheringham, 3; William Bradley, 4; John Mason, 5; John Fettiplace, 6; Francis Draper, 7; Wiliam D. Crofts, tenor, who also conducted the peal. This is the first recorded peal to be rung on the eight bells.

In 1974, the ringers decided to mark the bicentenary of this peal and to celebrate the occasion with a peal attempt. After making arrangements, which included the cancellation of the regular weekly practice, the band arrived in the tower on the evening of Thursday, September 26, 1974 somewhat apprehensive as to whether or not the attempt was viable. Although for several years the object of ringing a peal to mark this bicentenary had spurred the local ringers forward the band arriving this particular evening were just a little awe struck as they ascended to the belfry. In the event a very good peal, again 5280 changes of Oxford Treble Bob Major, was rung by: Elaine Hollingworth, treble; Arthur J. Brown, 2; Florence Adcock, 3; John Robinson, 4; Monica Robinson, 5; Roger Hardy, 6; Frank Cooke, 7; and Brynley A. Richards conducting the peal from the tenor. The peal was brought home in three hours and eight minutes and was the first peal of Oxford Treble Bob Major to be rung by each ringer. Only fellow ringers will appreciate the sheer hard work and determination that was put in by each member of the band to reach this high standard.

This was achieved in spite of a major setback some twenty months earlier, when in the early hours of Friday, 26th January, 1973 the tower was damaged by fire. The alarm was raised at midnight when smoke was seen emitting from the tower and spire. The fire was located by the fire brigade to a wooden cupboard situated in the tower and containing the clock's weights. The fire was tackled by erecting a platform and injecting water through the louvres. The clock and clock chamber were extensively damaged. In the ringing chamber the bell ropes were consumed and the furnishings and fabric blackened. Fortunately the bells escaped serious damage but the steel bell frame suffered slight damage. Following the ringing practice on the previous evening the bells had been left in the "rung up" position. This necessitated, on Friday morning, the tower captain, Mr John Robinson in the company of a fireman, ascending the tower and pushing each bell over in turn in order to lower them within the frame and make them safe.

In 1979, Canon Robert Warburton had to call a halt to the bells being rung on account of the bell-frame being found to be in need of urgent repair. On closer inspection it was found that the eight bell clappers needed overhaul and bushes and bearings replacing. The sixth clapper proved to be unreparable and had to be replaced together with a new crown staple, shank and clapper pin. In addition all the bells were lifted and their bearings checked and greased. The wheels were checked and repaired as necessary as were the tie-rods. In the clock room new diverter roller pulleys were fitted and encased. Much of this ancillary work was undertaken by the local ringers in support of Mr. Roger Hardy, tower keeper, and Mr Fred Adcock, captain of the ringers working under the watchful eye of Mr. Fred Pembleton the local bell-hanger responsible for the complete overhaul.

On the occasion of the East Derbyshire and West Nottinghamshire Association attaining the fortieth anniversary in 1927 a peal of 5040 changes of Grandsire Triples was rung on the bells. It was a composition known as Thurstans' Five Part. The peal, conducted by Joseph Lord took exactly three hour to complete and the ringers were:- Wilson Allin, treble; Herbert G. Fretwell, 2; Thomas W. Hopson, 3; William Swain, 4; William Lancaster, 5; Joseph Lord, 6; Thomas Stimpson, 7 and Charles Carr covering on the tenor bell.

A further peal of Grandsire Triples, this time Holt's Original conducted by L.W. Jaques ringing the treble was rung in two hours and fifty-two minutes for the same association on Thursday, April 27, 1932. The other ringers being, H. Allsop, 2; T. Bettison, 3; E.C. Gobey, 4; J.F. Milner, 5; J. Robinson, 6; C. Carr, 7 and C Randall covering on the tenor bell.

The weight of the bells is:-

Treble	4cwt.	1qr.	19lbs.
3rd.	5cwt	1qr	2lbs
4th.	5cwt	2qr	12lbs
5th.	7cwt	0qr	26lbs
6th.	8cwt	1qr	2lbs
7th.	11cwt	0qr	5lbs
Tenor.	16cwt	0qr	11lbs

The Belfry of St. Edmund, Mansfield Woodhouse

The Gardening Bell. Awarded Sunday Service Ringing Certificate.
Tenor weighs over eighteen hundredweights. Lion and Griffin on crown of Treble.

The church of St. Edmund once boasted a timber spire but this sadly burned down in 1304 and the present steeple erected in its place. The western tower, supported by angled buttresses rising to the level of the parapet which add further support to the broach spire that rises straight off the eaves. The spire is ornamented on each cardinal face by bold centrally placed double vented lucarnes, similar to a dormer. A second tier being placed so near the apex that from a distance they appear as a decorative finial and incorporating the weather vane. On the east face, the clock dial is fixed above the two light bell opening and breaks through the base line of the spire thereby masking the sill of the lucarne. A small west door leads into the tower and a south-west spiral stair leads to the ringing chamber.

The tower contains a fine ring of six bells with the tenor bell, in the key of E, weighing 18cwts. 1qr. 23lbs. In addition the old third bell has been replaced and now hangs above the six as a service bell. There is also a plain old sanctus bell. The bells are inscribed:-

Treble   + JESUS
           On the crown of the bell, a lion and a griffin.
           H.D. and Nottingham coat of arms on the waist.

The lettering is in Gothic capitals. The initials on the waist are those of Henry Dand who was in partnership with Henry Oldfield of Nottingham. (See chapter 4) The initial 'H' is ornamented with a lion's head and the D with a heart being pierced with a spear. The medallion bears the Nottingham coat of arms.

The lion and griffin stamped upon the crown were often used as supporters of the Royal Arms of Queen Elizabeth I (1558-1603). The griffin, or sometimes referred to as the dragon, was an imaginary animal with a lion's body and eagle's beak and wings.

In addition to the inscription and medallions is a border of ornament depicting acorns and leaves and one of grotesque figures.

2nd.   GOD SAVE HIS CHURCH
           P. Wilson, I Hooke Churchwardens. 1698.

This bell was cast at the Oldfield foundry in Nottingham and is thought to be one of Willian Noon's bells.

3rd.   In thanksgiving for the church restoration
           1986 – 1988
           D.B. Stevens, Vicar
           R.B. Grinter R.J. Lee Churchwardens
           (Mark of John Taylor & Co.) Recast 1988

The old third bell now used as a service bell is inscribed:-

> IHC. SCA MARIA O.P.N.
>
> Fleur de lys G.H. mark.

The inscription "I.H.C. St. Mary pray for us"is in lower case letters and the fleur de lys. The letters O.P.N. are an abbreviation of orate pro nobis.

The founder's mark is that of George Heathcote of Chesterfield who cast bells in the town from 1525 until 1558. This was a favourite inscription of this founder, (see Teversal, and the relative chapter.)

4th.   INTACTUM SILEO PERCUTE DULCE CANO 1749
               Thomas Hedderly. Founder.
               Woodhouse Willey, Churchwarden (on waist)
               (Taylor medallion) Recast 1988

Prior to being recast the name of Woodhouse Willey was scratched upon the waist of this bell as though omitted at the time of the original casting. One cannot help but wonder what story lies behind this action and also behind the inscription "Untouched I am silent, strike me and I ring sweetly". The bell is, like a lady, decorated with ornament round the waist and lip. Strangely for a lady perhaps, but it is on this bell that funeral knells were tolled, the tenor bell being reserved for Royalty. It is ironical that when Hedderly cast the bell he used the old stamps Oldfield had acquired depicting the Royal Heads of a King and Queen.

5th.   RING IN LOVE OF TRUTH AND LIGHT
               Charles Webb, Vicar.
               W. Warner & Joseph Harrison
               Churchwardens 1892.

The parishioners subscribed the cost of this bell in order to complete a peal of six. When this bell and the tenor were cast in 1892 the bells were hung in a new timber frame. In 1988 this frame was removed and replaced with a metal frame by Frederick Pembleton when he was rehanging the bells.

Tenor   IN MEMORY OF FRANCIS HALL DIED 1888
               MARY ANN HALL, HIS WIFE. DIED 1871
               1892.

Captain Francis Hall and his wife are commemorated by this bell which was donated by Mr. W. W. Hall.

Known locally as "The Gardening Bell", it was rung for many years at six in the morning and again at noon from St. Valentine's Day, (February 14th) through until Michaelmas (September 29th) to inform workers on farms and in gardens the time. In addition the day of the month was indicated by tolling the

The ringers of St. Edmund's affiliated to the East Derbyshire and Nottinghamshire Association on June 1st, 1914 when they invited all members to ring the bells, take tea and play bowls. Mr Munks being heartily thanked for the use of his green.

Hanging in the ringing chamber is a beautiful illuminated certificate which was awarded to the same band of ringers by the Association in 1915 under the Sunday Service Ringing Scheme. Three certificates were awarded annually, one each for eight bell, six bell and five bell towers. The object of the scheme being to improve Sunday Service ringing by means of competitive annual assessment. Unfortunately it fell victim of being launched at the onset of the first World War and as a result was plagued with difficulties and was abandoned after only three years. The certificate, the only six bell one in existence, is delightfully executed, depicting Southwell Minster in a cameo at the top left whilst the right hand cameo is of St. Edmund's. It bears the signatures of the local team, Alfred Munks, Charles Rogers, Arthur Munks, W. Hardwick, John Radford, Henry Rogers, Walter Mason and Robert J. Sheppard. The Rev. S.J. Galloway became an Honorary Member. For the record this band were awarded the Certificate of Merit for three successive years, 1914, 1915 and 1916.

On May 8th, 1979 it was with regret that Arthur J. Brown died at the age of sixty-nine years. Arthur served as a ringer for fifty-two years and had been tower captain since the Second World War, during which and afterwards he served full time in the national Fire Service until his retirement. Arthur's forthright deliberation on ringing affairs were often controversial but his steadfastness about Sunday Service ringing was paramount as was his dedication to the training of beginners which was no easy task on the bells of St. Edmund's. It was fitting that on October 25th, 1978 he conducted his first peal, of Grandsire Doubles, on the bells he had cared for so diligently.

In 1980 the clock hammer mechanism was overhauled and re-roped. A new hammer removal lever was connected to operate from the ringing chamber.

As previously alluded to the bells were rehung in 1989 and the third and fourth bells recast. A new metal frame was installed and designed for eight bells. Who knows, it might yet be filled!

George Heathcote's 16th Century Inscription on the Old Third Bell

The Belfry of St. Giles, Matlock

Fifteenth Century Tower. Peal of nine bells.
Passing Bell tolled on Christmas Day. Pre-Reformation Bell preserved.

The tower of St. Giles is the oldest remaining part of the church. The embattled tower ornamented with four handsome crocketed pinnacles, and supported by diagonally placed buttresses, that rise almost to the parapet in receding stages, was built in the fifteenth century. Central to both the south and west face is the prominent clear white dial of the clock. The tower, divided in three stages, has on each face of the upper bell-chamber, two light louvred openings, a stage lower on the west can be seen the small window giving light to the ringing chamber and to the right of this the upper of two small slit windows giving light to the turret stairway within the south west corner. On the west, above the door is a three light window, which since the removal of the internal galleries allows much light into the body of the church. At the base of the south face stands the facade of the old south porch bearing the date 1636 and the initials T.B and D.W. (probably churchwardens), having been rebuilt in this position sometime after its removal in 1871.

Inside, at the south-west angle of the basement is a small doorway leading to the stone spiral stair. The paneled door is worthy of notice as it seems to be coeval with the building of the tower. Also, against the south wall are the five panels removed from the front of the former west gallery. They give details of the different parochial charities.

It is known that for close on four hundred and fifty years three bells have hung in the tower, for we find that on September 19, 1548, in the first year of Edward VI's reign the following inventory was taken.

"Matlock, Sept. 19 - - - - iij bells; j handbell - ; sacringe bell. Edw. Walker, Edw. Madden iij li at changinge of the bells."

Today, the tower boasts the unusual in having a peal of nine bells. An augmentation to a fine peal of eight was undertaken in 1904 and the old fifth, a pre-reformation bell, was preserved and hung separately. This bell weighing nine hundredweight is in the key of A and bears the inscription "SCA MARIA MAGDALENA O.P.N." together with a fylfot cross. Without doubt this is the mark of the Heathcote Foundry that functioned in Chesterfield from about 1476 until 1647. Ralph Heathcote is credited with using the fylfot cross as his mark. However, there were several generations of Heathcotes bearing the Christian name of Ralph (see separate chapter) but the bell here was in all probability cast by George who took over the business from his father Ralph on his death in 1525. The family were tradesman of considerable importance within Chesterfield. Also, during the early part of the reign of Henry VIII (1509-1547) William Woolley of Riber, within the parish of Matlock, left certain lands which had been given to him previously by Ralph

Heathcote, bell-founder of Chesterfield. So here we have a glimpse of history in the making inasmuch that the 'old fifth' bell was in all probability cast to mark the coronation of Edward VI and was in the process of being hung in the tower in September, 1548 when the Inventory of Church Goods under Edward VI was taken. The inscription was often used by the Heathcote foundry and the last three letters O.P.N. are an abbreviation of "Orate Pro Nobis," which interpreted means "Pray for us." Today, this bell is possibly the oldest and the most interesting bell to be found in Derbyshire.

History does not record what happened to the other two bells hanging in the tower in 1548 nor do we have knowledge of the handbell and the sacringe bell mentioned in the inventory. But in 1626 a further bell was hung in the belfry followed by two more, hung in 1718 and 1767 respectively, which one would assume brought the peal of bells to six. Not so, because we find it took another twenty-four years, until 1791, for this to happen. This of course gives rise to the question, what happened to the two old bells. Were they recast in 1791 in which case the tower did posses a peal of six bells prior to that date or was their metal used as part of this casting? We probably will never know. The tower and bells escaped the major alterations inflicted upon the rest of the church in 1871 and waited until 1904 before Messrs. Mears and Stainbank of the Whitechapel Bell Foundry, London were engaged to augment the peal to a full octave by the addition of two new treble bells, and a seventh bell. Then in 1936 John Taylor and Co. of Loughborough rehung the eight bells, placing them on ball-bearings.

The peal of eight is inscribed :-

Treble	In memory of Robert Wildgoose, J.P.
	Praise the Lord O my soul and forget not all his
	benefits. A.D. 1904.
	Note F. Weight: 4cwts. 2qrs. 22 lbs.
2nd.	Ad Dei gloriam gratias pro Rectore referentes D.D.H.
	et C. Staples 1904.
	Note E. Weight: 5cwts. 0qrs. 24 lbs.
3rd.	Remunerabit calum benefactoribus meis.
	F. Walker, R.B. S.T., C.W. D.H., fecit 1718.
	Recast A.D. 1904.
	Note D. Weight: 5cwts. 3qrs. 27 lbs.

This bell, cast in 1718, bears the initials 'D.H.' which are possibly those of the founder Daniel Hedderly. The Hedderlys began their business in Bawtry and Derby long before Thomas took the business to Nottingham where it is known that he was casting bells in 1742. Daniel moved to Nottingham from Bawtry but what exactly the relationship was between Thomas and Daniel or the unfortunate Thomas, who died of apoplexy in 1785, some seven years after the death at the age of sixty-six years of Thomas senior I have not established. What is known is that Thomas senior refrained from placing the word "Nottingham" upon his bells until after the death of George Oldfield IV in 1747/8. So here we have a bell, possibly cast by Daniel Hedderly at some period before they were fully established in Nottingham.

4th. Rev. Geo. Holcombe Rector,
R. Mason, W. Goddard C.W. G.H. 1791
Recast A.D. 1904.
Note C. Weight: 6cwts. 3qrs. 22 lbs.

Like the third bell, this bell was cast by the Hedderlys but here we find the initial 'G.H.' inscribed. Without doubt these are the initials of George Hedderly who succeeded to the family business on the death of his elder brother in 1778. Toward the close of the century and in consequence of some family disagreement, George emigrated to America and the Nottingham foundry closed.

The rector, Rev George Holcombe, served St. Giles church and parish for fifty-six years from 1780 until 1836.

5th. John Woolley, Jno Wood, Churchwardens.
Lester and Pack fecit 1767.
Recast 1904. J.W. Kewley, Rector.
J. Sladen, W.N. Statham, Churchwardens.
Note B flat. Weight: 7cwts. 3qrs. 1 lb.

6th. Jesus be our speed, 1626.
Recast A.D. 1904.
In memoriam, Ann Hopkinson.
Note A. Weight: 8cwts. 2qr. 4 lbs.

Was this bell first cast in Chesterfield or in Nottingham? At this period both the Heathcote's and the Oldfields were very active bell founders. However, the inscription was a favourite one used by the Oldfields of Nottingham.

7th. "Praise our God all ye his servants."
The gift of Margaret Harrison of Dean Hill,
A.D. 1904.
Note G. Weight: 10cwts. 1qr. 6 lbs.

Tenor I unto those that liveth well,
Do toll their welcome passing bell.
G. Hedderly, fecit 1791.
Recast A.D. 1904. Marian Wildgoose.
Note F. Weight: 14cwts.

Benjamin Bryan, writing in 1903, a year before the augmentation to a peal of eight took place, gives interesting measurement detail of the old peal of six.

	Width:	Height:	Thickness:	
1st.	27½ins	20ins.	2¼ ins.	
2nd.	29½ins	21ins.	2ins	Bare. Skirted.
3rd.	31¼ins	22ins	2¼ins	Bare.
4th.	32¼ins	24ins	2¼ins	Bare.
5th.	37¼ins	.27ins	2⁵/₈ins	Note F.
6th.	41ins	28ins	3ins	Bare.

It will be noted that the fifth bell is given as being in the note of F, but if this refers to the pre-reformation bell that now hangs outside the octave, the present church guide gives the note of this bell as being in A.?

The tenor bell originally cast in 1791 became known as the passing bell and as such was regularly tolled at the death of a parishioner. In the year 1880, after much feeling and opposition had been roused, an Act was passed authorising the burial of

Nonconformist and others in Church of England burial grounds. The first interment in St Giles churchyard under the Act was made on Christmas Day 1880 when the body of Drill- Instructor, Sergeant O'Brien, who was a Roman Catholic, was buried. The officiating priest was Rev. Canon McKenna of Derby. The Rev. W.R. Melville, the rector of Matlock, caused the bell to be tolled at the time of the funeral.

A tradition is preserved that more than two hundred and fifty years ago a Mr. Davis took up residence in Matlock Bank on what was known as Davis's Lot. Before his death he expressed a wish that the bells of the Parish Church should be rung on the day of his interment. This was done, and the custom was continued upon the death of one of his descendants. An instance of its observance occurred on September 26, 1880, when John Davis, of Matlock Bank, was buried and the bells were chimed unmuffled while the ceremony was in progress.

The clock and its chimes date from 1889 and were a gift of Mary Ann Bailey, as a memorial to her husband, Henry Edwin Bailey. A brass commemorating this is to be found at the west end of the nave.

In the years preceding World War Two, St. Giles boasted a competent team of Sunday service ringers and their Friday evening practice afforded some of the best in method ringing. Members of the band at this period were, Harold E. Austin; John Blackham; Clifford Bradshaw; T. Raymond Greatorex; Fred Paulson, J. Henry Paulson and Victor E. Taylor.

On the Feast of the Annunciation, 1949, the daily ringing of the Angelus was again introduced.

The Belfry of Holy Cross, Morton.

Rector's lesson put in question! The great offender recast in 1884.
Octogenarian and Nonagenarian Ringers. Royal Peals rung upon the bells.

The embattled tower, surmounted with eight crocketed pinnacles has stood at the west end of the Holy Cross Church for about six hundred years. First it was attached to a twelfth century building then rebuilt about 1400. In 1840, this old edifice was completely demolished with the exception of the tower, in favour of the church we see today.

The tower, which is just over fifty feet high, is supported by diagonally placed buttresses that rise to above the two-light louvred bell openings. The west door is fitted into curious jambs with mouldings that stop abruptly about two feet above the ground, and also, the tracery of the west window above is possibly not the original as the base of the mullion will be found not to be in complete union. Other interesting external features are the four Norman gargoyles and built into the base of the south face are several stones with old markings. These are possibly part of a Saxon tomb. To the base of the south face can be seen a vertical line of pointing stretching through several courses of masonry and without any visible form of bonding.

In the 1950s the former rector, Canon F.P. Cross, G.C. was once conducting a class of children from the village school round the church. And, in describing the tower, he pointed out this 'defect', explaining that it is considered to be of very poor masonry practice. He decided to use it as an example to get over to the children the message that in whatever job one undertakes one should always follow the correct practice and by so doing execute a first rate job to the best of ones ability. In other words, to always do one's best. Afterwards, during the usual question and answer period, one bright ten year old remarked:-

"Sir, the tower may be jerry-built, but it's still standing."

The small window in the second storey of the south face gives light to the old ringing chamber. A duplicate on the east face gives a bird's eye view into the nave.

Inside, the tower arch appears to be of earlier date than the rest, and on either side, facing into the nave, are old hatchments. They bear the coat of arms of a member of the Turbutt family former patrons of the living in alternation with St. John's College, Cambridge. Until the 1970s the Turbutt family resided at Ogston Hall. In strong sunlight, patterns of coloured paint decoration can be traced on the plasterwork of this wall.

Entry to the small ground floor ringing chamber is by passing through a carved wooden screen. The screen was erected to the memory of Mrs Prior the wife of former Rector, Canon Prior to whose memory the choir stalls were erected in 1923. High in the west window are fragments of ancient glass. A low doorway splayed on

146

the south-west corner leads to the stone stairway giving access to the old ringing chamber, bells and roof. In the belfry floor is situated a small cellar which houses the central heating appliance. For a period of sixty years the organ stood in the tower before being removed to the north aisle. On February 19th, 1911 the ringers, having extended the five bell-ropes, once again stood to ring on the floor of the tower. In 1923 a new treble was installed to augment the peal of bells to six. They are inscribed:-

Treble   Jesus be our speed.
                Mears and Stainbank. Founders. London 1923.

This bell weighing 3cwts. 0qrs. 11lbs. and measuring $23^5/_8$ inches in diameter was erected in a metal frame which fits tightly alongside the oak frame, in which the other five bells hang, and beneath the east bell-chamber opening.

It was customary at this time and in earlier days before the onset of motor travel for the representative of the bell-foundry and the bell-hanger to be offered accommodation during the time they were employed in a belfry. I remember my parents recalling later that the bell-hanger had stayed with them for several days on this occasion.

2nd.   J.Taylor and Co. Founders. Loughborough 1884.

Prior to 1884 there were only three bells hanging in the tower but in that year Messrs. John Taylor & Co., of Loughborough were invited to inspect and submit estimates for repair and possible augmentation.

A contemporary account about the proposed augmentation as submitted by Taylor's reads:-

"The second bell being cracked, must necessarily be recast. Also the interval between the largest and smallest Bells is nearly a 4th instead of a 3rd, and therefore another Bell is required, which, with the recast one, will complete a peal of four.

The whole of the fittings, i.e., wheels, headstocks, gudgeons, bearings, clappers, &c., are in a most dilapidated condition, and are indeed so bad that it is quite unsafe to ring the Bells. ... There should therefore be an entirely new set of fittings and framework. ... In accordance with the foregoing we respectfully submit to you the enclosed estimate:- The first (£72.1s) to include recasting the cracked Bell and hanging the three Bells complete with entirely new Fittings in a new Oak frame-work arranged for four Bells. The second estimate (£43.10s) is for the proposed additional Bell with necessary Fittings complete."

In the event two bells, now the second and the fourth, were added to complete a peal of five.

3rd.   God Save His Church.

This was the treble of the three old bells and has probably hung in the tower for upwards of four hundred and fifty years. The 1884 account refers to it thus:- "The Treble or Least Bell in the Tower is the most musical in the ring. It is the work of a good Founder, whose memory is preserved only in the quality of his work. It has no founder's mark, but bears the following inscription in beautiful Lombardic characters which prevailed about 1540: 'God save his Church'. The main members of the letters terminate in cusped openings. The letters are on plaques about an inch square." Some authorities credit the casting of this bell to the Heathcote foundry situated in Chesterfield from 1476 until 1647. This may well be so and the year 1540 would fall within the period when George Heathcote (1525-1558) was casting bells there. However George was keen to place upon his bells an elaborate shield design for his bellmark being also careful to incorporate the fylfot cross and his initials. This does not appear on this bell.

Others who have inspected the bell place it as being cast about 1630 but likewise consider it to be a Heathcote bell. This would place it as being cast in Chesterfield by Godfrey Heathcote. The interesting point here being that Godfrey had two sons working in the business with him, Godfrey and Ralph. Godfrey Jnr. died before his father at some date between 1628 and 1638. Father died in 1643 leaving son Ralph to run the foundry. After 1643 Ralph used his own mark. Father Godfrey had on taking over the foundry from his father Ralph reintroduced the fylfot cross as his mark. This leaves one to assume that as there is no trace of a bellmark on the bell it might possibly have been cast by one or other of the two sons whilst in the employ of their father.

The Churchwarden's accounts of this period show an item of 2/- (10p) being paid to the landlord of the nearby White Horse Inn to provide supper for the churchwarden, clerk and ringers on St. Hugh's Day, November 17th 1592. This would suggest that the tower contained several bells and therefore, as we know the tenor was cast earlier than 1592, and that the fifth was recast in 1635 it is fair to assume that the third bell was cast by one of the Heathcote family in Chesterfield at sometime before 1592. In the same accounts are items paid for ringing Curfew.

In the floor of the north aisle, near the Soldiers' Altar, is a decorated tombstone to the memory of Ralph Heathcote, Rector of Morton who died in 1738 and to his wife Elizabeth. In the Chancel a brass tablet records the memory of Grace Heathcote, their daughter. It is worth placing on record that they are all direct descendants of the bellfounding family.

4th.   J. Taylor and Co. Founders. Loughborough 1884.

5th.   J. Taylor and Co. Founders. Loughborough.
            1635 Recast 1884.

Known as the great offender this bell being cracked was recast in 1884 and our contemporary account has this to say:- "The Second Bell is the great offender; and although it is the youngest of the tree sisters, has collapsed many years

148

ago. A great crack extends from her lip through the sound-bow, almost to the middle of her waist. She has nothing to say for herself, only to tell us of the year of her re-founding, '1635', and on reference to the Churchwardens Accounts all we find there is, 'Ite, paid for castinge the bell and all other charges aboute it, £5.6s.2d.'. She seems to have been the work of an indifferent Founder, and her pitch when new was probably not much different from what it is now, and it is now nearly unisonous with the Tenor, i.e., about a 4th below the Treble. This singular gap in the musical scale Mr Taylor proposes to remedy by the insertion of two new Bells between the First and Third, making a ring of Four." Hence the present fifth being recast and the fourth bell being installed newly cast.

What a history. If we could only trace this bell to its original founding. Was it put in the tower when the tower was built? Where was it cast and by whom? Could it have been cast close by the church by some itinerant founder? If not how was it transported? Who first chimed it? When was it first rung full circle? What a great pity we do not know the answers. It is precisely these very reasons that have prompted me to endeavour to compile this account in order that some interesting snippets of our belfries will be recorded for all time.

Tenor   + S + S + S +   Founders mark.

Returning to the 1884 account we find this bell referred to as:-

"The Third or Tenor Bell is singularly interesting. It is the earliest in the Tower, and was probably re-cast at the re-construction of this part of the Church about 1500. It has round its haunch or shoulder the letter 's' repeated four times, with a cross between each. With these is the stamp or Founder's mark, usually assigned to Richard Mellors, a wealthy bell-founder of Nottingham. He was Mayor of that town in 1506, and died shortly after his mayoralty. His wife, Dame Agnes Mellors, founded the Nottingham Free School. In her deed of foundation, dated 22nd Nov., 1513, which may be seen in Deering's History of Nottingham, she terms herself Widow and Vowess."

The mark of Richard Mellors is a shield charged in the centre with a cross, the base of which is forked and surrounded with a circle. On the dexter side of the cross is the letter 'R', and on the sinister side a bell, and in chief are two crowns.

With the addition of the treble in 1923 we have here at Holy Cross Church a unique peal of six bells. The treble is heavier than the second bell and the fifth bell is heavier than the tenor. Their diameter and weight are as follows:-

Treble	Dia. $23^5/_8$ins.	Weight. 3cwt.0qrs. 11lbs.
2nd	Dia. 24 $^1/_8$ins.	Weight. 3cwt 0qrs. 4lbs.
3rd	Dia. $27^1/_{16}$ins.	Weight. 3cwt 3qrs. 12lbs.
4th	Dia. $27^1/_4$ins.	Weight. 4cwt 1qrs. 2lbs.
5th	Dia. $30^1/_2$ins.	Weight. 5cwt 1qrs. 14lbs.
Tenor	Dia. 31ins	Weight. 4cwt 3qrs 7lbs.

In 1911, at the time when the bell-ropes were lengthened to allow ringing to take place from the ground floor, an old custom of chiming the treble at the conclusion of

Matins was resumed. The reason for this is lost in time. Mention was also made of Curfew having been rung in times past but this has not been rung in living memory. But not so the early morning ringing on Christmas Day and Easter Day. The bells would peal out at 6.30 a.m. on these Festivals and continue until the commencement of the 7 a.m. Holy Communion Service and then at its close peal out again prior to the second Holy Communion Service at 8 a.m. The ringers then dashing home for breakfast before returning to ring before Matins at 10.30 a.m. This custom was kept going until late in the 1950s.

Morton has been singularly fortunate in gathering together on several occasions good bands of dedicated and loyal bell-ringers.

At the time of the founding of the East Derbyshire Association in 1887 a very dedicated band was in being. With the bells having been augmented three years previously this band was at the forefront of introducing change ringing in the form of Doubles, that is change ringing on five bells, into the belfry but for some reason best known to themselves they hesitated before becoming affiliated to the new Association. Several invitations were extended to them before they took up membership in 1895 only to withdraw two years later. It was 1906 before they rejoined. By 1910 the following members of the band had affiliated: Philip Maltby, Sidney Holdgate, Albert Lindley, A. Statham, H. Wheeler and W. Lindley.

Mention ought to be made at this point of the encouragement Holy Cross ringers received from the rector, Rev. James William Maltby. He was instrumental in augmenting the three old bells. He saw the possibility of forming a band from his parishioners and by so doing institute some vibrant activity within his church. Later, he drew pleasure from entertaining bell-ringers at the Rectory, particularly on New Year's Eve when by all accounts a bountiful supper was laid on at his expense.

James the son of Rev. William Maltby, was born at Pleasley Rectory, April 4, 1829. Educated at the Rev. Nathan Habberstey's private school in Wirksworth and at St. John's College, Cambridge, he was the originator of the second St. John's Boat Club, which became in two years second on the river and was then merged into the Lady Margaret Club. Formerly Curate of Thrumpton, Radcliffe on Soar and Gotham, Nottinghamshire, which he held whilst still in deacon's orders, by special permission of the then Dean of Lincoln. This was a circumstance unique in church history. He was Curate of Clifton before taking up the living at Morton.

At the time of the installation of the new treble in 1923 another competent band of Sunday Service ringers was established at Holy Cross and received much encouragement from the rector, Canon Prior. In the Association's report for 1929 we find the following members listed:- F.W. Knowles Jnr., F. Clarke, Vaughn Cox, William Swain, Ernest Mallender, F. Wheeler and B. Wheeler.

Between August 1924 and January 1931 twelve peals of 5040 changes were rung on the bells by this band and two competent conductors, Fred. Knowles and William Swain, emerged.

William Swain went on to ring about fifty peals and of these he conducted nine. At the age of thirteen he began ringing and along with W. Wheeler and Albert Wheeler joined the Association in 1911. He joined the Midland Counties Association in 1926 and became a founder member of the Derbyshire Association of Change Ringers, now known as the Derby Diocesan Association, in 1947 when the Chesterfield District was formed. As a devotee of the exercise he gave seventy-one years of faithful service. He was responsible for training many and perhaps his greatest achievement was during the Second World War when, due to wartime restrictions being placed on the ringing of church bells, he taught change ringing to a new band at Clay Cross. Practising upon handbells, this band became proficient at ringing changes, then by securing the clappers of the tower bells at St Bartholomew's, to keep the bells silent, they gained rope handling experience before the ban was lifted in time for Christmas 1943. It was but a short period before this new team were competent on the tower bells. In fact they rang a peal of 5040 changes of Bob Minor on November 25, 1944.

Fred Knowles was born at North Wingfield, but having moved to Morton, he joined the band in October 1912. Following the augmentation to six bells in 1923, Fred rang in the first nineteen peals on the bells of which he conducted twelve. In 1927 the East Derbyshire and Nottinghamshire Association appointed him to be instructor of a new team at St Werburgh's, Blackwell, following an overhaul of the bells. Within two years most members of this team were ringing peals. Fred went on to ring fifty-five peals of which he conducted twenty-two. In celebration of his ninetieth birthday in November 1986 he celebrated by joining the local band and ringing the treble. He remarked at the time that he would like to return and ring it again for his century. He almost made it - sadly though, he died on April 18th, 1996.

At the end of hostilities in 1945 the seed for another new band of ringers was sown by the rector, Rev W.L. Latham. This time for a young band formed initially by boys attending the weekly Sunday Bible Class.

In these austere post war days of rationing, very little in the way of public transport and almost none after 9 p.m. there was little to occupy teenagers in the village. So, the Rector's foresight in arranging for a group from his Bible Class to take up campanology was met with enthusiasm.

Teaching was somewhat haphazard, inasmuch that there was no appointed tutor. William (Bill) Swain, Fred Clarke and Vaughan Cox lent a hand when shift work and other commitments allowed but in the main the new band fended for themselves. Albeit they received every encouragement from the ringers of Clay Cross, Tibshelf, Blackwell and Shirland and were invited to attend their practice night. It was not long before a natural leader emerged within the band. Brynley Richards took naturally to the roll and I am sure that all the band at that time would endorse this remark and join with me in recording that it was through his sheer determination to see the young band succeed that brought them to one of the finest minor ringing bands in the country at that period. They had their first pull on a bellrope on February 5th, 1946 and within eighteen months rang in their first peal as follows:-

On Friday, August 1st, 1947, in three hours, five minutes,
A Peal of Minor, 5040 Changes,
being four extents of Plain Bob and three extents of St. Clement's.

Kenneth F. Greaves (Aged 16)	Treble	R. Michael E. Richards (14)	2nd.
E. Glyn Holdgate (16)	3rd.	Peter H. Wright (16)	4th.
Eric J. Sterland (16)	5th.	Brynley A. Richards (16)	Tenor.

Conducted by Brynley A. Richards.
First peal by all the band.
A compliment to the ringer of the treble who is serving
with the Royal Air Force. (Apprentice Cadet.)

These ringers together with Harold Franklin, Edwin Gough. Frank Lindley, Denis Lindley, Michael Wright, Keith Stirland, Ronald Frost, Selwyn Gough, David Palmer, Howard Hill, Stuart Towndrow and later joined by Shirley Carlin (nee Froggatt) kept the bells ringing regularly for services for upwards of two decades. During this period National Service, working rota and marriage took members away from the parish. Sadly three of the ringers have died, Frank Lindley, Denis Lindley and Harold Franklin. They are remembered with affection for their dedication and loyalty to the team. At the time of his death in February 1995 Harold Franklin was Churchwarden at Chesterfield Parish Church and took an active part in the ringing there.

During the years numerous peals were rung both for the East Derbyshire and Nottinghamshire Association and the newly formed Derbyshire Association. On Thursday, November 20th, 1947 the bells pealed out to commemorate the wedding that day of H.R.H. Princess Elizabeth and the Duke of Edinburgh :-

A Peal of Treble Bob Minor, 5040 Changes.
Consisting of two 720's of Oxford, three of Kent
and two of Kent and Oxford Spliced in
two hours and twenty seven minutes.

Harold Franklin *	Treble	E. Glyn Holdgate	2nd.
Peter H. Wright	3rd.	R. Michael E.Richards	4th.
Eric J. Sterland	5th.	Brynley A. Richards	Tenor.

Conducted by Brynley A. Richards.
* First Peal.   First peal in methods by all.

And, twenty five years on, to mark Her Majesty's and the Duke of Edinburgh's Silver Wedding Anniversary on Monday, November 20th, 1972 the bells again pealed out. But on the Saturday previous:-

A Peal of 5040 Changes of Plain Bob Minor.
Being seven different extents:
C.C.C. nos. 1.2.21.23.25.26 and 27
in 2 hours and 34 minutes.

David Palmer *	Treble.	E. Glyn Holdgate	2nd.
Peter H. Wright	3rd.	Harold Franklin	4th.
Eric J. Sterland	5th.	Brynley A. Richards	Tenor.

Conducted by Brynley A. Richards.
* First peal. First peal in method by all.

During this period the Association Jubilee Shield was awarded the team on four occasions, 1948, 1949, 1950, and in 1953. The rules governing this award were based simply upon regular Sunday Service ringing throughout any one year. Sadly, with the changing pattern being established regarding services generally within the church awarding the shield became impractical to maintain and it now hangs in the tower of St. Helen's, Selston.

Mention has already been made of the valuable and dedicated assistance given by William Swain but nothing gave his fellow ringers more joy than on Wednesday, January 30th, 1980 when they rang a peal in honour of his 83rd birthday and to celebrate his 70th year as a ringer. Sadly, on June 6th, 1981 the bells were again rung - this time in memoriam.

The churchwardens' accounts relate numerous payments for the upkeep of the bells and to the ringers in times past. One interesting record now in the parish chest is a diary of small events that occurred in the belfry week by week. Entries include what was rung for service, by whom, special events and minutes of the ringers meetings. This record, started by Canon Prior was continued until late into the 1950s.

In 1980 the bells underwent a major overhaul. The work being carried out by Fred Pembleton, himself a most proficient ringer at St. John the Baptist Church, Ault Hucknall. All the bells were lifted and bearings checked and greased. A set of ground rollers and pulleys made. The clappers re-bushed and refurbished. A new timber headstock made and fitted to the third bell. The wheel of the treble was re-aligned and new support straps fitted to the second and fourth. New sliders and stays were provided for the second, third, fourth and tenor. The total cost being raised by local subscription.

On November 20, 1947 the bells of Morton rang out in honour of the wedding of H.R.H. Princess Elizabeth and the Duke of Edinburgh. A year later they rang out in honour of the birth of their first son, Prince Charles. In 1972 H.M. The Queen and H.R.H. Duke of Edinburgh celebrated their Silver Wedding and the bells of Morton again rang out as they did twenty-five years later in thanksgiving of their Golden Wedding. On each occasion a Peal of 5040 Changes was rung, and four of the ringers had the honour and good fortune to take part in each of the four peals.

The 600 year old belfry of Holy Cross, Morton seen grom the south west. One of its six bells dates from 1500.

At a height of over 100ft the belfry of St Lawrence, North Wingfield is twice that of Morton's belfry. In this treeless view' the dial of the old clock that was replaced in 1893 can be seen.

The Belfry of St. Lawrence, North Wingfield

Tower arch gallery, erected and removed. Theft of clock's weight in 1633.
Child's coffin lid built into tower. Parishioners of Staveley donate bell?
Oldest bell - poorest casting! Midland Railway ran to Wingfield time.

The fine Perpendicular west tower of St. Lawrence Church, North Wingfield commands its hill top setting by rising further, to a height of over one hundred feet. Angled buttresses support almost the full height and terminate only on reaching the frieze and string course beneath the battlements. This frieze, of portcullis alternating with uncharged shields, surmounts, on each face, a pair of well proportioned two light louvred bell openings. At the angles of the battlements traces of former pinnacles can be found. Large gargoyles look down from each cardinal face and are joined on the north and south by the illuminated round dial of the clock. Simple string courses accentuate each storey of the tower and in the lower one small windows give light and air to the ringing chamber. A dripstone over the west doorway terminates in two heads, one bearing a ducal crown, the other a bishop's mitre.

Inside, the tall tower arch shows to advantage the west window. One of the top lights contains the figure of a monk, depicted in yellow and white glass, bearing in the left hand a book and in the right a rosary. On the north wall a small brass memorial to Geoffrey Laird Jackson, a captain in the Rifle Brigade, who was killed near Arras at the age of 23 years, on April 9, 1917. It is to his memory that the tenor bell was recast. On the south wall hangs an illuminated panel recording a peal of 5120 Changes of Kent Treble Bob Major. The peal, taking three hours and ten minutes to complete, was rung on the bells on Saturday, September 24, 1924. It was conducted by William H. Wain, and the ringer of the treble was Miss Doris Dilkes, a local lady, and probably one of the first ladies to ring in a peal at St. Lawrence.

The tower arch to the nave was blocked off in 1717 by the erection of what has been described as an ugly and obtrusive gallery. It was most probably erected to meet the demand for extra seating and had on its front a central panel informing that the then curate gave £10 toward its erection. The gallery remained in situ for upwards of one hundred and eighty years.

Several ancient stone coffin lids are to be found built into the fabric of the church. A small one, measuring only two feet in length, and possibly that of a child, is situated in the west wall of the bell chamber between the apex of the two louvred bell openings. It lies upon its side and bears a carving. A shaft rising from a base of two steps with a motif at the top of four curves, each of which almost forms a circle or an acute crescent. These are placed symmetrically, as upon a four petalled flower. A small lozenge, bearing a cross, is central too and touching each of the four crescents. It must be of a great age.

A more recent addition, set into the north wall of the ringing chamber, are two inscribed stones, set side by side, giving details of the eight bells. The ringing chamber walls accommodate several charity and peal boards together with a number of framed old photographs. These date from early in the century and show groups of ringers. An illuminated certificate informs that the ringers of St. Lawrence were awarded the certificate in three consecutive years, 1914,15 and 1916, for their achievements. The award was made annually by the East Derbyshire Association of Change Ringers to the affiliated band of ringers making the best progress during the year. Three awards were made, one in each group of towers with five, six and eight bells. The ringers were: T.P. Tarlton; J.F. Butler, captain; W. Butler; F. Thompson; A. Butler; W. Martin; W. Waddington; W. Barker and Tom Allibone. The certificate is beautifully executed and carries two miniature panels depicting Southwell Minster, in whose diocese North Wingfield was, and the church of St. Lawrence in watercolour.

The present clock was installed in 1893. Its round illuminated dials being positioned considerably higher in the tower than the previous one on the south side had been situated. That had a black diamond shaped dial and covered what is now the south window of the ringing chamber. At the end of 1996 the old hand wound mechanism was replaced by a system driven by electricity. The case that allowed the clock weights to rise and fall stands in the north west corner of the tower. On the frame supporting the clock's works is a small plaque inscribed: J. Smith & Sons, Midland Steam Clock Works, Derby.

Since 1902 the tower has contained a peal of eight bells.

In 1878 the Rev. George W. Darby became rector and immediately put forward a scheme to restore the bells, the six bells and frame being in a dilapidated state. On the few occasions that the bells were rung it was with the utmost difficulty. Five of the bells were re-tuned and one was re-cast. This was the old bell dating from 1617. They were next rung on March 18, 1879, having been hung in a new oak frame.

At Christmas 1880 some misunderstanding arose between the ringers and church officials that resulted in the ringers withdrawing their services. The nature of the dispute is lost in time but resulted in the Rector asking Mr Tom Allibone to form a new band. Tom Allibone obliged, and continued as a ringer at St Lawrence Church for over forty years. He became the third secretary to the East Derbyshire Association of Change Ringers in 1894 and remained in the office until elected as President in 1920. He continued in this office until his death in 1926.

The augmentation to eight bells in 1902 by Messrs. John Taylor and Co., of Loughborough necessitated the old six being re-tuned and the erection of a new iron frame of the type known as an 'H' frame. The cost of the two bells and the re-hanging was born by the generosity of Mrs. Bright, the Darby family and Miss Ward, who donated one bell to commemorate her late father, Mr. Jno. Ward. The work included repair to the masonry and the fitting of a lead floor beneath the bells to help deaden their sound from within the belfry and most especially the ringing chamber.

To piece together the history of the present ring of eight bells is inconclusive when taken from any one source. However, by using the inscriptions of the bells to be found on the two stone tablets let into the north wall of the ringing chamber together with the valuable reference to be found in Rev. J. Charles Cox's Notes on the Churches of Derbyshire, publications in the Bell News and Ringers Record of 1902 and an article that appeared in the Derbyshire Courier of February 12th, 1910 of a chat with Tom Allibone the following can be concluded.

Treble   O come let us sing unto the Lord.
                Given by Eliza P. Bright. 1902.
                Diameter: 2ft 4ins. Weight: 5cwt. 3qrs. 7 lbs.

2nd.   My song shall be of mercy and truth, 1902.
                Given by Ellen Ward in memory of her father,
                John Ward, OB, July 30, 1891. Age 67.
                Diameter: 2ft. 5ins. Weigt: 5cwt. 3qrs. 23 lbs.

Both the treble and second carry a decorative band depicting intertwined leaves and were cast by John Taylor and Co.

3rd.   This bell was given by the parishioners of Staveley,
                &c on Wm. the Marquis of Hartington's coming of age,
                the 21st. May, 1811. T. Mears, London. Fecit.
                Diameter: 2ft. 8ins. Weight: 6cwt. 1qr. 18 lbs.

An explanation of this particular inscription is best given by Rev. J. Charles Cox in his notes:- "It is singular to find this bell at North Wingfield, as we cannot imagine for a moment, that the parishioners of Staveley were sufficiently generous to present a bell to North Wingfield. On referring to the account of Staveley Church, it will be seen that the tower of Staveley has a bell with precisely the same inscription, and another presented at the same time by the Rector. We can only conclude that a third bell was ordered of T. Mears at this date for Staveley, but being found unsuitable, was subsequently transferred, either from Staveley, or direct from the foundry to North Wingfield." Mr. Tom Allibone's theory being similar in every instance, adding only that probably this bell was not in tune for Staveley.

4th.   God save His church. 1617.
                Diameter: 2ft. 9¼ins. Weight: 6cwt. 3qrs. 27 lbs.

The founder's mark of George Oldfield, a cross of calvary with his initials 'G' and 'O' flanking the shaft, and surmounted by a crescent moon and a star, are cast upon a raised plaque almost two inches square.

5th.   This bell is undated and without inscription.
                Diameter: 3ft 1ins. Weight: 8cwt. 3qrs. 0 lbs.

Cox describes this bell:- "a poor piece of casting with many bubbles." Tom Allibone believed it to be of fourteenth century origin.

6th.   J. Taylor & Co., Founders, Loughborough. (Recast) 1878.
Diameter: 3ft. 2ins. Weight: 10cwt. 3qrs. 26 lbs.

This bell, first cast in 1617, was cracked. It had inscribed round the haunch:-
Thomas Stevenson, Richard Millward, John Breilsford, John Dobb. 1617. In a
lower line, the word, 'Wardens,' and beneath that the founder's mark of
George Oldfield.

Over three hundred years ago the ringers of North Wingfield entertained the
ringers of Ashover on Oak Apple Day, May 29th, 1688. Among the contemporary
writing of Leonard Wheatcroft of Ashover is a verse describing this visit in which
he names the ringers: Henry Royles, Robert Mottershaw, George Brent, John
Pendleton, William Mottershaw, Tommy Clay, John Marsh, William Ashmore, John
Brelsford, Edward Clay, John Wheatcroft, and Will Brown. John Brelsford is most
probably the same John Breilsford whose name appears in the inscription on the old
sixth and who in Wheatcroft's verse gets singled out for his striking:-

"John Brelsford often rings behind;
(He will pull far apart.)
Besides, there's honest Edward Clay
Will make his bell to start."

Each ringer mentioned was taken to task or praised for his performance upon the
bells and a full account of the ringing, as adjudicated at the time by Leonard
Wheatcroft, can be found in chapter 5 on belfry jingles, rhyme, verse and hymn.

7th.   + IN MULTIS ANNIS RESONES CAMPANA JOHANIS.
Diameter: 3ft. 4ins. Weight: 10cwt. 3qrs. 4 lbs.

This bell is undated. The inscription, in Lombardic letters, is carried round the
haunch. The initial letters of the words Multis and Resones being surmounted
with crowns. In the same line as the inscription is a cross formed of four
radiating fleur-de-leys, followed by a small coin. On my visit, in the company
of Tom Stocks the tower-keeper, this coin appeared much worn to my
untrained eye and to be without markings but the Rev. Charles Cox, writing in
1876, had this to say. "The reverse of this coin being presented. It has a cross
pate extending through the legend with three pellets in each quarter. The
legend is much worn but he believed it to read 'CIVITAS DUREME', and that
the coin is a penny of the fourteenth century, struck at Durham." This is a fine
old bell of beautiful tone in F#. Some authorities date the bell, c1450, whilst
Tom Allibone believed it to be a thirteenth century bell. A decorative border
adorns the shoulder.

Tenor   Anthony Legat, Will Holland, George Shaw, Peter Dowker,
Friends to this bell. 1661.
Wardens.
Recast 1922 in memory of Geoffrey Laird Jackson,
Captain, Rifle Brigade. Killed in action near Arras,
April 9th. 1917.
A.J.B. Ellerton, Rector. T. Allibone, Parish Clerk.

158

Following the date are the three 'pips' of the rank of Captain. (Capt. G.L. Jackson was the eldest son of Brigadier-General G.M. Jackson, chairman of The Clay Cross Company)

This bell, cast by George Oldfield for Chesterfield Parish Church, in 1661, rang out from beneath the Crooked Spire, calling parishioners to Service for over one hundred and fifty years before being removed to North Wingfield in 1820. It was the seventh bell of the octave. In 1819 this old peal of eight at Chesterfield was removed and replaced by a peal of ten. At North Wingfield it replaced the old tenor bell, cast by Daniel Hedderly in 1749. This bell had a flaw and was no longer ringable.

In the parish register for 1749 an entry recording the settlement for Hedderly's bell reads:- "Received the 18th of October, 1749 of the then Churchwardens (that is to say) Will Hopkinson, Tho. Boller, Will Parsons and Hen. Rooth, the sum of Twenty-seven pounds and eighteen pence, being in full of all demands for casting the great bell, fusing Metal and Hanging the said Bell. I say Received the same in Full. Per me, Daniel Hedderly.

Test. Robert Parsons, J. Snibson, Clerk."

It would be interesting to find a relevant entry in respect of the transfer of the 'Chesterfield' bell which was most probably undertaken by Thomas Mears on completion of his work on the new ring of ten at Chesterfield.

This 'Chesterfield' bell was recast in 1922 by John Taylor & Co., Loughborough. At the same time all the bells were rehung on ball bearings, the clappers re-bushed and pulley wheels renewed.

An Ellacombe chiming apparatus was also installed. This is a system whereby the bells can be chimed from a central clavier. It operates by means of wires attached to a hammer placed alongside each bell and, as at Wingfield, the wires descend from the bells to an accommodating frame in the ringing chamber. At chest height additional hand grips are placed over the wires which are arranged in descending musical order of the octave. On engaging the apparatus the 'ringer' can then operate each hammer and chime tunes upon the bells. The octave are in the key of E.

In 1892 the question of a permanent memorial to the late Rev. G.W. Darby was discussed and it was finally agreed upon the installation of a new clock, the previous clock apparently having proved unreliable for the past twenty years. The work was completed and the new clock set in motion by the late Rector's daughter, Miss E.M. Darby, on July 31st, 1893. Tom Allibone in his capacity as tower keeper and ringer took charge of the new clock.

Church bells and everything connected had a great fascination for Thomas Allibone. Born at Braunston, a small agricultural village in Northamptonshire, his early pursuits were gardening and following the plough. This he began to do at the age of eight. As a young man he obtained employment on the Midland Railway, and, on coming to Clay Cross station in 1875, he became a signalman, an occupation he followed until his retirement.

Having joined North Wingfield Church at the time he came to the district he was able to recall in his later years many happenings of his day. His duties as Parish Clerk and that of tower keeper and ringer together with his interest and activities as secretary to the Association for twenty-six years is considerable. The effort put into Association work over those years had a marked effect upon its growth and members, and even today members have a lot to thank him for.

One brief glimpse into the man behind the office so to speak is perhaps best described through the following story. Being a railway man and proud of it, punctuality was of the utmost importance. This he carried out with the utmost care in his duties as tower keeper. When the church acquired the new clock in 1893 it came under his charge. Standing as it does overlooking a considerable stretch of what was then a major railway line he saw to it that it chronicled the time exactly. Engine drivers on the Midland Railway were known to adjust their watches by it, such had its reputation for accuracy become.

Other interesting snippets from Tom's memory is the occasion one of the large bells fell from within its frame with a terrible clatter, startling those ringing at the time. Several times he recalled clappers dropping out of the bells. He started a group of handbell ringers, who used to give performances in the neighbourhood. They used twelve handbells, given by Mr. Darby, at the outset, but these were augmented to thirty-five. He assisted at over 1900 burials, about 670 weddings, and about 2800 baptisms.

In 1927 members of the East Derbyshire Association of Change Ringers gifted a pair of brass candlesticks, for use in St. Lawrence Church, as a token of their esteem and in recognition for the life of Thomas Allibone.

Five years previously, on Remembrance Day, Saturday, November 11th, 1922, a public tea was held and the parishioners were delighted to hear the bells ring out once more. The whole peal had been overhauled and the tenor bell recast. The Ven. Archdeacon Crosse officiated at the dedication after which Brig.-General Jackson ascended the tower with the Parish Clerk (Mr T. Allibone), and sounded the tenor. The hymn "Let our bells ring from the steeple" was sung by the choir and congregation. After tea the bells were rung well into the evening by mixed bands of local ringers and visitors.

In 1887, six North Wingfield ringers, Thomas Allibone, Wm. Hopkinson, Thos. Day, J.P. Tarlton, Geo. Tarlton and George Hunt became founder members of the East Derbyshire Association of Change Ringers. They had been encouraged by the Rector, Rev. G.W. Darby, who along with other local clergy had been instrumental in pioneering the formation of such an organisation for bell-ringers.

The bell-ringers of South Normanton. Rev. J.C. Massey with his team in 1894. Eight members of the Hill family were regular ringers.

Rev. T.N. Evans with his team in 1952.
(Standing l to r) M. Slater, K. Hemm, A.B. Judge, C. Turton, S. Alvey, P. Wainwright. *(Seated l to r)* H. Doughty, L. Hill, Rev. T.N. Evans, J.W. England.

Swanwick ringers, circa 1914.
(Standing l to r) T. Stimpson, B. Walvin, F. Hill, P. Straw, H. Cartiledge,
C. Walvin, G. Walvin. *(Seated l to r)* H. Hill, H.G. Fretwell, C Wiggington.

Ashover ringers, circa 1905.
(l to r) Allan Tomlinson, Tom Dent, George Eastwood and Rev. J.B. Nodder. *Seated front left*
Harry Hopkinson and George Garner.

Fred Watkinson "Who Taught me to Ring. in 1912.

Alfreton ringers try out their new handbells, 1902.

Alfreton ringers after the 1970 bell restoration.
(l to r) J. Vintiner, K. Chadburn, Mrs D. Vintiner, A. Holdgate, A. Walters, H. Leggoe,
H. Painter, Mrs. J. Taylor, G. Holdgate, D. Rice.

Association members join in a lively discussion about the qualities
of variant Doubles Methods during a 1972 meeting in the belfry
of St. Katherine's, Teversal.

Members of the East Derbyshire and Nottinghamshire Association of Change Ringers gather by the Parish Hall in Ashover before their A.G.M. on Easter Monday, 1947. Member, George Dwelley of Clay Cross *(front row left)* took this photograph using delayed shutter release.

Two years later, 1949, members gather at Selston for dinner.

Ringers meet at Sutton in Ashfield, late 1930s.
(Standing l to r) Tom Clarke, Jack Bleby, Ernest Wilson, Wilson Allin, John W. England.
(Front row l to r) Neil Partridge, Tom Bettison, Cyril Heathcote.

Six members of the Warsop team who won the Southwell Diocesan Guild's
Crawford cup competition in 1989. *(l to r)* Frederick Flint, Nicholas Parkes, Joan
Crosby, Brynley Richards, Mandy Freeman, Christopher Richards.

August, 1953. Wedding peal in progress at Blackwell.

Ringers *(l to r)* George Hancock ringing the 5th bell; Glyn Holdgate, tenor; William Swain, treble; Harold Franklin, 2nd; Arthur Smithson, 3rd; Walter Davies, 4th.

Morton bell-ringers and friends on the first of many annual ringing tours stop off at Ashbourne for tea, July 19, 1952.

Tom Hopson taking a training session with six young learner ringers at South Wingfield about 1968.

In 1951 Tom Hopson introduced his daughter Anne and her friends Anita Woolfenden, Judith Brown and Elizabeth Radford to bell-ringing at St. Martin's, Alfreton.

A decade apart these two pictures show the band of bell-ringers at St. Helen's,
Selston in the 1970s and 1980s.

Ringers at S.S. Peter and Paul, Mansfield, 1960s

The band who rang a bicentenary commemorative peal on September 26, 1974, thereby duplicating the first recorded peal of 5280 changes of Oxford Treble Bob Major to be rung upon the bells on September 26, 1774. Ringers (l to r) Roger Hardy, John Robinson, Frank Cooke, Monica Robinson, Florence Adcock, Brynley Richards, Elaine Hollingworth, Arthur Brown.

Two annual ringing outings of the 1980s.

A presentation is being made to Arthur Smithson of Blackwell to mark his long service to bell-ringing and his retirement as President of the East Derbyshire and West Nottinghamshire Association of Church Bell Ringers.

The new treble bell for Kirkby in Ashfield being cast at the foundry of John Taylor and Co, 1973.

By the end of July the bell had been installed by the local volunteers and was dedicated by the Bishop of Southwell, Rt. Rev. Denis Wakeling, on Sept. 9, 1973.

The East Derbyshire and West Nottinghamshire Association of Church Bell Ringers celebrated its centenary on Oct. 29, 1987. A visual exhibition made a tour of libraries and churches throughout the area. At a celebration, held in Ashover, the honour of cutting the centenary cake, made by Mrs Wendy Heading, was given to the oldest member, Frederick Knowles of Morton *(second from left)* in his 91st year, and a bell-ringer since 1912.

Kirkby in Ashfield
was the venue for the E.D.W.N.A. Centenary Dinner in October 1987. Some
members and guests enjoy the after dinner speeches.

Forty years on and former bell-ringers at Morton Holy Cross Church in 1947 honour their wives. Seated in front of their respective husbands are *(l to r)* Mrs Joan Sterland, Mrs Betty Wright, Mrs Enid Franklin, Mrs Susan Holdgate, Mrs Margaret Gough, Mrs Joan Richards, Mrs Trudy Richards.

The East Derbyshire and West Nottinghamshire Association group by the door of St. Barnabas, Linslade, Bedfordshire after ringing at the church whilst on tour. July, 1976.

The band of ringers at St. Mary and All Saints Church, Chesterfield, about 1920.
Standing l – r: W. Bennett, B.A. Knights, F.E. Smith, Rev J.F. Amies, G.A.Thompson, W. Allwood, J. Flint, S. Thomas. *Seated l – r:* F. Jacobs, W.M. Crossley (Churchwarden), Canon F.L. Shaw (Vicar), A. Knights, G. Hollis.

By 1910 these ringers had been joined by R. Hall, J.T. Butler, Jas. Thompson, W. Wain, Thos D. Allibone, W. Butler, and A. Butler. 1916 saw them joined by W. Martin, W. Waddington, W. Allwood, W. Barker, W. Rooth and Miss Jessie Wain. In this same year the Association's certificate awarded under the Sunday Service Ringing Scheme was awarded the St Lawrence Ringers for their outstanding achievements during the previous year. And as we read earlier the certificate still hangs in the belfry.

Six months after the installation of the new trebles the first peal of Major was rung on the bells:-

Saturday, November 8th, 1902.
A Peal of 5040 Changes of Bob Major,
in three hours and ten minutes.

W. Hopkinson Jnr.	Treble	J.P. Tarlton	5th.
J. Milner	2nd.	T. Clough	6th.
R. Hall	3rd.	W. Hopkinson Snr.	7th.
W. Butler	4th.	J.T. Butler	Tenor.

Conducted by J.T. Butler.

During the next thirty-seven years the ringer of the fifth bell, John P. Tarlton, rang in over one hundred peals. Many of them were rung here or in local towers and often in the company of Arthur Knights and his son, A. Percival Knights, with the occasional peal being conducted by the second son, Benjamin A. Knights of Preston. The peals being composed by Arthur and mostly conducted by Percival.

Arthur Knights was a great composer and few men could, at that period, lay claim to the authorship of more peals than he produced. He composed peals in many methods, but Treble Bob was his particular interest. Composing about four hundred and thirty original peals of Treble Bob Major and over three hundred of Treble Bob Royal. He had composed a great many peals in other methods, too. It is reckoned that nearly one thousand, two hundred of his compositions have been rung. Although a regular visitor to North Wingfield it was however one of his greatest disappointments, that before his death, in 1939, he was unable to see the restoration of ringing at Chesterfield Parish Church.

Typical of peals rung on the bells at this period were :-
Saturday, May 5th, 1928. 5024 Kent Treble Bob Major.

Arthur Knights	Treble	John P. Tarlton	5th.
Fred. Knowles	2nd.	William Swain	6th.
F. Hector Bennett	3rd.	William T. Palmer	7th.
William Wain	4th.	A. Percival Knights	Tenor

Composed by Arthur Knights. Conducted by A.P. Knights.

Saturday, October 31st. 1931. 5120 Oxford T.B. Major.

Arthur Knights	Treble	Norman C. Lewis	5th.
Miss Kath.Burchnall	2nd.	John W. England	6th.
Miss Grace Burchnall	3rd.	William T. Palmer	7th.
John P. Tarlton	4th.	A. Percival Knights	Tenor.

Composed by Arthur Knights. Conducted by A.P. Knights.

161

On Saturday, October 8th, 1904 a long peal consisting of 6144 Changes of Plain Bob Major was rung on the bells. It took three hours and forty-seven minutes to complete. Composed by Arthur Knights, it was the first time this extent had been rung, and to this day it stands as the greatest number of changes to have been rung consecutively upon the bells. The ringers were :-

W. Butler	Treble	J.T. Butler	5th.
Joshua Millner	2nd.	Francis H. Kay	6th.
James Thompson	3rd.	W. Hopkinson, Snr.	7th.
Herbert Day	4th	John P. Tarlton	Tenor.

Conducted by Wm. Butler.

The first peal of Grandsire Triples to be rung on the bells took place on Tuesday, September 26, 1905 when 5040 changes were rung in three hours and fifteen minutes. This peal, a variation of Parker's twelve part, afforded five of the ringers (marked +) their first peal in the method:-

James Thompson +	Treble	John T. Butler +	5th.
William Butler +	2nd.	Francis H. Kay	6th.
John P. Tarlton	3rd.	Herbert Day	7th.
Ernest Butler +	4th.	Thomas Clough +	Tenor

The records give no conductor of this peal.

Before leaving this period in the life of St. Lawrence mention is due of the then Rector, Rev. C.J. Boden. His encouragement of ringers was second to none and his help in the support of ringing guilds and associations caused him great pleasure. He became Treasurer of the East Derbyshire Association of Change Ringers in 1898. In 1902 he was elected President for two years. Then, during the First World War, he was elected for a second term as President from 1914 until 1916.

After the Second World War ended another strong band of bell-ringers took charge of Sunday Service ringing at St. Lawrence. Led by William H. Wain, whom we first noted in the 1928 peal above, and very ably supported by his wife, they set about building up the post war band. Among these ringers were Jack Brewster, Albert Turner, Harry Johnson, George E. Hancock, Derek and Walter Davis. On Wednesday, June 14th, 1950, the following peal of Minor was rung on the back six bells.

A Peal of Treble Bob Minor, 5040 changes.
Comprising three extents of Oxford and four of Kent Treble
Bob, each being called differently.

Albert Turner +	Treble	Frank Robey *	4th.
George Hancock *	2nd.	Harry Johnson +	5th.
Derek Davis	3rd.	Jack Brewster +	Tenor.

Conducted by Derek Davis.
+First peal. *First peal of Minor. First peal as conductor.

The experience of visiting the ringing chamber can, to the unwary, give rise for concern as to safety. The oscillation of a peal of bells to some extent causes movement and is echoed throughout the structure. In no other local belfry can this effect be monitored more than in the tall tower at St. Lawrence. To sit in a corner of the ringing chamber and allow one shoulder to lightly rest upon each of two walls simultaneously whilst the eight bells are ringing, picks up the full impact of the movement. The effect can create an alarming and bewildering sensation to the onlooker but they can rest assured all is well and the structure perfectly safe.

Finally, over three hundred and sixty years ago someone stole the weight belonging to the church clock for we find in the parish registers the following;-

"1633. Upon the first day of August, or thereabouts, their was a great clock plum (weight) stolen out of the steeple, which was eight or nine stone waight; some stronge body did steal yt, or else it could not have been carried away, for I could not lift it with one hand. At the same time there was a kaye left in at Booth (?) Savage house (the chantry house), which did unlock th chapple door when they pleased to goe and ringe when I was out . . . . and many times the church doores was left open when I did never know of it, for by this means allso by going into the chappel windos and breaking the . . . door into the chancell at there pleasure. The church was made common, and doores left open alnight manie times."

"1633. This parish church steiple at North Wingfield white lymed in September."

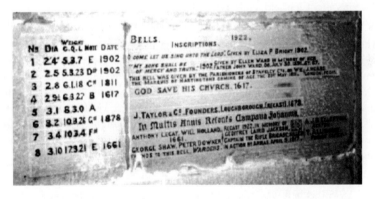

Set into the wall of the Ringing Chamber at St. Lawrence Church, North Wingfield, are two stones carved with details of the eight bells.

The Belfry of SS. Peter and Paul, Old Brampton

Diamond Jubilee Clock. Sheriff re-cast Bells.
Change Ringing introduced in 1887. Bellfounder buried in churchyard.

Here at the church of SS Peter and Paul, Old Brampton we find one of the earliest broach spires in Derbyshire. It is in the shape of an octagon with large broaches, and has a low placed tier of dormer openings. A tier of small canopied openings above complete the adornment on each cardinal face.

Below the broaches, which is where the spire joins the tower, there is no intervention of a parapet only a narrow string course. On the east face of the tower are to be seen traces of where a former high pitched roof to the nave was positioned. Standing high in the tower are the louvred two light bell-chamber openings, whilst below, on the south face, the dial of the clock, installed to commemorate Queen Victoria's diamond jubilee in 1897, tells all who pass the time of day. But, beware, the dial shows there to be sixty-three minutes in every hour. One wonders if the good ale served at the George and Dragon opposite had any bearing on the signwriter's minor misdemeanour! Below the clock dial a small lancet window allows light into the ringing-chamber.

The tower was built in two stages. It is known that by 1253 the lower part of the tower was built, for on July 21st that year, Bishop Brenden, suffragan to the Bishop of Coventry and Lichfield, consecrated the Chapel at Brampton and we are told that along with the two aisles the lower tower had been added to the existing building.

The spire was erected about a century later in 1353 after the tower was completed. A change of both colour and texture of the stone in the upper portion of the tower determines the two stages of building. Later additions are the angled buttresses. Note how those on the east extend out into the nave. Since the doorway in the south wall of the tower was filled-in during 1868 the tower has been entered via a spiral flight of external stone steps leading from a door in the north wall. At the head of these stairs, the lintels of the new and old openings have been formed by using old gravestones. Among the carvings traced on them are crosses and the hilt, guard and blade of a sword.

Over the east gable of the nave is a bell-cot in which hangs a Sanctus Bell. Around 1875 this bell was missing from its bell-cot and was believed to have been removed to the adjacent parsonage by a former incumbent. It was later restored to its rightful use and position.

Inside, the tower arch to the nave was completely blocked with masonry until 1868 when this and an adjacent west gallery was removed. This removal allowed the west window, with its figures of Faith, Hope and Charity to be viewed from the nave. The ringing room, much reduced in size by the encroachment of the casing of the clock's works, affords little room to spare for the ringers of the six bells.

The four largest bells have origins going back several centuries and the second bell dates from 1887. This was the year of Queen Victoria's golden jubilee. It was also the year following major building work being carried out at the church. So, it is fair to assume the addition of this Treble bell and the augmentation to a peal of five bells was accredited to one or other, if not to both events. The inscription we see today gives no indication only the year, 1887. Be that as it may, thirty six years later in 1923 this bell along with the four old ones, was recast. Another Treble bell was commissioned and a peal of six bells returned from the bell-founder and hung in the tower. The six bells are inscribed:-

Treble. These five old bells were recast
and rehung and this bell was
added by Edwin Clay Barnes
Sheriff of Derbyshire
1923
*   *   *

DOMINE DIRIGE NOS

On the reverse waist, Taylor, Loughboro.

2nd. 1887 on the inscription band and flanked by a
pattern motif.

On the reverse waist, Taylor, Loughboro.
Recast 1923.

3rd. Jesus be our sped.
Initials 'H.D.' high on waist.

On the reverse waist, Taylor, Loughboro.
Recast 1923.

4th. In Nomem Jesu. Interspaced with motif.
Initials 'H.D.' high on waist.
On reverse waist, Taylor's logo as 3rd.

5th God save His Church.

On reverse waist, Taylor's logo as 2nd.

Tenor. Jesus be our sped.
Initials H.D. on waist.

On reverse waist, Taylor's logo as 3rd.

With the exception of the Treble bell all the inscriptions are within the inscription band. The fourth and tenor bells have the words interspersed with beautiful decoration whilst the third has a founder's decorative stop. Interesting initials 'H.D.' appear high on the waist of the third, fourth and tenor bells. These could be the initials of Henry Dand a bellfounder who was in partnership with Henry Oldfield (II) of Nottingham. In 1591 he cast a bell for Shrewsbury Abbey Church. The inscription, "Jesus be our sped", was often used by the Oldfield Foundry and on the original casting of the third and tenor bells they executed it in fine Lombardic capitals. The inscription of the fourth, also cast on the original bell in Lombardic capitals, is less common, "In Nomen Jesv", which I am told translates into "In the name of Jesus." For the inscription "God save His Church" on the fifth bell the original founder used small Gothic capitals.

1923 was the year Edwin Clay Barnes was High Sheriff of Derbyshire and in commemoration of this the five bells were re-cast and the Treble bell added. John Taylor and Company, Bell-founders, of Loughborough, carried out the casting and the rehanging. They give the diameter and weight of each bell as:-

Bell:	Treble	Dia.	25¼ inches.	Weight,	3cwt.	1qr.	12lbs.
	2nd.		27½ "		4 "	0 "	13 "
	3rd.		30¼ "		5 "	1 "	8 "
	4th.		31³/₄ "		6 "	0 "	0 "
	5th.		34⁷/₈ "		8 "	0 "	17 "
	Tenor		39¾ "		12 "	0 "	9 "

The addition of a fifth bell into the tower in 1887 gave the opportunity for Change Ringing to be introduced into the belfry. Joseph Mee, Snr. and his son Joseph, together with George Marples, Joseph Keighly, Elijah Bradbury, Edward Hancock, Harry Marsden and Alfred Green took up the challenge and soon a very enthusiastic and competent band of ringers was established. So great was their enthusiasm that they, along with ringers from Ashover, Clay Cross, Crich, North Wingfield and South Normanton, joined together with their respective clergy to form the East Derbyshire Association of Change Ringers.

At the first meeting of members of the new Association to be held at the tower in June, 1889, the Rev. G. Shipson was elected a Vice President.

In the churchyard, adjacent to the east window, is the grave of Ebenezer Smith. Ebenezer, together with John Smith were partners in a foundry business in Brampton known as the Griffin Foundry. They were famous for their many different industrial castings and are known to have cast a few bells. Their most famous work being the re-casting of the Bonaparte bell for Ashover in 1814.

The Belfry of St. Matthew, Pentrich

Old bell exchanged for new one. Three bells in tower in 1552.
Legacy gives ringing new impetus. Saxon monolith discovered.

In the reign of Edward VI the inventory of the Church Goods Commissioners contains three items about bells at St. Matthew's Church, Pentrich. They list: "j - hand bell, iij - bells in the stepyll and j - sacrying bell." The inventory was taken on 5th October, 1552 by "Barnard Brande, mynyster."

Of the hand bell and the sacring bell we have no further knowledge but of the three tower bells, two are still ringing out over the village, whilst the second of the three bells listed was replaced after being found beyond repair in 1869. But more of them later.

The short embattled tower has its lower part dating from Norman times. This is indicated by the great thickness of the walls, almost four feet thick, and the absence of a stone stairway. All this is substantiated inside by the small round-arched doorway leading from the nave into the ground floor ringing chamber. The upper portions of the tower date from about 1430 with the bell chamber openings and other external detail being Perpendicular in period. In 1875 the organ was removed from the west end of the nave to the east end of the north aisle. No mention is made of the wall painting we see today above the tower doorway although reference can be found to the tower wall being plastered at the 1859 restoration. Could it therefore be that the painting was executed shortly after the organ was removed and the wall became open to full view?

Today the tower contains a ring of six bells but behind this simple statement lies an interesting story. First let us look at the inscriptions and details of the present six bells:-

Treble	Sing to the Lord a New Song.	
	Whitechapel. 1993.	
	Weight: 4cwt. 2qrs. 3 lbs.	
2nd	J. Taylor & Co. Founders Loughborough. 1869.	
	Weight: 5cwt. 0qrs. 9 lbs.	
3rd.	Jesus.	
	H.D.	
	Weight: 3cwt. 0qrs. 24 lbs.	
4th.	1715.	
	Bell-mark of Richard Sanders.	
	Weight: 5cwt. 0qrs. 1 lb.	
5th.	Ave Maria Gracia Plena.	
	Richard Selyok, Nottingham.	
	Weight: 5cwt. 3qrs. 4 lbs.	
Tenor.	J. Taylor & Co. Founders Loughborough. 1869.	
	Weight: 10cwt. 1qr. 17 lbs. Note G.	

Let us begin almost up-to-date by looking at the story behind the new Treble bell. Cast in December 1993 at the Whitechapel Bell Foundry in London this bell will most certainly be one of only a few to be newly cast in the last decade of this century for use in Derbyshire. And it is almost a dream come true for the people of Pentrich.

The story begins in the 1950s. In celebration of the eight hundredth anniversary of the consecration of St. Matthew's Church the local ringers were joined by members of the East Derbyshire and Nottinghamshire Association on Saturday, June 10, 1950 to ring the bells in celebration. This proved to be one of the last occasions on which the bells were to be rung in over forty years, although there was at least one occasion in the 1980's when some misguided young ringers foolishly took ropes into the tower and rang the bells. But, returning to the 1950s.

The wooden frame being attacked by woodworm and with the bell fittings becoming dilapidated the bells were deemed unringable. There was little chance of the parish tackling such a major restoration project so the matter was put in abeyance. In this state the situation lay for thirty years until early in the 1980s the Parochial Church Council decided to have the bells inspected. Quotations for their restoration were obtained and deemed to be too costly.

A member of the Parochial Church Council at the time was a lady who had fond memories of the bells ringing out over the parish. Sadly, this lady, Miss Enid Bryan, died in 1987 but in her will was a most generous gift. Miss Bryan generously left the sum of £10,000 so that "the bells could be heard loud and clear again" as in her youth.

In 1988 revised quotations were obtained and alas there would still be a significant shortfall of funds. At an estimate of £20,000 there was still a need to match Miss Bryan's generous gift from other sources. The P.C.C. were somewhat reluctant to promote the matter and four years of debate and indecision followed. Eventually, after promise of much help using local volunteer labour and thereby making a substantial reduction in costs the P.C.C. decided to launch the project on the firm understanding that when cash ran out the work ceased.

It was decided to replace the old frame with a new one that would accommodate six bells and that the existing five bells be re-tuned and rehung. The forward thinking of providing a frame for an additional sixth bell was at that time little more than wishful thinking.

Using local transport and local labour the old timber bell frame was dismantled and the five bells removed via Messrs. Eayre and Smith of Melbourne to the Whitechapel Bellfoundry in London for re-tuning. The Eayre and Smith specification for a new steel frame was put into production by Mr. Brosch of Lichfield with the volunteer team continuing with the ancillary work.

Another volunteer team, drawn from the steel erectors of Butterley Company took over the assembly within the tower but before they could start erecting much restoration of the stonework within the tower was needed. The re-tuned bells were brought back to the tower and hung in their new frame. Again as much work as possible was carried out by the volunteer teams as was the painting of the frame, the building of new timber floors and later the final refurbishment of the ringing chamber. The effect of this superb volunteer work saved the project an estimated £7,500. The project leader was Derek Clough who was ably assisted by John Bate. Ted Martin, Maurice Greasley, Norman Davies and many others who will for as long as the bells sound forth be remembered for their fortitude and skills.

Whilst the work was progressing others were busy winning support by way of publicity, fund raising and contacting known charities asking for any help available. Radio Derby transmitted a live interview at Christmas 1993 and several local newspapers ran features on the efforts being made by the volunteers. One paper highlighted that there was still a shortfall of funds and to everyone's amazement a gift of £1000 was received anonymously within a week.

The cost of a new treble bell had been estimated at around £5000 and this alone had made the idea of ever getting it somewhat of a dream. But, with a grant from the Sharpe Trust toward the restoration element of the project and grants from the Barron Bell Trust and the Pilgrim Trust via the Council for the care of Churches the opportunity of completing the restoration and re-hanging of the old peal of five began to look a real possibility.

Then came the offer of grants in varying size from the Derby Diocesan Association of Church Bell Ringers, The East Derbyshire and West Nottinghamshire Association of Change Ringers and through the Central Council of Church Bell Ringers a grant was made available from the Manifold Trust. With a substantial amount toward the cost of the new treble promised the Derby Diocesan Association offered an interest free loan covering a greater part of the balance needed. This clinched the pipe-dream and the bell was cast at Whitechapel in December 1993. Again volunteers made short shift of transporting the bell to Pentrich where it was hoisted and hung in the new frame early in 1994.

The climax came on Saturday, April 30th. 1994 when the six bells rang out from the ancient tower once more in honour of a wedding. The following day they were dedicated by Rt. Rev. Peter Dawes, Bishop of Derby.

Two of the old five bells are subject to a preservation order on account of their age. The fifth bell is thought to have been cast about 1525 by Richard Selyoke of Nottingham and some give the date of the third bell as being cast about 1575 by Henry Dand who also cast bells in Nottingham.

However, as we read in the opening paragraph, the Church Goods Commissioners inventory of 1552 lists Pentrich as having three bells in the tower. We know that the second bell of the three was cracked and unringable by 1869 when it was replaced. More of that bell later. On the surface all appears to fit nicely into place regarding the fifth bell, cast about 1525, and the third cast about fifty years later. But, the date of the Commissioners inventory falls almost midway between the dates we today believe the two bells were cast. Let us look closer and bring in what little we know about the bell founders Selyoke and Dand.

The Selyoke family, sometimes found spelt Seliok, were known to be casting bells in Nottingham during the latter half of the fifteenth century and the first half of the sixteenth. Over this period Richard Selyoke and his son John operated the business. It is known that one or other of them became Mayors of Nottingham four times, in 1497, 1498, 1505 and 1548. From these dates we can safely assume that John Selyoke was mayor in 1548. With less certainty that Richard Selyoke was mayor on the three earlier occasions. The assumed date of the casting of the fifth bell fits nicely into Richard and John Selyoke's life span and there is absolutely no doubt that one or the other cast it. We know that the attaining of the office of Mayor usually is the honour awarded after many years of civic service, or at least it was in times past, so it is fair to assume that in 1525 Richard would be in today's parlance, a senior citizen, John on the other hand would be quite young. With the mayoralties covering a period of fifty years one is led to ask, could there have been an earlier generation? This we know not, but, we do know that the fifth bell was cast by one or other of the Selyoke's and that it must have been hanging in St. Matthew's tower at Pentrich when the Commissioners made their inventory in 1552.

Like the Selyokes little is known of Henry Dand who cast the third bell. For many years it was thought that he was in the employ of another bell founder in Nottingham, Henry Oldfield. This now seems to be less likely, or at least in his later life, because in 1591 records show that he cast a bell for Shrewsbury Abbey. He had a daughter Frances who in 1567/8 married Robert Quarnby. This is significant inasmuch that the Quarnby family were connected through marriage to another long standing family of bell founders in Nottingham, the Mellors. It is known that when Henry Dand re-cast some of the Mellor bells he always faithfully copied the Mellor bell-mark and placed his own initials, one at either side. Incidently, in 1587 he was fined for not attending church! These brief notes all point to the date of attributing the casting of the third bell as being correct. But, how does this fit in with the Commissioners' inventory? It doesn't. This leaves the question, was the third bell recast by Henry Dand and if so why did he not in accordance with his usual practice reproduce the original founder's mark? We may never know.

These two brief accounts of the founders of the third and fifth bells add more interest and further the joy when one realizes the same bells are still heard ringing out from the tower today. What a document they would produce if only they could recount almost four centuries of the village's happenings. As for instance, what exactly lies behind the local jingle handed down from before the enclosure of land measures, "Offerton Kettles, Pentrich Pans, Shirland Brave Ringers and Morton ting tangs".

1869 saw the removal of the second bell mentioned in the Commissioners' inventory. In that year it was decided to add two bells and augment to a ring of five. John Taylor & Co. bell-founders of Loughborough were asked to cast a new treble and a tenor bell. The second bell, being no longer ringable, was at the suggestion of Messrs Taylor, replaced by a bell previously cast for St. Peter's Church, Inkberrow, Worcestershire. It had been cast for that tower in 1715 by Richard Sanders of Bromsgrove. At St. Peter's, Inkberrow today is a peal of six bells. They are comparable with St. Matthew's bells, being tuned in the key of G and with the Tenor bell weighing just thirteen pounds heavier.

The work was planned so that the five bells would be on one level and at the same level as the old three, bearing in mind the extremely thick walls of St. Matthew's tower this was quite a squeeze but after the removal of much masonry from the interior of the extremely thick walls the new oak frame was fitted and the five bells hung within it. It is somewhat ironic that much of the interior stonework needed to be rebuilt before the new frame carrying the six bells was installed in 1994. This new frame is of course on two levels.

Obviously with the introduction of five bells into the tower came the introduction of Change Ringing. Although a keen interest in the bells must have existed at the time of the five bells being hung nothing is known about the ringers. In fact we need to move on thirty years before reference to a local team is found. On Saturday, July 22,1899 a meeting of the East Derbyshire Association of Change Ringers was held at St. Clement's Church, Horsley and seven ringers from Pentrich were made members. It is unfortunate we have no names but on Saturday, July 14, 1900, over thirty members of that Association visited Pentrich and rang the bells. Afterwards they were all entertained to tea by the Vicar, Rev. W.T. Ledward. In 1910 an Association report lists ringers H. Walters, F. Lamb, B. Hall, R. Clarke and W. Bates as members. The Association continued to hold meetings at the tower at intervals until 1950. After which the bells became unringable and remained in this condition until the restoration project began.

Upon the installation of the peal of six bells an appeal was launched to interest members of the congregation into becoming bell ringers. Several took up the challenge and made very good progress. But, unfortunately other commitments proved more demanding and the group floundered after a comparatively short time. However, Mr. Robin Gentle persevered, took over as tower-keeper and with outside help is able to maintain a regular weekly practice. Should any reader feel they would like to try their hand at the Art and Science of Bell Ringing they would be most welcome. Just contact Robin or simply turn up and make yourself known to him at practice. This invitation is of course open to anyone and at any belfry.

Finally, during the refurbishment of the tower a Saxon monolith, probably an early grave cover, was found by the volunteers in use as part of a lintel over one of the belfry windows.

The Belfry of St. Helen, Pinxton

Low built buttresses. Gabriel Bell inscription re-cast.
Two to eight bells in three years. Pioneering belfry D.I.Y.

Within the most unusual and singularly interesting tower of St. Helen's hangs a peal of eight bells. They were placed there about thirty years ago. Prior to 1968 the tower contained two bells. One was of considerable age bearing the inscription "AVE GRATIA PLENA DOMINUS TECUM." Sadly this bell was severely cracked. The other bell carried a self-explanatory inscription, "Thomas Mears of London, fecit 1803".

The tower itself is peculiar for its "brick on end" shape with its east and west sides being much narrower in width than the north and south.

It is evident, both on the interior and on the exterior, that the upper part of the tower, though composed of old material, has been rebuilt. About 1750 a larger church was built at right angles to the old one and it is probable that the upper part of the tower was rebuilt then. This is the theory of Dr. Cox, writing in his Churches of Derbyshire in 1875. Nikolaus Pevsner, however, gives 1897 as the date of rebuilding the upper part which leaves the reader wondering when in fact the upper portion of the tower was rebuilt.

Another source of 1897 gives an interesting account about the construction. "About the year 1600, the idea was conceived of raising the four walls of the vestry so as to form a tower, which was carried out and resulted in the present shape. The original integrity of the transept without a vestry or tower is proved by the continuity of the stone courses of the lower portions of the tower with the adjoining work to the north of it."

So, the oldest part of St. Helen's church are fragments within the base of the tower. Returning to Dr. Charles Cox let us recall what he wrote in 1875. "This tower, and its adjacent fragment of old work, are not a little puzzling; but the most likely conjecture that occurred to us was this, that the part of the old church that now opens out of the chancel, occupied the same relative position to the body of the original church, to which it served as a transept, or chantry for the side altar, at the time when the Early English lancet windows were in vogue; that the doorway, that now leads into the tower, then opened into the churchyard; and that the tower was an after-thought, the church having previously only had a western bell-turret, and that it was built on to the end of this chantry as the most convenient and least expensive place. This, too, might account for the peculiarity of its oblong shape, for had it been built of an equal square with the previous existing wall, it would have been so large as to be quite out of proportion with the rest of the church."

Reaching only to the height of the first storey are two buttresses supporting the south wall. The bell-chamber openings are square-topped whilst the tower roof rises

172

slightly to a point above the plain parapet. There is no external doorway the tower being entered through a small doorway, not six feet high, on the north side of the tower and leading directly from the church. The ringing chamber being reached by a wooden stair, through a trap-door and the ringers taking up their positions, in order to ring the eight bells, by standing almost in two rows of four, facing each other along the north and south walls.

Ravaged by the death watch beetle in 1965 an appeal was launched to enable restoration work on the tower to be undertaken. A further scheme was adopted aimed at providing a light peal of eight bells for the tower. Two years later a new peal of five bells was installed. These were hung in a new frame made to accommodate eight bells. An order for three further bells was placed with Messrs Taylor and Co. of Loughborough.

Behind this achievement, in just two years, lies a story of much local organisation and enthusiasm. The rector, Rev. W.L. Gwyther and members of St. Helen's congregation, some of whom happened to be engineering craftsmen at nearby collieries, together with the ladies of the church, not only raised the necessary cash but undertook much of the bell hanging and frame construction within the tower, thereby saving considerably the amount of money needed to be raised. Today, D.I.Y. is a common household term but in 1965 it was just not understood and certainly something rather unique and not undertaken on projects such as bell frame building and bell hanging.

By 1968 the three bells cast by Taylor's had been hung in the tower, the treble bell having been donated at a cost of £167 by the Derby Diocesan Association of Church Bell Ringers. This work completed the octave. A wonderful achievement in just three years. Because of their lightness and the short draft of rope the bells are a little difficult to handle when one is first introduced to ringing them but this is quickly adjusted to and an early problem of excessive noise within the ringing chamber has been overcome by the adoption of sound control techniques.

The bells are inscribed and weigh as follows:-

Treble   1968
           Given by the Derby Diocesan
           Association of Church Bell Ringers.
           Diameter: $17^{1}/_{8}$inches. Weight: 1cwt.1qr.17lbs.

2nd.   1968
           Ronald Lloyd Gwyther
           Rector of Pinxton 1968.
           Diameter: 19inches. Weight: 1cwt.2qrs.15lbs.

3rd.   1968
           G.H. Cotterill.
           Diameter: 20inches. Weight: 1cwt.3qrs.0lbs.

The above inscriptions are upon the waist of each bell. The bellmark of Messrs Taylor & Co. is placed between the figures nine and six of the date stamp on each bell. The name G.H. Cotterill on the third bell is on the reverse waist.

4th.   * John Taylor & Co * Loughborough * 1966
In Memory of
William Smith 1868 - 1964
and
Ada Smith 1875 - 1946.
Diameter: 21½inches. Weight: 2cwt.0qrs.9lbs.

5th.   * John Taylor & Co * Loughborough * 1966
Diameter: 23¹/₈inches. Weight: 2cwt.1qr.25lbs.

6th.   + ave gracia plena dominus tecum
1966
Diameter: 24½inches. Weight: 2cwt.3qrs.9lbs.
The inscription from the ancient bell is reproduced round the inscription band. As with the first three bells, Messrs Taylor's have inserted their bell-mark within the date cast upon the waist.

7th.   * John Taylor & Co * Loughborough * 1966
Diameter: 27 inches. Weight: 3 cwt.3qrs.21 lbs.

Tenor   * John Taylor & Co * Loughborough * 1966
Ronald L. Gwyther, Rector
C.P. Farnon; J.E. Searson Churchwardens.
Diameter: 31inches. Weight: 5cwt.2qrs.8lbs.

The bells are tuned in the key of C.

Before leaving let us return to the old cracked bell. You will recall it was inscribed, "Ave Gratia Plena Domicus Tecum." Pre-Reformation bells, particularly throughout the Midlands, frequently carried a not unsimilar Latin inscription, "Ave Maria Gratia Plena Dominus Tecum," which translates, "Hail Mary, full of grace the Lord be with thee." Bells frequently bore this inscription which is the short form of the Angel Gabriel's message. This inscription gave rise to the bells bearing it to be known as Ave or Gabriel bells. In medieval times these bells were tolled for the daily Angelus in the early morning and evening. Upon hearing the bell tolling the people were ordered by the Church to repeat the words.

Judging from the number of church bells found within a wide circle of Nottingham that carry this inscription it seems almost certain that such bells were cast in that town. The inscriptions are nearly always in small black lettering as found on the old Pinxton bell, and widely spaced so that they encircle the bell. Linking this with the early known Nottingham bell founders we have John Selyoke and Richard Selyoke, Richard Mellors all of whom became Mayors of Nottingham between 1497 and 1506.

Coupling this with the remark of Dr. Cox about the old church having a western bell-turret one is left wondering if the old bell was first hung in that turret. You will recall that the second old bell was not installed until 1803, some years after the upper storey of the tower had been rebuilt. An interesting topic for future research.

The installation of eight bells has been popular with peal ringers and many peals have now been rung on the bells. Sunday service ringing is a somewhat different story. Sadly, a number of young bands have been trained over the years but after a period it is often found that young ringers need to move away. This depletion has a knock on effect resulting in it always being a struggle to keep the bells ringing regularly for services. Mr Gordon Riley, the present tower captain and a churchwarden, is constantly working at training ringers in an effort to keep the band together at St. Helen's.

The cracked pre-Reformation bell and its 150 year old neighbour
Being removed from St. Helen's Belfry, Pinxton in April 1966.

The Belfry of St. Michael, Pleasley

Fine gargoyles peer from boundary tower. Ancient stones built into belfry.
For hanging ye great bell...£2. In two Provinces, Canterbury and York.

The fourteenth century embattled tower of St Michael's, Pleasley stands on a hillside almost on the county boundary of Derbyshire with Nottinghamshire as defined by the little River Meden. One of the five bells hanging in the tower has called the faithful to prayer for close on five hundred years and it is now over a century since the peal of bells was augmented to five.

The western tower is of the Perpendicular period and was added to a building whose origins existed in the Norman period. The embattled parapet is adorned at the angles by four short crocketed pinnacles and a fine pair of gargoyles project through the roof string course on both the south and north face. The well proportioned, two light bell openings sit comfortably on a further string course at bell chamber height. Below this string course the tower is supported by diagonal three step buttresses. The graceful three light west window is of moderate proportion as is the doorway beneath, and now filled in with masonry.

Inside, the tall narrow arch to the nave is open and supported by two plain pointed corbels. There is no screen, and the open floor of the belfry, being raised from that of the nave by three steps, is not used, as one might expect, by the ringers. The bells being rung from the ringing chamber above, to which access is gained via the narrow doorway in the south-west angle.

In the belfry, on the west wall, are two stones bearing portions of an incised cross. These are of great age and were broken and used when the tower was built. The ringing chamber is lit by a deeply recessed window on the south face. The lintel of this window being formed from a fragment of stone previously used as a coffin lid. The slab, now about two feet wide and four in length, has, down the centre, double incised lines that probably formed the stem of a cross. To the sinister side a crudely executed symbol of a key can be traced.

On Sunday, March 17, 1816 an earthquake struck and as a result the pinnacles upon the tower were afterwards stoutly secured with iron clamps and other iron stays fitted at the north west angle. According to Lysons the earthquake made "a large chasm in the church steeple." An aged eye witness is quoted by Dr. Cox as saying the description given erred on the side of exaggeration, but it was true that "a slight fissure" was made and that the pinnacles were somewhat shaken. Further damage done by the earthquake was to the adjacent rectory chimneys.

The five bells are inscribed:-

Treble	mar ga re ta

Diameter: 29 inches. Weight: 4cwt.1qr.0lbs.

This treble bell dates from about 1520 and was cast by a member of the Selyoke family of Nottingham. The inscription is rudely executed in large Gothic letters.

2nd.   God save His Church   1618
          Diameter: 31¾inches. Weight: 5cwt.3qrs.2lbs.
          This bell was cast in Nottingham by Henry Oldfield.

3rd.   God save the King. C J M H Churchwardens 1675.
          Diameter: 34½inches. Weight: 6cwt.3qrs.18lbs.

Like the second bell, the third was also cast by a member of the Oldfield family of Nottingham, George the son of Henry (II), who had died within two years of casting the second bell. The Oldfields cast many local bells and were in the bell-founding business in Nottingham for close on two hundred years.

4th.   John Taylor and Co. Founders. Loughborough. 1897.
          Diameter: 38⅝inches. Weight: 10cwt.3qrs.4lbs.

Tenor   John Taylor and Co. Founders. Loughborough. 1897.
          Diameter: 43½inches. Weight: 15cwt.2qrs.7lbs.

Both the fifth and the tenor bells carry a band of decoration in the form of grape and vine-leaf. 1897 was the year of Queen Victoria's Diamond Jubilee, a year when many bells were hung to commemorate the event. I have not been able to establish if these bells do in fact commemorate the occasion.

Early in the eighteenth century we find an item of interest in the parish accounts of 1724: "For hanging ye great bell....£2." As the bell referred too was newly cast in 1675 one wonders why this bell alone needed to be rehung almost fifty years later?

Little is known of the bell ringers of Pleasley. We know not if the old three bells were hung in a frame suitable for ringing them in changes or whether a suitable frame was erected in the tower in 1897, at the time of the augmentation to five.

We do know however that four years after the augmentation both the churchwardens became honorary members of the East Derbyshire Association of Change Ringers and paid a subscription of 2/6d each. The Association's minutes do not record the number of ringing members until 1910 when the following ringers at St. Michael's are listed :- Frank Haynes, Fred Hardy, A. Mugglestone, C. Rogers, T. Wint, Jos. Mugglestone, E.A. Rogers and Thos. Rogers.

It is recorded that King Edward I, who was known for his extensive travel about the Kingdom, visited Thomas Bek at Pleasley Manor on Wednesday, February 18th, 1293. Edward's reign lasted thirty-five years from 1272 until 1307 and during this period the manor and church of Pleasley were held by Thomas Bek who held the important office of Lord Treasurer. Almost seven hundred years later, on July 28, 1977, H.M. Queen Elizabeth II passed through Pleasley whilst on a visit in celebration of her Silver Jubilee to Derbyshire and Nottinghamshire. In loyal greeting the five bells of St. Michael's rang out.

As this is being written the five bells are all but silent. They are, I understand, simply tolled for services, instead of being rung in full circle. This is on account of the bell-frame working loose and giving rise for concern. The P.C.C. is in the process of having a survey carried out and is awaiting the outcome before making a decision about the future.

An interesting and unique situation arose in 1983 with regard to the geographical position of St. Michael's, Pleasley. Pleasley, being situated on the county boundary of Derbyshire with Nottinghamshire, which also forms the boundary of the Diocese of Derby with Southwell, had, under the appointment of the Bishop of Derby, John Goldsmith as Priest in Charge from 1981. Under a scheme of reorganisation adopted in 1983, John Goldsmith was, in addition to the benefice of St. Michael's, appointed to be Priest in Charge of St Barnabas, Pleasley Hill. With Pleasley Hill, being almost a continuation of the same residential area as the parish of St Michael's this made good sense. However, as the parish of Pleasley is in the Diocese of Derby and that of Pleasley Hill is within the Diocese of Southwell a unique situation in church history was instituted. The incumbent being responsible at Pleasley to the Archdeacon of Chesterfield, the Bishop of Derby and the Archbishop of Canterbury, whilst at Pleasley Hill he was responsible to the Archdeacon of Newark, the Bishop of Southwell and the Archbishop of York. This situation continued until 1987 when, at the next interregnum, the ecclesiastical parishes were again separated.

Taking this aside one step further, and applying the same position with regard to the East Derbyshire and West Nottinghamshire Association of Church Bell Ringers, it makes it that this Association is in the same unique situation, in that it not only bridges two counties and two dioceses, but also two Provinces, Canterbury and York.

The Belfry of All Saints, Ripley

Queen Victoria Memorial Bell. Ringing persona portraits removed.
1901 Augmentation to an octave. "Ring in the Christ that is to be."

Built in 1821, at the south-west angle of the church, the tower of All Saints, Ripley stands just off the market place and only a few paces from the busy shopping street. The lower stage of the belfry forms a spacious porch to the church. A small door in the north west corner of this porch invites any bellringer up to the ringing chamber from where the bells can then be reached by means of a ladder.

> "Ring out the old, ring in the new,
> Ring out the false, ring in the true."

Until some few years ago the ringing chamber had a decorative frieze beneath its ceiling depicting these lines by Alfred Lord Tennyson and taken from his In Memoriam. This quotation was somewhat fitting as Tennyson (1809 - 1892) was contemporary with the building of All Saints tower. At the same time as the words on the frieze were removed so were a series of portraits of noteworthy bell ringers. To the ringing fraternity at large they were something rather special, interesting and unique, but alas no more. Beginning with the south wall the portraits hung as follows.

Arthur Percival Heywood, M.A. J.P.	Duffield.
Rev. H. Earle Bulware, M.A.	Stanhoe, Norfolk.
W.T. Sevier,	Gloucester.
James William	Washbrook.

West wall;

Thomas Hattersley,	Sheffield.
Henry Bastable	Birmingham.
Joseph Henry Hardcastle,	Bradford.
George Newson,	London.
Rev. Edward W. Carpenter, M.A.	Hon. Sec. Kent County Assoc.
Charles Henry Hattersley,	Sheffield.
Rev. Charles D.P. Davies M.A.	
John William Taylor Jnr.	Loughborough.

East wall;

W. Hertford Baker,	Hertford.
George Dorrington,	London.
Charles Jackson,	Hull.
Henry Bright,	Woolwich.
Capt. Arthur Penistone Moore,	Waytread, Suffolk.

Sir Arthur Heywood took up change ringing seriously in the 1880s and nothing was allowed to interfere with his Sunday service ringing at nearby Duffield. As a prolific ringer of peals and a substantial benefactor to the belfry at Duffield he became aware of the urgent need for a body to watch over and protect the rights, privileges and interests of the bell-ringer. To this end he pioneered the founding of the Central Council of Church Bell Ringers in 1890, and was elected its first President. He involved himself on the theoretical side of change ringing, devising a Method known as Duffield. It was originally composed for ten and twelve bell peals but later adapted for ringing on eight bells. In 1899 he was Sheriff of Derbyshire.

A similar story lay behind each of the gentlemen whose portraits hung in the ringing chamber. What a pity they are lost but let us not dwell but take a look at the bells.

Five of the eight bells date from 1866 with the other three having been added in 1901. They were all cast by John Taylor & Co. of Loughborough and are inscribed:-

Treble	John Taylor & Co. Founders. Loughborough. In Memoriam Queen Victoria A.D. 1901. Diameter: 28⁷/₈inches. Weight: 6cwt.0qrs.21 lbs.
2nd.	John Taylor & Co. Founders. Loughborough. Serve the Lord with gladness. A.D. 1901. Diameter: 29⁷/₈ inches. Weight: 6cwts 1qr.8 lbs.
3rd.	John Taylor & Co. Founders. Loughborough. Be joyful in the Lord. A.D. 1901. Diameter: 31⁷/₈inches. Weight: 7cwt.2qrs.8 lbs.
4th.	J. Taylor & Co. Founders. Loughborough. 1866. Diameter: 35½inches. Weight: 8cwt.0qrs.12 lbs.
5th.	J. Taylor & Co. Founders. Loughborough. Subscribed for A.D.1866. W.G. Ketchley P.C. J. Wood A.C. W. Jessop, W. Frost, Wardens. Diameter: 37¾ inches. Weight: 9cwt.0qrs.9 lbs.
6th.	J. Taylor & Co. Founders. Loughborough. 1866. Diameter: 38³/₈inches. Weight: 9cwt.1qr.16 lbs.
7th.	J. Taylor & Co. Founders. Loughborough. 1866. Diameter: 42³/₈inches. Weight: 12cwt.0qrs.22 lbs.
Tenor	Taylor & Co. Founders Loughborough. 1866. Diameter: 473/8 inches. Weight: 16cwt.2qrs.8 lbs. Tuned to the note of F.

The tower of All Saints Church, Ripley remained empty and the congregation waited patiently for forty-five years before the peal of five bells was installed. From their inscriptions we learn that the present fifth, sixth seventh and the tenor bells were subscribed for. The slightly differing inscription upon the present fourth bell leaves one wondering if it was a gift. In 1901, when the three front bells were added we find that the treble and the second bells were the gift of Mr. A. Leslie Wright, Vicar's Warden and his wife. The cost of the third bell being raised by the bell-ringers together with a public subscription to cover the necessary bell work. As in 1866 Messrs John Taylor & Co. of Loughborough were entrusted with the work which included casting the three light bells and returning and rehanging the old five at a total cost of £307.

A contemporary report of the dedication appeared in Bell News on Saturday September 21, 1901 when the enthusiasm of the local ringers was praised. The report went on to say that the bell provided by the ringers would be known as the Queen Victoria Memorial Bell but a later reference, this time in Kelly's Directory states that the three bells were added in commemoration of the coronation of Edward VII.

The ecclesiastical parish of Ripley that we know today was formerly part of the larger parish of Pentrich. Following the well recorded disturbance that became branded "the Pentrich Revolution," in 1817, the vicar of Pentrich, John Wood, seized upon the situation to further a subscription toward the "intended Chapel of Ease at Ripley." In a circular of 1819 he states that the smallness of church accommodation at Ripley "has occasioned a neglect of religious duties and morals, the lamentable effects of which during the last two years are but too well known, and have rendered it an imperious duty upon the well-disposed inhabitants to take some means of stemming the torrent of irreligion and disaffection." Ripley church was built in 1821.

With the augmentation of the five bells to eight in 1901 it is obvious that a competent band of change ringers existed at the tower. How soon after the installation of the five bells in 1866 a competent band was formed is not recorded. We do know that in 1895 the ringers joined the East Derbyshire Association of Change Ringers and invited members to meet at the tower on October 17th, 1896. Unfortunately, the Archbishop of Canterbury, Dr. Edward White Benson, died that week and out of respect the bells were rung half-muffled.

Half-muffled ringing again took place at the end of February 1915 following the death of a ringer of thirty years standing, Francis H. Key of Moorwood Moor, who had contracted an illness and died after only 15 days. Francis was fifty years of age and an accomplished change ringer. He walked miles to take part in his ringing and to help and teach young ringers, in fact, he introduced and taught method ringing to the band at St. Helen's Church, Selston. He was laid to rest in Ripley Cemetery when four brother ringers, T. Stimpsom (Swanwick), G. Brown (Crich), W. Booth and W. Hawksley (South Wingfield) acted as pall-bearers. Half-muffled ringing took place throughout the day on the Sunday following when touches of Triples and Major methods were rung by H. Day, H. George, A Bowmer, C. Pilcher, J. Bourne, F.W. Hill, F. Hill, A. Hutchinson and S. Sander.

Several of these ringers were regular members of the All Saints band of ringers throughout their lives and responsible for maintaining the bells in excellent order until well after the end of the Second World War. In the late 1940s W. Beresford, G.A. Bowmer, R. Graham, Frank Hill, G. Lavender and F. Murfin were regular Sunday service ringers. On Wednesday, August 4th, 1948 a Peal of 5024 changes of Double Norwich Court Bob Major was rung on the bells taking three hours and one minute to complete. It was composed by Sir A.P. Heywood and conducted by Jack Bailey. The ringers were :-

Miss D. Templeman	Treble	Frank F. Hill	5th.
Jack Bailey	2nd.	Keith Hudston	6th.
Edward C. Gobey	3rd.	Denis R. Carlisle	7th.
Francis R. Lowe	4th.	William A. Parsons	Tenor.

This was the first peal rung on the bells for the Derbyshire Association of Change Ringers which had been founded in 1946.

Early in the 1960s the band was made up by a number of lady ringers, Vivien Cheetham, Jean Hunt, Dorothy Plant, Margaret Allen, Susan Elliott, Barbara Peat, Doreen Land, Veronica Walters, Miss A. Bradley, Janet Mathews and Miss A. Mather who were joined by David Brown, Ian Sparham, A. College, D. Fleming, J. Asher, David Ashley, David W. Bailey.

At the annual meeting of the ringers in May 1980 Jean Bestwick was appointed Tower Captain and Mollie Oldknow, Secretary and Hazel Quarmby as Treasurer. They were ably assisted by Keith Eaton, Philip Ottewell and Stuart Scarborough. A special thank you was expressed to Philip Ottewell, his father and to Stuart Scarborough for all the unseen work they undertake in the tower, maintaining the bells, clock and attending to the flying of the flag.

The exterior of the tower in 1986 was showing some signs of decay and from the churchyard it was observed that the clock dial on the east face was in need of repair and crumbling around its rim. No fingers were in position and it was a very sorry sight. The three other clock dials were in working order. The dials are placed within the stone framework of the bell chamber openings, taking up the topmost section with the two frames of louvres forming the lower section of each opening. Beneath the plain battlemented parapet and without pinnacles is a plain frieze recessing on to each face. The moulding of the recess carries nine decorative bosses.

Let us return to the words written by Alfred Lord Tennyson :-

Ring out, wild bells, to the wild sky,
The flying cloud, the frosty light:
The year is dying in the night;
Ring out, wild bells, and let him die.

Ring out the old, ring in the new,
Ring, happy bells, across the snow:
The year is going, let him go;
Ring out the false, ring in the true.

Ring out the grief that saps the mind,
For those that here we see no more;
Ring out the feud of rich and poor,
Ring in redress to all mankind.

Ring out a slowly dying cause,
And ancient forms of party strife;
Ring in the nobler modes of life,
With sweeter manners, purer laws.

Ring out the want, the care, the sin,
The faithless coldness of the times;
Ring out, ring out my mournful rhymes,
But ring the fuller minstrel in.

Ring out the false pride in place and blood,
The civic slander and the spite;
Ring in the love of truth and right,
Ring in the common love of good.

Ring out old shapes of foul disease;
Ring out the narrowing lust of gold;
Ring out the thousand wars of old,
Ring in the thousand years of peace.

Ring in the valiant man and free,
The larger heart, the kindlier hand;
Ring out the darkness of the land,
Ring in the Christ that is to be.

Sir Arthur P. Heywood, Bart. of Duffield.
An expert ringer, composer and conductor.
Founder and first President of the
Central Council of Church Bell Ringers

The Belfry of St. Leonard, Scarcliffe

Thirteenth century spire removed. Bell from submerged church hung.
Lady Constantia's bequest.

The one hundred and fifty year old tower of St. Leonard's provides a delightful aspect as it is approached down the main street. We are told that the old thirteenth century tower was surmounted by a spire very similar in character to that still found at Bolsover. In 1842 it was considered unsafe, and too far out of repair to allow restoration so it was dismantled and the present tower built.

Some leading authorities on the subject held the view that had the improved taste in ecclesiastical matters that existed at the turn of the nineteenth century existed at the time of rebuilding it would either have not been taken down or at least have been rebuilt as closely as possible to the former one. Be that as it may, we find today a substantial and very interesting belfry.

Built on the south-west angle of the church with access to the ringing chamber and the bells being gained from an external stair. There is a clock and five bells. The oldest dating from about 1500 and the other four being cast in this century. There is a sixth bell, the old second, which is preserved within the church alongside the canons of the old third and fourth bells, the metal from these two bells being used in the casting of the present fourth bell in 1962.

The five bells in the tower are inscribed :-

> Treble   Given by George Godber
> in memory of his parents
> William Godber 1825 - 1900
> and
> Amy Godber 1832 - 1912
> of Palterton
> R.I.P.
> 1938
> Diameter: 28 inches. Weight: 4cwts.1qr.7 lbs.

The main inscription is upon the waist with the date on the reverse waist. The date being bisected with the bellmark of John Taylor and Co. On the inscription band a decorative border.

> 2nd.   In memoriam
> John Godber
> Late of Palterton
> 1938
> Diameter: 30½ inches. Weight: 5cwt.1qr.23 lbs.

As with the Treble the inscription is on the waist with the bisected date being on the reverse and decoration circling the inscription band.

3rd.   John Taylor & Co * Founders * Loughborough *
         Leicestershire
         Diameter: 32½ inches. Weight: 6cwts.1qr.27 lbs.

There is a grape and vine pattern encircling the bell and the founder's name is cast within the inscription band. This bell was cast in 1901 for the church at Derwent Woodlands and came to St. Leonard's, Scarcliffe in 1938 when that village, together with its neighbour, Ashopton, was being dismantled prior to being submerged beneath the waters of Ladybower Reservoir.

4th.   Recast January 1962
         Diameter: 36 inches. Weight: 8cwts.3qrs.0 lbs.

These simple words appear upon the inscription band and below, on the waist, is the bell-mark of the founder, John Taylor & Co.

Four bells hung in the old tower for upwards of two hundred and fifty years before the tower was dismantled in 1842. One of them being almost four hundred years old at the time. This old bell bearing the inscription "Sancta Maria ora pro nobis" in small Gothic letters of rough workmanship stands today on the floor of the church. It carries the founder's mark of a cross and the initials R.C. A bell at Shirland bears a similar inscription with the word "Johas" substituted for "Maria", and both bells may have been cast by Robert Crouch (1437-60) in London.

Two other very old bells coexisted with the "Sancta Maria" bell but in 1962 the metal from these two bells was used in the casting of the present fourth bell. The canons constituted an ancient system of casting a group of loops on the crown of the bell, in order to allow the threading of metal straps. The straps are then used for securing the bell in position onto the head-stock. The two canons are preserved and on display in the church together with the c1500 bell. The inscriptions upon the two re-cycled bells was:-

(a)   God save His Church
         T S G S W Revil W Hall Wardens 1698

(b)   Gloria in excelsis Deo. I.H.S.

The first of these two bells was most probably cast in Nottingham at the Oldfield foundry, the inscription being a firm favourite with that founder. The second of these two bells was cast in Chesterfield, probably early in the seventeenth century, by Ralph Heathcote whose mark appeared on the bell. It consisted of a shield on which his initials R.H. surmount a fylfot cross. Ralph (III) the son of Godfrey was baptised in 1592. His grandfather Ralph (II) had discontinued using the fylfot cross as his mark in favour of a crown prior to 1577 but Godfrey reintroduced it later and the tradition was continued by Ralph (111) until the Heathcote family stopped casting bells at their foundry in Chesterfield about 1647.

Tenor   "Hinc venio retro
          Cum silis noie Petro."
          Diameter: 40¼ inches. Weight: 10cwts.3qrs.3 lbs.

The rhyming legend is in Lombardic characters. There is a bell-mark depicting the letters R.B. under a crown. Ralph Heathcote (II), who is alluded to above, used a very similar mark but bearing his initials R.H. He was casting bells before 1558 when he took charge of the foundry in Chesterfield on the death of his father George and continued casting bells until his own death in March, 1577/8.

On the gable of the nave is a bell-cote measuring about two feet by one in which hung the sanctus bell until late in the nineteenth century.

When the common lands were enclosed in 1726 four acres were set apart to provide the parish with bell-ropes from the rent.

Another five acres of land is mentioned on a fixed slab above the ancient monument to Lady Constantia within the church. It is inscribed:

"Left by the Lady Constantia,

Five acres of land purchased for the purpose of ringing curfew at Scarcliffe for ever. Three acres and three roods now in the occupation of John Coupe and let at an annual rent of three pounds seven shillings and sixpence, and known by the names as follows- Moor close, one acre three roods; Twenty Lands, one acre and eighteen perches; and Honey Croft three roods and twenty two perches. Also one acre and one rood known by the name Cock-Stye now in the occupation of John Jeffrey and let at an annual rent of one pound two shillings and sixpence, 1832."

It is this bequest of Lady Constantia that gives rise to the legend that she and her infant son lost their way in neighbouring woods, and were in danger of perishing from cold and fatigue, when the welcome sound of Scarcliffe bells was heard and guided her back to the village.

The Belfry of St. Helen, Selston

Annual sermon from tower roof. Custodian of Jubilee Shield. Christmas Day handbell ringing. Seven bell peal for a period. Clock bell purchased for 5p.

It was in 1622 that the first dated bell was cast and hung in the tower of St. Helen's Church at Selston. But, it was to be almost three more centuries before the art of Change Ringing was introduced into the tower. This came about only after the peal of three bells was augmented to six in 1905.

Six ringers of the St. Helen's band in 1905 formed not only part of the first company of local Change Ringers at the tower, but they were also elected as members of the East Derbyshire Association of Change Ringers. This took place at a meeting of that Association's members held at Pentrich on December 9th, 1905. Not only did this open up a new horizon for the Selston bell ringers but it also opened up a new beginning for the Association. This was for two reasons. St. Helen's ringers became the first tower in Nottinghamshire to join the Association and they subsequently and unwittingly were the reason for a change in the title of the Association. It should of course not be forgotten that at this time, and in fact until 1927, Derbyshire was part of the Diocese of Southwell and consequently, in ecclesiastical terms, no boundary existed between Derbyshire and Nottinghamshire. On this basis it was quite a natural progression for the Association to spread eastward from its origin in 1887 at Clay Cross. Today the Association is known as the East Derbyshire and West Nottingham-shire Association of Church Bell Ringers and covers some thirty-six towers stretching from Crich and Darley Dale in the west to Edwinstowe and Warsop in the east.

For almost five centuries the tower of St. Helen's has stood at the west end of its church and witnessed many events. None more than the major restoration work and extension to the church building that was undertaken almost a century ago. The tower dates mainly from the fourteenth century along with its diagonal buttresses. The top battlemented section is of fifteenth century work. The two-light bell openings, the west window with modern figures of Our Lord, Nathaniel and Philip and the doorway below are well proportioned. On the battlements of the south face are the letters 'I' and 'M', (Jesus and Mary) also a shield and the letters 'T' and 'S'. The shield bears a bend between a pierced mullet and a small ring. The arms indicate that the Samons of Annesley Woodhouse may have been involved with the building as they were with St. Mary's, Nottingham. This would certainly explain use of the initials 'T.S'.

Another interesting mark, cut into the masonry toward the base of the south wall of the tower, is the mark used by Ordnance Survey as part of their national grid system for mapping.

Passing inside we find the tower opens into the nave through a fine arch and access to the upper ringing chamber, bells and roof are via the small door situated in the south west corner.

Under the tower is an incised slab of unusual character and believed to be a memorial to a knight dating from 1289 or before. It bears a wheel-like ornament at the top with a sword on the left side. In a frame hang the royal arms.

Of recent date, and loaned to St. Helen's bell-ringers for safe keeping, hangs the Jubilee Shield of the East Derbyshire and West Nottinghamshire Association of Church Bell Ringers. The shield was awarded annually to the affiliated tower attaining the highest number of points for Sunday Service ringing. Regrettably, the scheme had to be discontinued and as St. Helen's ringers were the last recipients the Association asked if it could be placed in the tower.

To digress for a moment it may be of interest to future ringers to explain briefly why awarding the Jubilee Shield ceased.

About church services much discussion could take place and much midnight oil could be burnt, but not here. However, with the emphasis being placed on family worship traditional matins and evensong have become secondary, and in many churches have been lost and or abandoned. In former days ringers dutifully rang the bells prior to matins and evensong but sadly this is no longer possible in many churches. For many years the Association awarded the Jubilee Shield using the ringing at these two services to determine the quality and dedication of a resident band of ringers and to assess that band's progress in the field of Change Ringing. A system of points was awarded covering a period of one year. Of these points the greatest number was given for regular Sunday Service ringing as that was the main objective in awarding the shield. It was a form of encouraging and promoting Sunday Service ringing. A problem arose with the general change in the Service pattern, particularly with evensong, and it was found that participating towers could no longer compete on a fair system of ringing for 104 services each year plus additional festivals and occasions such as confirmation services and mid-week events. The Association looked at all possible alternatives but with great reluctance discontinued the award. On the large shield will be found small ones engraved with the year and the award winning tower and a full list of these awards is listed elsewhere. This list in itself gives an insight into the strength of ringing teams in the area over many years.

Since 1985 the tower has housed a peal of eight bells and for a period of about a year prior to then a peal of seven bells were rung. To have an odd number of bells hung for Change Ringing is somewhat unique, although one other local tower, that of St. Giles Church in Matlock, boasts nine bells hung in this manner.

The eight bells are inscribed:-

Treble   EIJSBOUTS ASTENSIS ME FECIT ANNO MCMLXXXV
          James Rawson 1862 - 1949

In 1985 this bell was hung to complete the octave. It was donated in memory of the life of James Rawson by his sons Les and Gerald. A small founder's mark is on the reverse waist.

2nd.   OMNIA FIANT AD GLORIAM DEI
          In memory of Vera, wife of
          Ed. Wood 1968.

On the waist is a large medallion depicting three bells, a crown entwined with foliage. This is the mark of the Eijsbouts a most celebrated bell-founder from Denmark. This bell was hung in the tower in 1983. The frame in which it hangs was fabricated in section to a similar design to the frame that bells three, four and six hang. This old frame having been placed in the tower in 1905 by Barwell of Birmingham.

3rd.   Childrens Bell 1905
          The children did well and purchased this bell.

4th.   Bible Union Bell 1905
          Let my music be heard
          In praise of the word.

5th.   Gabriel I S   (date unknown)

6th.   Church Council Bell 1905
          For this church restored
          Give thanks to the Lord.
          Charles Harrison Vicar
          William Hardy James Rawson Churchwardens.

7th.   I sweetly toling men do call
          To taste on meats that feeds the soule   1622

Tenor   God save his church 1704
          William Wood Francis Cheetham Wardens

The "Gabriel Bell" is of unknown date and most probably was cast many years before its near neighbour which tells us it was cast in 1622. In 1704 a third bell was installed but another two hundred years were to pass before the peal was augmented to six.

At a meeting of the Vestry on Easter Monday 1904 plans were approved for the restoration and enlargement of St. Helen's. The accounts listed donations and gifts already promised and the meeting asked for a further £1000 to be raised plus a further £100 so that the much needed restoration work on the church's bells could be undertaken and so put them in full working order.

The account goes on to say that Feast Sunday (the nearest Sunday to July 6th) will be the last day on which services are held in the church in its present form. Then the following request was made; "Who will give as a permanent speaking memorial, for a peal of six bells. Bell No 1 £41; Bell No 2 £44; or Bell No 4 £62. To oblige additional donors the peal can be extended to eight. As the number of donors is limited the first offers will straight away be accepted. Dilatory donors beware!"

From this appeal we learn that it was the intention to add two new treble bells, use the then treble or "Gabriel Bell" as number three and to insert a new bell in as number

189

four, leaving the 1622 bell as five and the 1704 bell, weighing 14cwts, as Tenor.

In July of each year is held the service known as the Tower Service, this is when the Vicar, by local tradition, delivers a sermon from the roof of the tower. It coincides with Feast Sunday when in former times much merriment took place. When the tower service was first started I have been unable to trace but it was restarted after 1937 when the Rev. Schofield became vicar.

Nowadays, an invited preacher often gives the sermon and various youth and church organisations assemble for the service which takes the form of the Sunday School Anniversary.

Close by the tower and under the shade of a lofty lime tree lies Dan Boswell, King of the Gipsies. The broken stone, now flat upon his grave, with few words to be seen, bore an epitaph curious enough to be remembered;

> I've lodged in many a town.
> I've travelled many a year.
> But death at length has brought me down,
> To my last lodging here.

An interesting little incident which happened in the days when tower bells were not allowed to be rung, except in the emergency of invasion, during the 1939 - 1945 War, was remembered by Mrs M Spears, (nee Schofield of the Old Vicarage), and published in the October issue of the Parish Magazine of 1979.

> "One Christmas when the bells were silent, waiting for the invasion signal, and only altar candles were permitted in a building incapable of blackout, as I opened the door to go in for the 8.00a.m. service I thought I was dreaming. The faint sound of bells! Then I saw the ringers with their handbells standing under the tower at the west end, welcoming the great day. No music has ever surpassed it in my memory."

Handbells can be rung to Change Ringing methods in the same way as tower bells. They can, of course, also be rung to music and many teams of very keen musical handbell ringers exist throughout the country raising money and entertaining.

Change ringing on a set of handbells however calls for a different approach. To begin, each ringer operates two handbells, one in each hand. The ringer then simulates the tower bells being rung by introducing a wrist action in the movement of each hand-bell. This defines both the handstroke and the backstroke. These two strokes are essential to the ringing of changes and are automatically produced by tower bells as they oscillate within the bellframe. Once this action is accomplished and perfected the ringer then introduces the ringing of rounds whereby the team ring all the bells in order down the musical scale. They next launch into the ringing of a Method (a unique sequence of arithmetical changes for a given number of bells) taking great care to strike each bell in its allotted place and at the same time ensuring

190

that rhythm and pace is not lost. Obviously the Method to be rung is agreed beforehand and a conductor appointed to call the touch or peal. Bearing in mind that the handbell ringer is ringing two bells, each of which is methodically progressing through a predetermined sequence of changes, of which no two must be repeated throughout the touch or peal, then it will be seen that a great deal of concentration and mental energy is demanded of the handbell ringer. Selston is very fortunate, at this period, in having among its bellringers those who can be rightly honoured as being amongst the leading Change Ringers of handbells in England. It is therefore very fitting that over fifty years ago the faint sound of handbells ringing at the base of the tower heralded Christmas. Very few towers can boast such a long association with the ringing of handbells. It is also worth recording that recently the ringers have spent £300 from belfry funds, much of which is raised from the fees of ringing for weddings, to have the twelve handbells refurbished. The bells, having been reburnished and fitted with new leather caps and handles, together with the renewing of the felt pads and a complete overhaul of clappers and fittings now look and are in pristine condition.

In 1974 a clock bell was donated to St. Helen's by the National Coal Board on payment of a nominal fee of 1/- (5p). Formerly the clock's bell at Pye Hill Colliery it had been cast in 1902 by John Taylor & Co. of Loughborough and weighed approximately 1cwt. The purpose in accepting the gift was to use the metal to help in the future augmentation of the peal to an octave. The gift was commemorated by the ringing of a Quarter Peal consisting of 1260 Changes of Plain Bob Minor (six bells) on Sunday, April 14th, 1974, by members of the local band, with Margaret Webb ringing the Treble; John Hutchinson 2nd; Elizabeth Lounds 3rd; A Leslie Rawson 4th; Adrian Dempster 5th and Stanley Harpham ringing the Tenor. The Quarter Peal was conducted by Adrian Dempster.

In the event the metal from this clock bell was not used when the six bells were augmented, first to seven in 1983 and then to eight in 1985. Messrs Eayre and Smith, who were awarded the order for the two new bells, agreed instead to take the clock bell and make an allowance for it in their contract. This resulted in the Pye Hill Colliery bell being taken to the bell-hangers yard at Melbourne. Some time later a private buyer, Mr Phil Gay, was found to be wanting such a bell to hang in a private belfry he was installing at his home and so the bell now hangs as the tenor bell of Mr Gay's light ring of bells in Staffordshire.

When the clock bell was acquired it was found that a small bell also formed part of the 'deal'. This remains at Selston and has served on several occasions as a receptacle for fund raising.

In the previous year, 1973, members of the band had accomplished the ringing of the first Peal to be rung on the tower bells in almost forty years. This is what a contemporary news report of November 23rd had to say:-

"For the first time since 1935 a band of local bellringers have rung a peal at Selston St. Helen's Church. The peal of 5040 Changes of Plain Bob Minor was rung in three hours on Sunday afternoon and was half-muffled for Remembrance Sunday. This was a great achievement for all six ringers as it needs continued concentration to complete the peal, but particularly so for John Hutchinson who rang Treble in the band and is only 11 years of age.

John is the youngest ringer ever to have rung a peal at Selston Church, and possibly in the East Derbyshire and West Nottinghamshire Association of Church Bell Ringers. By any standard it was quite a feat for one so young to have completed the peal.

Fifteen year old Janet Slaney and sixteen-year-old Elizabeth Lounds were in the band with Moureen Dempster, Stanley Harpham and Adrian Dempster who rang the Tenor and was conducting his first peal.

The Rev. H.V. Simmons, Vicar of Selston and Westwood, congratulated the ringers, who afterwards were served with tea at the vicarage by Mrs. E. Simmons.

The Selston bellringers are trained by Leslie Rawson, of Selston, who is captain of the Tower and has been ringing the bells of Selston Church for over fifty years."

Unfortunately this report is not completely accurate regarding the date of the previous peal. There was a peal rung on the six bells in 1935 as stated. It was rung on Monday, March 4th and was a peal of Treble Bob Minor, 5040 Changes, being one extent of Cambridge Surprise and three extents each of Kent and Oxford Treble Bob. It was rung in three hours and one minute by:-

Thomas H. Hand *	Treble.	Charles H. Cottam	4th.
Franke Cooke*	2nd.	A. Leslies Rawson	5th.
F. Gerard Rawson	3rd.	Cyril Jacques	Tenor.

Conducted by Frank Cooke. * First peal.

On February 19th, 1936, a similar peal was rung on the bells and then on Wednesday, July 13th, 1960, the bells sounded out in honour of the 85th birthday of Wilson Dobb. Sadly, almost three years later on Wednesday, July 10th, 1963, the bells rang again. This time they were half-muffled in memory of Wilson Dobb who had been a ringer at St. Helen's for over sixty years. Wilson had been a former President (1930-1939) of the East Derbyshire and West Nottinghamshire Association of Church Bell Ringers.

The first peal to be rung on the six tower bells took place on Saturday, October 16th, 1909. It took three hours and one minute to complete the 5040 changes of Plain Bob Minor. Conducted by Williamson Wharmby it was the first peal rung by the other five.

Arthur Elliott	Treble	Charles H. Cottamm	4th.
Harold C. Harrison	2nd.	John Dobbs	5th.
James E. Anness	3rd.	Williamson Wharmby	Tenor.

Many ringers complete fifty years of ringing service to the church and it is usually a memorable occasion. This was the case in May 1975 when during evensong Cyril Jacques was presented with a clock, suitably inscribed, in recognition of his loyalty to St. Helen's belfry from 1925 until 1975. Cyril had also completed sixty years as a chorister at St. Helen's. The band commemorated the event by ringing a Quarter Peal of Kent and Oxford Treble Bob Minor in his honour. Cyril together with Gerard Rawson rang their first Peal, 5040 changes of Plain Bob Minor, together at Selston on Saturday, September 6th, 1930, and conducted by J.W. England.

William Swain	Treble	Cyril Jacques	4th.
F. G. Rawson	2nd.	F. W. Knowles	5th.
Arthur Smithson	3rd.	J.W. England	Tenor.

1975 brought in the fiftieth anniversary of Leslie Rawson being elected as tower captain of St. Helen's and his fifty-fifth year as a ringer. He also reached the age of 75. On October 16th, the event was honoured with a Peal of 5040 Changes of Minor on the bells and rung by:-

John A. Rhodes *	Treble	David C. Lester	4th.
Elizabeth I. Lounds	2nd.	Leslie C. Smith	5th.
Maureen A. Dempster	3rd.	Adrian Dempster	Tenor.

Conducted by Adrian Dempster. * First peal.

Mention has already been made of handbell ringing at Selston and the skills involved. The following marks but the first milestone in that field.

East Derbyshire and West Nottinghamshire Association
Of Church Bell Ringers
On Wednesday, March 10th, 1976, in two hours, eleven minutes,
At 210 Nottingham Road, Selston, Notts.
A Peal of Plain Bob Minor on Handbells, 5040 Changes.

Bells:	1st. and 2nd.	Elizabeth L. Lounds *
Bells:	3rd. and 4th.	Adrian Dempster.
Bells:	5th. and 6th.	David C. Lester. *

Conducted by Adrian Dempster.
* First peal on handbells.
First peal on handbells as conductor.
First peal on handbells for the Association.

A parson has it in his position to make or break a band of bell ringers. He can either encourage, reject or at worst show apathy. But, when encouragement is shown, the result will be monumental and a really first class team of ringers will almost always be established in any tower thus encouraged. The parson does not necessarily need to be a ringer although the exercise as a whole would welcome more clerical ringers. For sixteen years the ringers of Selston had in its Vicar, Rev. H.V. Simmons, a great encourager and when he died on March 3rd, 1978, the ringers rang the following peal not only as a mark of their esteem, but as friends, and as a thanksgiving for his life and ministry at St. Helen's from 1962. The peal was rung "open", that is, without a muffle being placed upon the clapper of each bell.

On Sunday, March 12th, 1978, in two hours, 47 minutes,
at the Church of St. Helen, Selston.

A Peal of Minor, 5040 Changes,
being two extents each of Cambridge Surprise, Oxford Treble Bob,
Kent Treble Bob and one extent of Plain Bob.

Cyril Jaques	Treble.	J. Neville Parkin	4th
Maureen A. Dempster	2nd.	David C. Lester	5th.
Elizabeth A. Lounds	3rd.	Adrian Dempster	Tenor.

Conductor Adrian Dempster.

That peal was twenty years ago and at least four of the ringers are still active in the belfry. Elizabeth has changed her name, through marriage, to Elizabeth A. Murray and is joined in the tower by her daughter together with the two daughters of Maureen and Adrian Dempster. They are joined by Miss S. Kelly and Miss J. Tew and Mr. R. Tew.

The Central Council of Church Bell Ringers was founded in 1890. It was pioneered by a Derbyshire ringer of Duffield, Arthur Percival Heywood, M.A. J.P. who had the foresight to see the need of such an organisation. Today it is still the recognised body for embracing all aspects relating to our belfries. It is made up of members from all affiliated Guilds and Associations. The East Derbyshire and West Nottinghamshire Association affiliated to the Council in 1927 and is allowed one representative elected on a triennial basis. Adrian Dempster is the current elected representative, an office he has been re-elected to for the past eighteen years. He is the Chairman of the Tower and Belfries Committee and as such travels throughout the country assessing and advising Parochial Church Councils on work they are proposing to have undertaken in their belfries. This is an honorary position, and because of the upsurge in proposed renovation work, due to the availability of the Millennium Commission's Grant Aid Scheme set up in 1996, Adrian is extremely busy.

Finally two snippets. Access to the tower roof has always been an hazardous venture and not least so for the unacquainted preacher at the tower service who was required to climb over the bells. However, in 1997 life for him and for the visitor has been somewhat eased by the erection of a wooden stairway over the bells. The cost was born by the ringers and should serve for many generations to come. The other item is of more interest to bell-ringers. When the augmentation took place in 1985 it was decided to try the then new material, polypropylene, in place of hemp as the main component of bell-ropes. This has been found agreeably suitable in the main as it does not get affected by the atmospheric changes like a rope made of hemp. Therefore it does not get stiff during wet weather periods and its wearing qualities are very good which means virtually no splicing is needed. However it is not too kind on the ringers' hands and many are splicing in a hemp tail-end section to overcome this. Like all change there is valid argument both for and against but for my choice a bell-rope made of good quality hemp, with a pure wool handgrip, called a Sally, takes some beating. But let us not forget, it was here at St. Helen's belfry that the ringers tried the new material almost fifteen years ago. Another local first.

194

The Belfry of St.Leonard, Shirland

Incised cross used as lintel. A Monastic fifth bell?
Mysterious re-casting in 1757/8. Bell Acre and the noonday Angelus.
Belles paint bells! 1689, Ringers visit Ashover.

The fine west tower of St. Leonard's Church, Shirland, was built about 1500A.D. in the late Perpendicular style. An embattled parapet, supporting eight crocketed pinnacles, grace the top and long diagonal buttresses support the walls. Large and well proportioned two-light, louvred, bell chamber openings stand high above the bells and a single clock adorns the west face. Four large gargoyles protrude, one on each cardinal face, and the west window leads the eye down to the small west door. Two small windows over the nave and another on the west admit light into the old ringing chamber. Three slit windows serve the stone spiral stairway in the south-west corner.

Inside, the view of the tall pointed tower arch into the nave was, until the turn of the century, bisected by a gallery within the tower. High on the north wall is a huge painted charity roll. Unfortunately, this is not legible from the floor and is in need of restoration work if its full story is to be revealed. In 1972 the bell ropes were lengthened to allow ringing to take place from ground level but the Tower Captain, Mr Richard Whittle, has, a few years ago, returned the ringers to the old ringing chamber above. Access is via the stone spiral steps which after almost 500 years are showing the effects of continuous use, but this danger is to be rectified as the surface of the steps are refaced.

Within the ringing chamber is housed the clock's works. The present clock dates from 1890 and was made by G. & F. Cope of Nottingham. For many years it was wound daily by hand. It is now powered by electricity and this has allowed the removal of the old weights and the huge housing case. In turn this has given more room and allowed the ringers to return aloft to ring the six bells. There has been a clock installed in the tower for upwards of 250 years as entries in the Churchwardens accounts for 1733 endorse. We find an item of five shillings (25p) being paid to BINJEMAN RODGERS for MENING clock. Then in 1752, MR. HOBSON for painting ye dial, one shilling and sixpence (7½p).

Two small windows, mentioned earlier, that admit light into the ringing chamber contain an interesting feature. In the recess of each window, on the stones used as lintels, can be seen marks of an incised cross. These were noted and mentioned by Rev. Charles Cox in his "Notes from Churches of Derbyshire" published in 1875 as follows:-

> "On measuring we ascertain that these two stones had formerly made a single slab about six feet long by two feet broad. It is a plain incised cross with a pedimented base, the ends of the limbs being slightly floriated. There is a space of four inches between two parallel lines which form the stem. This points to the existence of an earlier church here, for this memorial slab appears to belong to the thirteenth century."

In the bell chamber hangs a peal of six bells. For a period of almost 260 years from 1713 until 1972, when the treble bell was added, a peal of five bells rang out. Until 1907 these five bells hung in a timber frame but this was replaced by metal during the major overhaul in that year. The new treble, also hung in a metal frame, was cast in Loughborough by John Taylor & Co., but the old five were cast by a most interesting group of bell-founders in Nottingham. The oldest bell, c1510, is the fifth and was most probably cast by Selyoke. Briefly, as the subject is covered in a separate chapter, two independent bell foundries existed in Nottingham and covered a period from about 1376 until 1795. They were private concerns operated by members of the Selyoke, Mellour, Oldfield and Hedderly families. Some of the families carried on their bell-founding through several generations and many of their bells can be found in local belfries. Henry Dand, founder of the Tenor, was foundry foreman of Richard Mellour and later became a partner with Henry Oldfield the second about 1590. The founder of the third bell, William Noone was also a foreman in the employ of Oldfield.

The details and inscriptions of the six bells is:-

Bell:	Date:	Founder:	Diameter:	Weight:
Treble	1972	John Taylor & Co.	25 inches.	3cwt.0qrs.27lbs.
2nd.	1713	Hedderly	27¼ ins".	3cwt 1qr 19lbs.
3rd.	1710	Wm. Noone	30¼ ins	4cwt 2qrs 16lbs.
4th.	1618	Henry Oldfield	32¼ ins	5cwt 3qrs 4lbs.
5th.	c1510	Selyoke	33½ ins	6cwt 0qrs 21lbs.
Tenor	1560/98	Henry Dand	37⅝ ins	8cwt 0qrs 18lbs.

Treble   Ad Gloriam Dei   1972
                    John Taylor and Co. Loughborough.

This bell was installed at a cost of £350 and dedicated on November 22nd, 1972 by the Rt. Rev. Thomas Parfitt, Assistant Bishop of Derby. It is fitted with plain bearings at the request of the parish and was the last newly-cast bell to be despatched from the Loughborough Bellfoundry equipped with plain bearings.

2nd.   Floreat Ecclesia MDCCX111 I.H.
The inscription, placed round the inscription band, is interspaced with decorative blocks and above the sound bow, which is somewhat pitted, is a band of ornamentation which is a feature found on many bells cast by Hedderly.

3rd.   God save his church 1710
                    Pattern fillets separate the words. No Founder's mark.

4th.   + God save his church. 1618
                    Each word of this inscription lies on slightly raised blocks.

The inscription used upon both the third and fourth bells, which were cast almost a century apart in Nottingham, was a favourite inscription of the Oldfield family. The fourth bell whilst not bearing a founder's mark is attributed as being cast by Henry Oldfield II on account of the style of lettering used. Henry died within two years of casting the bell. He, like his father, also named Henry, is buried in St. Mary's Church, Nottingham. The third bell is attributed as being cast by William Noone who worked as foreman for the Oldfield's following the death of Hugh in 1672. Hugh's heir at the time was an infant son, George, and his wife, Alice, continued with the business during this period.

It is possible that Henry Oldfield II cast three bells in 1618 to augment the present fifth and tenor to a ring of five and that two of these bells were recast in 1710 and 1713, respectively. But, when one reads the churchwardens accounts for 1757 and 1758 we find mention of extra brass, four pounds, being bought and the taking down of the bells. We are left wondering if the two bells were again re-cast and enlarged and why. Could it have been to improve the musical pitch and tone of the five bells as a whole. And why were the old dates and inscriptions of 1710 and 1713 so faithfully reproduced and nothing added to record the project of 1757/8?

5th.   + Sancti Johes Ora pro Nobis. R.C.

This inscription is of rough execution in small Gothic letters. The component letters of Ora Pro Nobis being widely separated.

The bell-founder's mark follows within a shield and principally consists of a cross between the initials R.C. However the stem of the cross may be described as forked, although a further description could be that the stem of the cross carries to the right a design similar to the strickle used by the bellfounder when fashioning the mould prior to casting a bell. In addition there is a founder's stamp of an initial cross.

It is worth noting that although Selyoke is ascribed as the founder of this bell it is quite possible that this ancient bell may have been a monastic bell which was sold off at the Dissolution of the Monasteries. If this is the case, and I am grateful to the Curator of Taylor's Museum, Trevor Jennings for this information, then the bell might have been cast by Robert Crowch, 1437-1460, and hence the initials R.C. Crowch is generally ascribed as being a London Founder who it is thought made itinerant tours and casting his bells on site. About twenty five of his bells are scattered through the north of England. A similar inscription is to be found on a bell at Scarcliffe, but the word Maria is inscribed instead of Johes.

Tenor   Jesus be our sped   H.D.

These words appear round the inscription band and below the shoulder of the bell are the initials H.D. wrought one initial on each side of the founder's mark which consists of a Latin cross with a circle round its base. The mark is that of Richard Mellour for whom Henry Dand (H.D.) was foreman. The inscription is interspaced with decorative fillets and a founder's stamp depicting a Tudor Rose.

Between 1990 and 1991 all the fittings were overhauled and all six headstocks equipped with new gudgeons and fitted with self-aligning ball bearings, together with one new headstock and one side frame. All casting work was carried out by John Taylor's Foundry, with all on-site work being undertaken by Mr. Richard Whittle and the St. Leonard's team of ringers, Mr. Steve Clarke, John Daniel, Lee Whittle, Tammy Whittle, Sarah Barratt, Katherine Hush, Laura Thorpe and Dale Townsend. It is most appropriate at this point to recognise Richard Whittle's commitment in overseeing this mammoth task, obviously carried out with great enthusiasm. Also to record the huge savings made, the total cost having been drastically cut by half if not more. Even the girls donned overalls and were not afraid to get dirty as they set to with scraper and paint brushes etc.

Shirland has a long tradition with bell-ringing stretching back in time well over three centuries. From the writings of Leonard Wheatcroft, one-time Parish Clerk of Ashover, we learn that on Lady Day (March 25th) 1689, five bell ringers from Shirland visited Ashover and rang the bells of All Saints Church. He gives their names as George Wright, Henry Lees, - Farmery, - Revil and Mr. Miles together with the bells they rang and how they each performed.

Change ringing is thought to have its origins in Saxon times and was later widely promoted during the seventeenth century by Fabian Stedman a Cambridge printer who in 1668 published his "Tintinnalogia". With the augmentation of Shirland's bells to five in 1713 St. Leonard's ringers were keen to practice the new found art, as entries in the Churchwardens' accounts for the period endorse. Mr. Gladwyn Turbutt in his "History of Shirland and Higham", relates in great detail the items of which these are but a few concerning the belfry.

1712	For oyel for ye bells	1d.
	For mending ye 2nd bell and church gates	8d.
	For a bell rope	2s.2d.
	For dresing ye clock	3s.0d.
1729	Pd FFor Ropes and Glew	15s.4d.
1730	Paid for clock tenting	10s.0d.
	For a new bell wheell and old ones mending to Thos. Sidden	£1.11s.0d.
1733	Paid to Binjeman Rodgers for menin Clock	5s.0d.
1738	Paid ye Clark for Ringing Curfur	5s.0d.
1739	Samuel Wright for making door for the top of the steeple	5s.6d.
1740	Thomas Siddal for turning the great bell and finding wood for that purpose	£2.17s.6d.
	Cleaning and repairing the clock	8s.2d.
1743	Thomas Sidall for makeing a new bell wheel and other work at the bells	£2.6s.6d.
1745	James Radford for ringing 12 o'clock bell a quarter of a year due at May Day last	5s.0d.
1752	Paid to Mr Hobson for Painting ye dyal	1s.6d.

Mr. Thomas Siddall of Higham was the joiner responsible for the maintenance of the bells and his account as churchwarden in the autumn of 1757 and spring 1758 are interesting.

1757	for repairing the Bells for casting 11p of Brass for the fourth Bell and find four pounds of brass to make them larger	8s.2d.
	for taking the bell Down takeing the Gugans out turning them and puting it up and turning the Rowlers and brushing them	6s.6d.
	for a man to help me two days	2s.8d.
	for drink for them	1s.6d.
	for repairing the first bell and the wheel	2s.3d.
	pd for nals	10d.

1758	or repairing the Great Bell for casting	
	16p & ½ of Brass and bearing the waste	
	at 6d pr pound	8s.3d.
	for taking the wheel of and the bell down	
	the gugans out and puting them in and brushing	
	the Rowler	7s.6d.
	for two men to assist me	3s.4d.
	for drink when I let it down	1s.0d.

The payments on maintenance of the clock are recurring and one of the responsibilities of the parish clerk was to wind the clock, for which he was paid ten shillings (50p) a year. This was later increased to £1.

There are numerous payments made to the ringers for ringing at "Crismes" and "New Day" and on November 5th. Also to Joseph Radford for drink that the Ringers had at his house!

Another item taken from Mr. Gladwyn Turbutt's book refers to Bell Acre. "There is a field known as the Church or Bell Acre (O.S.(1916) 430 of 1 acre precisely), the rent for which was paid in the 19th century to the ringer of the angelus, Thus in the Ogston records copy of the 1829 Rate Book there is a pencil note against this field to the effect: 'John Hadfield has this rent free as a compensation for ring'g the 12 o'Clock Bell'. The Bell Acre Fund is still administered by the trustees of other parish charities."

A further item dating back to 1504 is most interesting:-
"In his will dated 1504 Hugh Revell leaves the church money to buy a 'banner cloth of Saint George's with a shaft to beyr hit on' as well as vestments and missal. This could be interpreted as implying that the church had only recently been re-built and that this banner was in fact a St. George flag to fly from a flagstaff on the new tower. If this were indeed so, then it would indicate that the tower, nave and side aisles date from about 1503, which would certainly accord with the late Perpendicular architectural style of the building."

This being so it nicely fits in with the date of the present fifth bell, c1510, being hung in the tower.

Two centuries later Change Ringing was introduced into the tower after the augmentation to a peal of five bells in 1713. Although we know that a keen band of bell-ringers practised at the tower in 1689, and were competent enough to visit Ashover, we do not know what exactly they rang. We do know that the skills of the Shirland ringers toward the end of the nineteenth century had progressed and peals extending to over 5000 changes were being attempted by the team. In the ringing chamber a peal board dated 1876 records:-

Bell Ringing at this Church.
A Peal of 5040 Grandsire Method
and rung in 2 hours, 37 minutes,
on February 15th, 1876

Treble	John Simkin,
2nd.	Henry Silkstone, Conductor,
3rd.	Richard Tagg,
4th.	William Lambert,
Tenor	John Lamb.

Mr. Lambert Snr. Timekeeper,
Joseph Hall Rector,
John Tagg Jnr. John Holmes Churchwardens.

Other peals of over five thousand changes have been rung on the bells. Of these one marked the Golden Jubilee of the founding of the Diocese of Derby. This was rung on Wednesday, May 18th, 1977. On other occasions the bells have rung out to mark victories, days of National rejoicing, festivals of the Church and regularly to call the faithful of Shirland to prayer. On November 5th, 1945 they rang out for an evening Confirmation Service conducted by the assistant Bishop of Derby, Rt. Rev. O'Ferrall, when several young men from Morton were being confirmed. Afterwards, at the invitation of the Rector, Rev. Edward H. Payne, they were taken up the tower to see the bells being rung. It being the first "Bonfire night" after the Second World War they were allowed to go out on to the tower roof to view all the bonfires around. Quite a sight after the austere days of blackout we had grown-up with. Unaware at the time, this event later proved for several of the confirmation party to be an unplanned introduction to the world of campanology. Little did we think that evening that on February 6th in the following year, 1946, at Morton, some of us would embark upon a lifelong association with the ringing, maintenance and history of church bells.

Many a Bride and Groom have received their first public acclaim from the bells and until recent times the sad toll of the Parting Bell announced to the Parish the death of some loved soul. The ringing of the Angelus or Noon Day Bell was for many years observed and formed part of the Clerk's duties as was the ringing of the Curfew each evening from Michaelmas through until Lady Day. Payment for carrying out these duties was £1 per annum for ringing the Noon bell and 5s.0d. for ringing curfew. This charming old ditty has been handed down which most probably had its origins in the days before the Enclosement of Land Act. One wonders who the brave ringers of Shirland could have been, and why? "Offerton Kettles, Pentrich pans. Shirland brave ringers and Morton Ting Tangs."

Bells all over the country used to ring out each November 5th, to remind people of the escape of the King, Lords and Commons from the Gunpowder Plot of 1605. In 1727 the ringers received the sum of 2s.6d. for ringing the bells to commemorate the Coronation of George II.

In 1893 St. Leonard's ringers affiliated to the East Derbyshire Association of Change Ringers and in 1910 the Rector, Rev. B. Hallows, became Association President. Many years later the office of Treasurer was held for eight years by Mr. Robert Mason who together with his wife Evelyn served the tower faithfully. The premature death of Mrs. Mason in 1955 following what appeared at the time to be an accidental minor scratch received whilst ringing, and which resulted in tetanus, was a severe blow. Robert however kept on with his ringing and particularly the teaching of learners at St. Leonard's until illness overtook him and compelled him to resign as tower keeper. Robert died in August 1975, having worked hard for and having had the pleasure of seeing the five bells augmented to six three years earlier. His favourite method remained Grandsire and Plain Bob Doubles and it was as a tribute to his life that representative members of both St. Leonard's team, and the Association, rang 1260 changes in the two methods, Jennifer Henshaw ringing the Treble, Arthur Smithson, 2nd; Wilfred Riley, 3rd; Glyn Holdgate 4th; Eric Sterland, 5th, and covering on the Tenor was Tom Hall.

Another Rector, Rev. Edward Payne, who served the Parish from 1928 until 1948 became an accomplished change ringer as did the band at this period, with Captain, Tom Newbitt and ringers Joe Shepperson, Bob Mason, Bert Lindley, Wallace Sinfield, Carl Row, Fred Sterland and Fred Lindley.

The Founder's bell-mark from the 5th bell ascribed to have been cast about 1510 by Selyoke of Nottingham. However, it is possible the bell was a monastic bell and sold off at the dissolution of the monastries. If this be the case, then the bell may have been cast by Robert Crowch (1437-1460) in London, hence the initials R.C.

1876 Peal Board at Shirland

201

The Belfry of St. Michael and All Angels, South Normanton

Seventeenth century King's Bell? Date Touches, order of the day.
Hill family, Ringers one and all. J.W.E. Diocesan Lay Reader, Ringer.

Today, the ringing of four thousand, six hundred and eighty changes on the bells at South Normanton, or on the bells in any other tower for that matter, would not merit inclusion in the Central Council of Church Bell Ringers records as a peal. The number of changes rung would need to exceed five thousand in order to meet with their rules governing peal ringing. Yet, in 1828 this number of changes was rung as a peal on the five bells at St. Michael's Church to welcome the return to the parish of the Rev'd. Doufton. The exact date on which the peal was rung is not recorded, nor is the method, only that it took three hours and fifteen minutes to complete and that it was rung by local ringers Thomas Moakes, John Hill, William Bailey, John Wilson and Thomas Kitchens.

The bells had been augmented to a peal of five some fifteen years earlier and with that augmentation came the introduction of Change Ringing into the belfry. One is left wondering if the method rung could have been thirty-nine extents of Grandsire Doubles? For the non-ringer, an extent of Grandsire Doubles consists of one hundred and twenty different changes. Then, so is an extent of the method Plain Bob Doubles and numerous other named Doubles methods. So at the end of the day we are none the wiser as to what method was rung on the bells in 1828. Suffice it to say that for any village band of ringers to attempt and to ring such a peal almost two centuries ago was quite an occasion and an achievement that reflects upon their skill and dedication to the art at that time.

The west tower of St Michael and All Angels Church is a good example of the Perpendicular period. It was most probably built about 1440 and by the same builder responsible for the building of the tower at South Wingfield. Being supported on the west by diagonal buttresses they have, as at South Wingfield, a pair of small upright shields used as ornament upon the second set-off. The embattled parapet is angled by four crocketed pinnacles which date from about 1812.

This is interesting inasmuch that two of the bells date from the following year, 1813, and church records reveal that Sir John Eardley Wilmot offered two bells and a clock to the tower on condition that four pinnacles were placed thereon.

The two light bell-openings and the larger west window are good examples of the style. A tiny west window gives the only source of daylight into the upper ringing chamber. The small west door is of much later date. Again, as at South Wingfield, it is doubtful if an original doorway existed. On the south face the clock's single dial can be seen.

The ringing chamber is somewhat cramped due to the clock's works and casing being housed there. Since 1902 six bells have hung in the tower. The five original bells hanging in an oak frame built on one level and supporting above the steel frame housing the 1902 treble bell. In 1902 the work of rehanging, providing the new treble and the recasting of the old third bell was undertaken by Messrs John Taylor and Co. of Loughborough.

The six bells are inscribed:-

Treble. Given by Catherine Wright
in memory of her brother John.
Both of Hilltop Farm. 1902
John Taylor & Co. Founder, Loughborough.
Diameter: 27½ inches. Weight: 4cwt.1qr.10 lbs.

2nd. T. Mears of London. Fecit. Sir Eardley Wilmot.1813.
Diameter: 30³/₄ inches. Weight: 4cwts.3qrs.19 lbs.
This bell was cast at the Whitechapel Foundry in London with a history dating from 1547 and of which Tom Mears and his family were an important integral part.

3rd. W.G.H. W.P.S. 1774. D. Coke Rector
Diameter: 32¼ inches. Weight: 6cwt.0qrs.0 lbs.

4th. Rev. Guy Bryan 1813
Bellmark of J. Taylor & Co. Recast 1902.
Diameter: 33 inches. Weight: 6cwt.2qrs. 0 lbs.
This bell was originally cast at the Whitechapel Foundry and carried in addition, T. Mears of London. Fecit.

5th. This bell is without inscription only being
ornamented with fleur-de-lys, a foliated cross and
a small regal crown or coronet beneath which the
Lombardic capital letters C.R.
Diameter: 36 inches. Weight: 7cwts.1qr.13 lbs.
This bell is thought to be a King's Bell dating from between 1630 and 1640 with the C.R. standing for Carolus Rex. Some give the probable founder as Heathcote of Chesterfield whilst Rev Charles Cox differs, claiming the mark to be that of George Oldfield of Nottingham. He also ascribes the bell as bearing the monogram I.H.S. but agrees on the bell as being cast in the seventeenth century.

Both of these probabilities are interesting. Ralph Heathcote, the last of the family to cast bells in Chesterfield, ceased casting bells about 1647 and he like his father, Godfrey, used as their bellmark a shield bearing the fylfot cross, with their respective initials in capital letters beneath. Two generations earlier Ralph Heathcote had used a small regal crown or coronet as part of his bellmark with his initials R.H. beneath. If therefore this bell was cast by them it must originate from before 1578 when the elder Godfrey took over the business on the death of his father Ralph. But then the initials are called into question as in fact they are when looking at Cox's assumption. He attributes the casting to George Oldfield. A point in favour of Cox is that George Oldfield took over the bellfoundry in 1620 after the death of his father Henry and continued to use his father's mark by simply cutting out the initial H and inserting his initial G. On some bells he used a curly G perhaps better described as a squiggly six as against one in Roman upper case. On this bell the curly G is used but that is where the similarity to the Oldfield mark ends. So it might well be after all that the bell was in fact a King's Bell confiscated during the civil strife and later sold on and therefore not cast locally.

Tenor   Geo. Dobb of Normentvm
           Gavseth this bell for to be rung 1654
           Diameter: 38 inches. Weight: 8cwt.3qrs.0 lbs.

The founder of this bell was George Oldfield referred to above and who cast bells in Nottingham for almost sixty years. It is unusual not to find his mark upon the bell. The bell is tuned to the note F#.

The Rev. John Cooke Massey was rector of Normanton from 1871 and in 1887 he was a prime mover in the formation of the East Derbyshire Association of Change Ringers. He held office as President from its founding until 1896 and ten ringers from St Michael's became founder members. It is unique to find that eight of them shared the same surname, Wm. Hill, Sam. Hill, Ed. Hill, Fer. Hill, G. Hill, Sam. Hill Jnr., John Hill and Geo. Hill. The other two ringers being Charles Taylor and William Bingham.

Toward the end of the nineteenth century the ringing of Date Touches was popular with some ringers. To do this calls for some degree of skill on the part of the conductor as he must compose the ringing in such a way that the bells ringing in rounds are then called into changes and then without duplicating a single change, allowing of course for the extents of 120 changes, the bells must be returned to rounds at the appropriate change. The following were rung on the bells in 1880 and 1890. These touches were of Grandsire Doubles rung with the fifth bell as the observation bell. Alas, again no exact date or name of the conductor is given, only the names of the ringers.

1880 Changes	1890 Changes
Rung in 1hr.15 minutes by	Rung in 1hr.10minutes by
George Hill Senr.	George Hill Jnr.
Samuel Hill Senr.	John Hill
Ferdinand Hill	Edward Hill
William Bingham	Samuel Hill Jnr.
Edmund Hill	George Hill Senr.

By 1928 another strong band of ringers practised at St. Michael's and it was six members of this band who attempted and rang the first peal on the six bells. Although only ringing the method Grandsire Doubles on the front five bells with the tenor covering. It took place on Monday, May 14th, 1928, taking three hours and three minutes to ring the 5040 changes. The ringers being Harold Doughty ringing the treble, Arthur R. Judge, 2; John W. England, 3; Melville Slater, 4; Harold Fradgley, 5 and Ernest W. Riley covering on the tenor. It was conducted by John W. England and consisted of 42 six-scores with ten different callings, and was the first peal by each member of the team and was recorded as the fiftieth peal rung by members of the East Derbyshire and Nottinghamshire Association.

On July 14th in the following year a peal of 5040 Changes of Plain Bob Minor was rung on the six bells in two hours, forty five minutes by Harold Doughty,

Treble; Wilson Allin,2; Harold Fradgley,3; Arthur B. Judge,4; Ernest A. Wilson,5 and John W. England conducting the peal and ringing the Tenor. This was the first peal of Minor rung on the bells and also by Harold Doughty and Arthur Judge.

A further peal, Kent and Oxford Treble Bob Minor in December that year and two peals during the following year, 1930, then an annual peal being rung until 1936 gives an insight into the progress made by the South Normanton ringers during this period. Firstly, in addition to the ringers already mentioned we find Cornelius J. Partridge, Alfred G. Gordon, Tom Clarke, Thomas Bettison and Joseph Swain taking part. Then the progress made by the team in the methods being rung is interesting. We have mentioned Grandsire, Plain Bob, Kent and Oxford Treble Bob. These are followed by Double Court, Single Court, College Single, Single Oxford and Cambridge Surprise. November, 1930, saw a peal rung in seven methods. November, 1931, a peal entirely of Cambridge Suprise Minor and in October, 1934 a peal of Double Court. Nine peals were rung on the bells by members of this band during the eight years from 1928 to 1936 of which John (Jack) England conducted eight and Tom Clarke one.

Jack England, as he was known to all, not only maintained a very high standard of ringing at St. Michael's but as Tower Captain, Chorister, Diocesan Lay Reader became most respected in the parish. Outside South Normanton he was greatly respected both in his daily work at local collieries and in the realms of bell-ringing. For sixteen years, from 1930 until 1946, he was Honorary Secretary to the East Derbyshire and Nottinghamshire Association of Church Bell Ringers. He then became the Association's President and held that office for eleven years from 1948 until 1959 before leaving the area.

It was whilst Jack was secretary to the Association that he was responsible for the compiling of an Order of Service for Bell Ringers. This was subsequently printed and has been in regular use by the Association's members, at their corporate services, for upwards of sixty years.

It was Jack, who as secretary steered the Association through the difficult days of the Second World War using what little spare time he could find, after working long shifts each day in the coal mines, to keep those ringers away from home on active service with the armed forces and those remaining at home in touch. Throughout these years, when church bells could not be rung other than as a public warning in the event of the country being invaded by the Axis forces, it was he who maintained contact with the ringers from all the Association's affiliated towers.

The Association members have by comparison with some other Guild memberships never been prolific peal ringers. However, it was Jack who set about collating all the peals known to have been rung for the East Derbyshire and Nottinghamshire Association. Having compiled and collated them in date order he set about entering the details of each peal in a peal book. This he did by his own hand using Old English script in red and black lettering. The book, listing the peals rung by members from 1901, is preserved by the Association.

Another of St Michael's ringers, Harold Doughty, served both the tower and the Association for a great many years.

In the early 1970s another keen local band emerged who on New Year's Day, Tuesday, January 1st, 1974 rang in their first peal; 5040 Changes, consisting of three extents of Kent Treble Bob and four extents of Plain Bob, rung on the bells in two hours and fifty minutes by Mrs Marjorie Brown, Robert Mewes, Kenneth Hemm. They went on to ring two further peals within a year assisted by Elizabeth A. Lounds, Maureen A. Dempster and Adrian Dempster of Selston.

Mrs Marjorie Brown has now completed (dare I reveal) well over twenty-five years as a ringer at St. Michael's. Marjorie, as I write, is still very active in the district ringing for services, attending practices, and has the inexhaustible desire to make progress with any of the Minor Methods she chooses to ring.

The Belfry of All Saints, South Wingfield

Gas lighting bracket retained. Peal of six bells since 1847.
Diocese 50th Anniversary Peal. Ringers visit Ashover in 1696.
Bellfounder, John Halton ?

Just over three hundred years ago John Halton gave a peal of three bells to All Saints Church, South Wingfield. These were hung in the tower that had been rebuilt by Ralph, Lord Cromwell, shortly after he acquired the manor of Winfield in 1440. Lord Cromwell was a man of great importance, having been Treasurer to the Exchequer under Henry VI, Warden of Sherwood Forest, and Constable of Nottingham Castle.

The tower, situated on the east bank of the river Amber, stands at the western end of the nave. It has an embattled parapet surmounted at each corner by rather crude crocketed pinnacles of a comparatively modern construction. Supported by diagonally placed buttresses the tower has no west door only a west window, a fine example of the Perpendicular period. Two light, louvred bell-openings pierce each cardinal face.

At the first set-off, or weathering, on the buttresses are small shields. The north west buttress has two shields, the faces of which are now worn plain by the ravages of weather whilst a single shield on the south west buttress carries indistinct lines. Similar shields are to be found at South Normanton where the tower is of the same age and design and attributed to the same builder. Further small shields are used on the interior to ornament the jambs of the tower arch.

Inside, the ringing room bisects the tower arch in the form of a gallery and is open to the nave. the old ringing room above, and the bells, are reached via a narrow stone spiral stairway behind the low doorway in the south-west corner. These stairs terminate at the bell chamber and access to the roof is gained by traversing permanently fixed wooden ladders over the bells and frame. The base of the tower serves as a vestry from which a short flight of wooden steps give access, through a trap-door, into the ringers' gallery. Dark stained boards form a high dado which attractively contrast the fitted red carpet, the gift of a parishioner twenty or so years ago.

Several long thin narrow pieces of board can be found hanging from the walls. These are unique inasmuch that they serve the ringer by showing the diagram or skeleton course of several Methods of Change Ringing. The term Method, when used by the ringer, indicates the composition of Changes about to be used in much the same way as sheet music is used by an organist. A relic of earlier days is the bracket gas light, complete with globe and mantle, by which the belfry was lit before the introduction of electricity. Prior to gas lighting the ringers would have relied on oil lamps and candles.

As the inscription on the fifth bell relates: "John Halton caused this ring of bells to be cast, 1693." This was a peal of three bells, the second, fourth and the fifth of the present six.

In 1736 Johannes Halton gave the tenor bell and there can be little doubt that he and the Halton family had been instrumental in providing the present third bell five years before in 1731. Upon the treble bell being added in 1847 South Wingfield became one of the first village towers in the locality to possess a ring of six bells.

In 1902 the treble bell was recast and all the bells re-hung in a metal frame of the type known as the 'H' frame. Constructed in sections resembling its name, this type of frame is most suitable for use in small towers. Although at All Saints the bells are hung on one level this system is widely used to hang bells on two tiers. One disadvantage is access for maintenance and painting. In 1976 the frame was wire brushed and primed, before receiving further coats of paint. This voluntary task was undertaken by Andrew Holdgate and occupied several weeks of his summer school vacation. It is typical of many voluntary projects undertaken by bell ringers generally in the maintenance of belfries.

Another feature that has been in use since 1902 is the Hasting stay. Being more complex than the conventional stay it has the advantage of not requiring wooden accessories in the form of sliders and guides thereby saving space. The base of a Hasting stay fits into a socket on the headstock, it then tapers throughout its length to be mounted at the other end by a dingler assembly. The length is critical because the finger of the dingler must engage exactly within the metal slider quadrant fixed to the frame. All stays are made from ash, which has just the right amount of resilience for the task of bearing the weight of the bell whilst being rested in the inverted position. Also, should the bell be over-pulled by the ringer the stay will compensate the over-pull to some extent, but if the pull should be too hard then the stay will break thus saving the bell from being wrenched out of its bearings and causing serious damage. For this very reason it is absolutely imperative that a non-ringer does not touch the bell-ropes when visiting a belfry.

Several decades ago, in the interest of economy and because sapling ash trees were readily available in the churchyard, several stays of the right length and diameter were chosen and cut from round ash saplings. These were used in preference to normal square section stays as cut from a large piece of ash. However, this exercise proved counter productive, and almost resulted in an expensive disaster. For it was soon realised that ash used in the round did not have the same amount of suppleness as the square ash stays cut from the section on account of the difference in the grain. In section, the grain is always straight and pliable whereas in the young round pieces, it is straight enough but being constituted of full growth rings it is not pliable enough. This in turn could lead to the bell being lifted from its bearing under certain circumstances. Fortunately this possibility was determined before any damage was done and the sapling stays rejected forthwith.

There are six bells tuned to the key of G and inscribed:-

Treble   GOD SAVE HIS CHURCH + ANNO DOMINI 1847 +
F. W. Christian + Vicar
H.E. Maltby   +
T. Cupit   + Churchwardens
Diameter: 25½ inches. Weight: 3cwts.1qr.22 lbs.

Beneath the inscription band is a decorative border of leaves and berries. On the reverse waist the medallion of John Taylor & Co. Loughborough, and beneath "Recast 1902".

2nd.   JESVS BEE OVR SPEDE 1693
Diameter: 26¼ inches. Weight: 3cwts.1qr.6 lbs.

3rd.   GOD SAVE HIS CHURCH 1731
Diameter: 29½ inches Weight: 3cwts.3qrs.25 lbs.

4th.   IHS NAZARENVS REX IVDEORVM FILI DEI MISERERE 1693
Diameter: 31¾ inches. Weight: 5cwts.2qrs.2 lbs.

5th.   JOHN HALTON CAVSED THIS RING OF BELLS TO BE CAST 1693
Diameter: 35¼ inches. Weight: 7cwts.1qr.6 lbs.

Tenor   GLORIA DEO IN EXCELSIS DONOVIT JOHANNES HALTON 1736
Diameter: 38 inches. Weight: 8cwt.3qrs.10 lbs.

Of the five old bells none of them bear a bellfounder's mark. This is unusual but not without reason. The bells were all cast in Nottingham at the Oldfields' foundry. The family of Oldfield being prosperous bellfounders there for about two hundred years. But, after George Oldfield, the second member of the family to be so named, died in 1680 the firm discontinued to use a mark. The reason being that two members of the family had predeceased George Oldfield and after his death George's daughter Alice carried on the business on behalf of her infant son who was also named George. This young George eventually succeeded to the business and cast many bells. After his death in 1748 the firm passed into the hands of the Hedderly family. It was Alice who decided, as a mark of respect, not to use the bellmarks and this was carried on by her son. During this period a founder by the name of William Noone appears on the scene and it is thought that he may have been in the employ of the Oldfields. With this in mind it is quite possible that the three 1693 bells in the tower could have been cast by William Noone.

The old churchwardens' accounts for the parish of Duffield have an interesting entry relating to the bells of South Wingfield. It dates from 1742 and reads: "Going to see ye bell weigh at Winfield, £0.0.6d."

It was customary when bells were being taken to and from the bellfoundry for them to be publicly weighed. The event was quite an occasion in any village with friends from neighbouring parishes being invited to attend. The only doubt that comes to mind on this occasion is the date. Assuming the bells had been put in good order after the addition of the new tenor bell in 1736 why was it necessary for a bell weigh six years later? Could it be that the work dated 1736 was not completed until 1742 or simply that the friend from Duffield forgot to claim his expenses immediately? On closer inspection of the snippets of information available it could be that neither of these ideas are creditworthy for it is just possible that one of Duffield's bells was brought over to South Wingfield for weighing. But more of this later.

No mention of the history of South Wingfield's bells would be complete without relating the local story of the fatal accident of the suitor who was thrown from his horse when startled by the sound of the bells. The story is coupled with a funeral garland, which, before being destroyed by a fire at the church in 1922, used to hang in the corner of the chancel roof. Made of white paper and decorated with rosettes and ornaments such garlands were carried in front of the funeral procession of maidens, and following the interment were hung in church.

This particular one was carried at the funeral of Ann Kendall of the Peacock Hotel who died on May 14th. 1745. Ann was the daughter of Mary and Peter Kendall, Peter being churchwarden at the time. It is said that Miss Kendall was most attractive and had a suitor, a young farmer from the village. The story goes, "that she loved him not wisely but too well." With the birth of a daughter and the subsequent refusal of marriage the problem preyed upon her mind and she died of a broken heart. The suitor, however, was shortly afterwards riding on horseback past the church when the bells started ringing. Startled by the sudden sound the horse threw its rider, who broke his neck in the fall.

A team of bellringers at South Wingfield was alluded to by Leonard Wheatcroft of Ashover just over three hundred years ago when five of them paid a visit to Ashover and rang the bells. This visit occurred on April 9th, 1696. From the verse that Leonard Wheatcroft wrote at the time of the visit we gather that Stout Mikell rang the treble bell, Brave Sidbury and Honest Thorpe rang two of the other bells whilst Master Halton and someone of the name of Clarke-son the other two. We learn as we read on that Master John Halton lived at Wingfield Manor, which of course is well known. It was the same John Halton who in 1693 had "caused the ring of three bells to be cast" and who instigated a fourth bell for the tower in 1731 and whom the tenor bell inscription of 1736 is a constant reminder.

John Halton, it is thought, had some connection with bell-founding. Earlier, mention was made of a bell weigh taking place at South Wingfield. This is an item in the All Saints, Duffield, churchwardens' accounts for 1742. In the same accounts for the previous year an item was paid for taking down a bell at Duffield so it seems that work on the Duffield bells was being undertaken at that time. Further, on

August 18th, 1742 another item, "pd. William Sowter for Enterteinment for Winfield ringers by Mr. Clives orders... 10 shillings," substantiates the connection between Duffield and South Wingfield. But, around 1726 one, J.M. Halton, is thought to have worked at a small foundry in Bawtry, for in that year he cast the fourth bell at Tuxford. However, North, in his book on the Church Bells of Leicestershire, held the view that he was foreman to Daniel Hedderly and that it was he who closed down the Bawtry foundry after the death of his master. But at St. Mary's, Ansty, Leicestershire we find on the second bell an inscription: "J.M. Halton cast us all. Anno MDCCXXIII (1723)." Further evidence in the possibility of John Halton being an agent or directly connected with bell-founding is brought together when we take a look at the history of All Saints Church bells, Derby, now the cathedral.

In 1712 an agreement was entered into between the churchwardens and John Halton, to the effect that the gentleman's brother Emmanuel Halton should recast the eighth bell. However, within the agreed period the bell was not recast and the wardens wanted to know why. In order that Emmanuel should not shirk in explaining, they served notice on John Halton, direct to his house, for him to appear at a parish meeting with his brother's reasons.

Unfortunately, no address is given, nor an account of what John Halton did or said at the meeting on June 24th, 1712,is recorded. But it was agreed that "the parish will allow the sum of seaven or eight pounds towards the new Castinge of the eighth bell." The bell was recast and Mr. Halton's account was settled on October 12th, 1713.

Turning again to Duffield churchwardens accounts for 1721 we find an item of £68.0.0d paid to Mr. Halton for further casting.

From these few items it would seem that John or Emmanuel Halton, either together or with John as agent, ran a business connected with the founding of bells. Whether this operated directly from South Wingfield and was in any way in union with the Haltons of Bawtry and Leicestershire is not established and a great deal more research is required before any such conclusion could be reached. Also to be considered is a possible connection between the Haltons and William Noon who died in 1732, and who may have cast the three 1693 bells alluded to.

The earliest peal rung on the bells for the East Derbyshire Association took place on Saturday August 6th, 1904 and consisted of 5040 Changes of Plain Bob Minor. It was rung in two hours and forty-eight minutes by W. Butler, W.G. Christian, B. Fletcher, J. Thompson, F.H. Kay and J.T. Butler who conducted the peal. As no reference is made in the recorded footnotes to this being the first peal on the six bells we must assume that earlier peals of similar length had been rung.

A peal rung on the bells twenty one years later on April 18th, 1925, is of interest in that Thomas W. Hopson rang the fourth bell to Plain Bob Minor and that it was his first peal. The other ringers were Wilson Allin, Rowland Huskinson, Cecil

211

Beckly, Hrebert G. Fretwell and George Allin who was conducting his first peal.

Thomas (Tom) Hopson began ringing at St. Martin's, Alfreton in 1912 where he was, apart from a period following this peal, when work took him away, a regular member of the Alfreton band. Records at St. Martin's show that over a ten year period, Tom's attendance for Sunday service ringing, annually averaged at one hundred and two services out of a possible one hundred and six. From the late 1950s he became involved with service ringing at South Wingfield and later became tower keeper and undertook the training of numerous young parishioners as ringers. On the occasion of his eightieth birthday in 1976, the ringers and congregation of All Saints presented him with a china bell, as a token of their esteem for his loyalty to both church and belfry over sixty four years. Relinquishing the office of tower captain he maintained a keen interest in the ringers and their progress until shortly before his death, at the age of 89 years, in March, 1985.

As with many towers, good bands of ringers flourish from time to time, and the period after the Second World War was no exception at All Saints. The Wheeler family provided almost a complete band and were capable of ringing Minor methods to a very high standard.

Another strong band existed both before and after the First War under the leadership of the Vicar, Rev. J. F. Morley. In 1912 and again in 1917 he was elected President of the East Derbyshire Association. Earlier, in 1903, the Rev. W. G. Christian had been instrumental in encouraging his church team of ringers at All Saints to affiliate to the Association.

During the period when the Wheeler family were responsible for the very high standard of Minor ringing a young band of equally enthusiastic ringers lived in Morton. Wanting to improve their method ringing some of the young men would cycle over to join in the mid-week practice at South Wingfield. At the same time, Herbert Taylor, who was a very competent ringer with the Darley Dale team, would often be on duty as signalman in the signal box adjacent to the main railway line on the south side of the railway bridge and well within earshot of the church bells. On the way home, it was quite usual for the young ringers to be stopped on passing under the bridge by Herbert and to be afforded a free and unsolicited adjudication of the evening's ringing. I hasten to add, that only the normal business of running a railway was allowed to interfere with the adjudication. Several of those young ringers were reminded of this little anecdote by Herbert on Easter Monday afternoon, March 31st, 1997, when at the age of 87 he and his wife came and listened to the ringing taking place at his home tower of St. Helen's, Darley Dale. The occasion being the one hundredth and tenth annual meeting of the East Derbyshire and West Nottinghamshire Association of Church Bell Ringers.

The Diocese of Derby was created in 1927 and to mark the fiftieth anniversary of its founding peals were rung at many towers in the diocese. At South Wingfield a

212

peal of 5040 Changes of Minor was rung on the bells. It consisted of two extents each of Oxford Treble Bob and Kent Treble Bob; and one extent each of Oxford Bob, St. Clement's and Plain Bob. The ringers were E. Glyn Holdgate, Arthur S. Smithson, Wilfred Riley, David C. Lester, Eric J. Sterland and Adrian Dempster who conducted the peal.

During the late 1970s a very good youth band flourished at the tower and did excellent work ringing for all the services over several years. Then, as is inevitable with a youth band, October comes round and suddenly everyone is missing. Gone off to college and university, or simply to work away. To those who teach this is quite daunting and comes as quite a shock. One can only stand and take stock, in hope that some of those good young ringers will find other towers in which to exercise their skills as campanologists, or at least, if not able to do so immediately, they will at some future date, realise what time and effort was put into their training and be prepared to return to a belfry and to pass on the skills they were once so freely given. As they know, all belfries are open to all ringers all of the time. As the millennium approaches and with the national call to have all church bells rung at noon on January 1st, 2000, this probably is a very good place to invite all who have ever undertaken the ringing of bells to return. You will be made most welcome.

SOUTH WINGFIELD CHURCH

The Belfry of St. Mary Magdalene, Sutton in Ashfield.

Spire struck by lightning. Peace bells. Ringers' penance by order of court.
Local ringer donates award. Three Association officials at tower.

The steeple of St. Mary Magdalene, Sutton in Ashfield, has withstood storm and tempest for upwards of six hundred years. Using local magnesian limestone, building was started in 1391, and took over eight years to complete. It is on record that in 1391 John de Sutton, a former Mayor and Member of Parliament for Lincoln, left a sum of money for the making and completion of a steeple at Sutton in Ashfield. This was to be attached to the twelfth century church that had been given to the parish by the Suttons of Thurgarton Priory.

By 1552 it is known that three bells hung in the tower. As the inventory taken during the reign of Edward V1 records:-

"Sutton in Ashfield. In the steple iii belles, one handbell."

When and where the three bells were cast we do not know; we can only hazard a guess that they had been hanging in the tower for some considerable time before the inventory was taken. These bells, of considerable age, were most probably re-cast during the next century, but more about this later. We do know that it was to be some three hundred and sixty seven years before the three bell peal was augmented to a ring of six. For this took place in 1919, immediately after hostilities ceased at the end of the Great War, and during the first year of peace as the inscriptions upon two of the bells so aptly recall. Today, the tower contains a fine peal of eight bells.

The embattled tower is supported up to bell chamber level by diagonally placed buttresses. The un-pierced spire, springing from behind plain battlements culminates in a fine orb finial. In 1867 the spire was struck by lightning. Masonry restoration involved not only replacing the damage but at the instigation of the architect, Mr. Fowler, the spire was raised three feet together with the erection of a weathercock and a lightning conductor. This work increased the height of the spire to ninety feet. If one takes a careful look, a course of a darker stone can be seen below the orb. The effect of the additional height has been to enhance the whole into a graceful octagonal steeple.

In the louvred two-light bell-openings the arch-curves are replaced by straight lines. Pevsner ascribes this modification to be a late feature of the period and which probably was, in part, responsible for the slow completion of the building work. Let into the string course at the base of the parapet are two short gargoyles on each cardinal face. A single lancet window on the west wall of the tower allows light into the ground floor ringing chamber. There is no west door. Notice also inside how the aisles protrude west on either side of the tower.

The three bells were increased to a ring of six in 1920 at a total cost of £862, which was raised by public subscription. They were hung in an iron frame. The tenor bell, weighing fifteen hundredweights, one quarter and eighteen pounds is tuned to the key of F. All the bells are hung on ball bearings and are rung from the ground floor of the tower, which at the time of the augmentation served as the baptistry. In 1904 a tower improvement scheme had been put in hand with the ensuing work planned to be undertaken in stages. The first section was completed in 1906 and included putting a new ringing chamber higher in the tower. The font, situated in the base of the tower was removed. However on the augmentation to six bells in 1920 the ropes were once again lengthened in order that ringing could take place from the ground floor. The bells are inscribed:-

Treble	Thanks be to God
	The gift of John Leeward Scott
	1946
2nd.	Come before Him and rejoice
	This bell was placed in the tower
	by public subscription
	1946

The two trebles were cast by John Taylor and Co. whose mark is placed on each bell.

3rd.	Timothy Gregory. John Moor.
	Recast 1900
	J.B. Hyde, Vicar
	C.H.B. Beecroft, John Briggs, Churchwardens.
	John Lewis James, Clerk.
4th.	Jesus + + Be Our Sped
	Recast A.D. 1900
	H. (The shield of Richard Mellor) D.
5th.	Glory bee to God on high.
	(G. O. Mark) 1656.
	Band of foliage and acorns.
6th.	To the glory of God
	and in memory of
	John and Mary Briggs.
	Peace 1919.

On the reverse waist the mark of John Taylor and Co.

lies between the numerals that make up the date of casting, 19+20.

7th.	1918 Victory
	Thine O lord is the greatness and the power
	and the glory and the victory.
	W. Allin, P.F. Block, H. North, W.R. Kidger.

John Taylor's mark and date as on the sixth bell.

Tenor.	1919 Peace
	Blessed are the peacemakers
	for they shall be called the
	Children of God.
	A.T. Cowen, Vicar.
	G.W. Briggs, W. Keeton, Churchwardens.

John Taylor's mark and date as on sixth bell.

The fourth bell, recast in 1900, dated from 1590 or earlier. It may have been one of the original three bells known to have hung in the tower in 1552. If this be the case then it is just probable that it could have been recast in 1590. What is of interest is the initials H. D. placed either side the shield of R. Mellours of Nottingham. The initials are those of Henry Dand, a bellfounder we have met with before, who you will remember was in partnership later with Henry Oldfield. The Mellours, Richard, or his son Robert, who took over the foundry after his father's death in 1507, most probably cast the fourth bell originally. Although it is feasible that Henry Dand cast it for the Mellours whilst still a young man. This would coincide nicely with the period before 1552 and mean that he did not recast it in 1590 as ascribed by some. We know that Henry Dand's daughter Frances married Robert Quarnby, who had succeeded earlier to the Mellour foundry, in January, 1567/8 and that it wasn't until later that Dand joined Henry Oldfield. Either way, the Mellour bellmark is, together with the cross and Tudor rose and fine decorative border of oak leaves and acorn, cast upon the bell. These were again faithfully reproduced when it was recast by John Taylor & Co. in 1900.

The fifth bell is somewhat rare. It was cast by George Oldfield during the Commonwealth period. Following the trial and execution of Charles 1 in 1649, Oliver Cromwell, beset by government difficulties became Protector in 1653 but was soon obliged to govern by major-generals. Three years into this difficult period and just four years before the restoration of Charles II the fifth bell was cast. A running border of foliage, berry and nuts between a sharply defined beaded edge, adorns and intersperse the inscription GLORY BEE TO GOD ON HIGH which is depicted by the use of plain capital letters.

Earlier mention was made of three bells being hung in the tower at the time when the inventory under Edward V1 (1547-1553) was made. A further return dated 1540 also confirms three bells in the tower. But, a Report made by the Commissioners of Henry VIII states that between 1533 and 1547 various items including two bells were seized by them from the church and sold. From this we can assume that bells three, four and five have ancient origins if one or other of them are not in fact the original bells to hang in the tower. But, we have already looked at the fifth, the Commonwealth bell, which most probably replaces one of the two bells confiscated. Then, between 1774 and 1820 an inventory was taken by Rev. Thomas Hurt which lists three bells as being hung in the tower of St. Mary Magdalene, Sutton in Ashfield. If, as many agree, the third bell was cast by Hedderly's of Nottingham, then the inventory must have been taken at the beginning of the period stated because George Hedderly closed the foundry down before the end of the century and emigrated to America. From this we may assume that the fourth bell is the original bell cast for hanging in the tower and that Henry Dand was most probably recasting it in the late sixteenth century whilst still having access to the decorative letters and stamps of the Mellours.

The treble of the three old bells, the one cast by Hedderly's, was recast in 1900 by John Taylor and Co. It is now the third bell of the octave.

We now come to the additions of 1919. The peace bells. In October 1920 a whole week was given over to ringing for the dedication of the three new bells, two memorial tablets and a belfry screen. All of which are dedicated to the memory of the men of Sutton in Ashfield who had died whilst serving their country during the Great War. Over seventy members of the East Derbyshire and Nottinghamshire Association of Change Ringers and many members of the Midland Counties Association attended to pay their respects during the week's activities.

It was during this augmentation that John Taylor and Co. cast another low sided section of frame to marry to the iron frame in which they had hung the three old bells in 1900. Then in 1946 they produced a further matching section of frame in which hang the two trebles completing the octave.

Three years before the first augmentation, and in spite of the tower only having three bells, the ringers had affiliated to the East Derbyshire and West Nottinghamshire Association at the annual meeting held at Tibshelf, St Mary's becoming the twenty fifth tower to affiliate to the Association. This probably came about through the keenness of Mr. W. Allen, a ringer of Sutton, who had become an honorary member of the Association in 1914.

From this affiliation came strong support for the Association both in the number of peals of Minor rung on the bells and in later support from three individual ringers at St. Mary's, namely, Cyril Heathcote, who became Association's Honorary Treasurer for twenty three years from 1937 until 1960. Benjamin Sollis who was Honorary Secretary for ten years from 1953 and Colin Evans who represented the Association at the Central Council of Church Bell Ringers.

Benjamin Sollis had quite a remarkable personality, full of character and very kind. A market gardener by trade and a keen cyclist and ringer in his spare time. After Ben was elected Secretary of the Association in 1953 he set about the task with great gusto and it was quite common place for him to cycle round the district and call upon incumbents personally to arrange the Association's monthly meeting. He was also noted for his long epistles, sent to members and others, spelling out in no uncertain terms his view of a particular subject considered by him to be in need of airing. These were not always received in a kindly fashion and from time to time gave rise to strong and lengthy discussion taking place at ringing meetings.

It was through the kind offices of another ringer, and the Association's treasurer, Cyril Heathcote, that a competitive shield known as the Jubilee Shield was instigated and donated. This shield was awarded annually by the Association to the most progressive affiliated band of ringers. It was in being for many years until a change in the service pattern at many churches rendered it impractical to operate the scheme. The shield now hangs, on loan from the Association, in the tower at St. Helen's, Selston, whose ringers were the last band to merit winning the award. A fuller account of the scheme can be found in the notes on St. Helen's. The ringers of Sutton in Ashfield were awarded the shield in 1938, and for each of the five years from 1956 to 1960.

On Saturday, October 16, 1948 the Association held a dinner at the Denman Head Hotel, Sutton in Ashfield. A large gathering assembled and were greeted by the President, Mr. John Hobbs. The toast, "The Association," was proposed by Mr. W. Lancaster the secretary of the newly founded Derbyshire Association of Change Ringers.

The bells form part of the church war memorial and were officially opened on October 24th, 1920. On Saturday, October 1st. 1921, the first peal was rung on the six bells.

The Church of St. Mary Magdalene, Sutton in Ashfield.
A PEAL OF MINOR, 5040 CHANGES,
being one extent (720 changes) of Oxford Treble Bob and
three extents each of Kent Treble Bob and Plain Bob, in
two hours and fifty five minutes.

Thomas Stimpson	Treble	William A. Parsons	4th.
Arthur J. Orgill	2nd.	Herbert G. Fretwell	5th.
Frank F. Hill	3rd.	Joseph Lord	Tenor.

Conductor Joseph Lord.

The peal was rung for the East Derbyshire and West Nottinghamshire Association as were a further nine peals during the years to 1940. Looking through the footnotes we find first peals being rung by Frank F. Hill (peal above), Wilson Allin, Jnr., Charles Allin, William H. T. King, Thomas Bettison, Cyril M. Heathcote, Frank Bradley and Jack Ginever. Clifford Bleby conducted his first peal on Tuesday, December 13th, 1938 to welcome the Rev. H. D. Wrigley and Mrs. Wrigley to the parish.

In 1930 the old three bells were re-hung on ball-bearings. A brass tablet, affixed to the south wall of the ringing chamber, commemorates: "To the Glory of God and in loving memory of Michael Haddon Heathcote and Mary Elizabeth Heathcote, the three treble bells in this tower were placed on ball-bearings. March 1930."

The last peal to be rung for the Association prior to the total ban being imposed on the ringing of church bells by the Government took place at St. Mary's in 1940.

On Saturday, April 6, 1940 in two hours fifty minutes
at the Church of St. Mary Magdalene, Sutton in Ashfield.
A PEAL OF MINOR, 5040 CHANGES,
Being one extent of Double Court, and three extents each
of Plain Bob, Oxford Treble Bob and Kent Treble Bob.

Jack Ginever +	Treble	Ralph Partridge	4

| Jack Bleby | 2 | Frank Bradley | 5 |
| Colin Evans | 3 | Clifford Bleby | Tenor |

Conducted by Clifford Bleby. + First peal at first attempt.
Rung as a farewell peal to ringer of second bell, who is
joining H.M. Navy and also to local ringers P. Eastland
and W. Stocks who have recently joined H.M. Forces.

Two new treble bells were added to the six in 1946. They were cast at Loughborough by John Taylor and Co. The treble was the gift of John Leeward Scott and the second bell was placed in the tower by public subscription. They each bear the date of casting and the bell mark of John Taylor and Co.

During the 1970s a complete overhaul of the bells and frame was undertaken by the ringers under the supervision of Mr. Frederick Pemberton of Ault Hucknall and Adrian Dempster of Selston. Since that time Fred has opened up in business as a bell-hanger. Adrian, under his cap as the representative for the East Derbyshire and West Nottinghamshire Association on the Central Council of Church Bellringers, has been elected to that body's Tower and Belfries Committee of which he is Chairman. This involves him spending much time giving specific and general advice on matters of tower maintenance, re-hanging, etc.

A small bell was given to the church by Mr Walton at sometime in the 1920s and was hung in one of the belfry windows. It is inscribed: "John Taylor & Co., Founder, 1878." Formerly it rang out at the old school in Newstead.

Over three hundred years ago, harsh rules were applied and any wrongdoing was severely punished. An interesting note concerning what was then considered to be the just punishment is extracted from the Act Books of the Archdeacons of Nottingham in respect of two Sutton bell ringers.

"7th June, 1638, Richard Parnham and Abraham Marriott of Sutton in Ashfield - for unreasonable ringing the bells in their Church upon New Years daie last past and which time there was a fire made in their Church and ale drunck there by the said Parnham and others as the common fame goeth and they (the Churchwardens) beleeve the same to be true. To do penance."

As the Rev R.F. Wilkinson, in his Church Bells of Nottinghamshire relates, "The penance probably meant standing in a white sheet in the churchyard during service on a Sunday, as a punishment and a warning to others. Many ringers in old days probably deserved to do penance for "unreasonable ringing and ale." Churchwardens were fairly broadminded, but evidently these two ringers overdid it altogether, and they were sentenced in the Archdeacon's Court."

The Belfry of St. Andrew, Swanwick

Twentieth century tower. Derbyshire's heaviest six.
Old bell-turret removed. Ringers withdrew their services.
They crowned a King when I did ring.

The church of St. Andrew's was erected in 1860, one year before Swanwick was constituted a consolidated chapelry by Order in Council. Hitherto, Swanwick had been an ecclesiastical district within the parish of St. Martin's, Alfreton. Built by Benjamin Wilson of Derby, at a cost of about £3000, St. Andrew's Church remained without a tower for over four decades but not without its bell. This was housed in a fine graceful turret built on the west gable of the nave.

In 1902, at a cost of around £5000, the tower we see today was built onto the north west corner of the church. Complete with five bells and a clock, it was erected as a memorial to Her Majesty Queen Victoria by FitzHerbert Wright, J.P., D.L., High Sheriff of Derbyshire. Queen Victoria had reigned for almost sixty-four years when she died on January 22nd, 1901, at the age of 81 years. Born Princess Victoria, on May 24th, 1819 she succeeded to the throne on June 20th, 1837, barely one month after her eighteenth birthday and some twenty-three years before the tower-less church at Swanwick was built. It is therefore a somewhat fitting tribute that the tower of St. Andrew's should serve as a timely reminder of Queen Victoria's long reign. The architects, Naylor, Sale and Woore were responsible for building the tower.

The tower is large in proportion and comprises a north porch, ringing room, clock chamber and a spacious bell chamber from which today a fine heavy peal of six bells peal out sonorously in the key of F over the parish.

The brevity of Nikolaus Pevsner, when reviewing the tower of St. Andrew's Church, Swanwick, in his volume on Derbyshire Buildings, could give rise to dismay. For we find it described as large, with ugly pinnacles and gargoyles. Let us therefore take a closer look and draw our own conclusion.

Commanding, as it does, the busy cross-road position in the centre of the village, it is viewed by a great number of people as they go about their daily tasks. Supported on each corner by angled buttresses that rise, in four set-offs, to a height level with the top of the three-light louvred bell-openings, they add much strength and character to the visual appearance and serve to draw the eye upward to the four large pinnacles rising at each angle. Each pinnacle is a square pier in design and capped by a miniature broach-like spire springing from a small crocketed gable. The visual effect is to give the structure a well balanced and majestic air. But, when viewed from a distance (Pentrich Road for example) the pinnacles take on a somewhat irregular and billowing appearance. Externally built of dressed stone the tower is internally lined with brick. Three recessed shields adorn the lower portion of each bell-opening, whilst above, the castellated parapet is further adorned on the centre of each cardinal face by the introduction of smaller pinnacles. Partially erected on small projecting piers these small pinnacles echo the same design as their counterparts at the angles. A string course at the base of the parapet ties in very nicely the four large gargoyles projecting at the angles with the corbel of each of the four small piers. A similar string course at the base of the bell-openings lie in sympathy with the third set-off of the angled buttresses. Below, on the east, north and west face of the tower is a clock dial sitting directly upon the masonry and highlighted by gilded numerals. On the north face, a two light ringing chamber window of fine proportion and on the west is a single light window. Both sit neatly upon a further string course and allow light into the spacious ringing chamber. The half round external turret on the west, with glazed slit windows, is the staircase which affords internal access to the ringing and clock chambers. An interesting and unusual small feature is that the stairs taking one aloft turn in an anti-clockwise direction.

Before entering by the imposing north door, notice the two shields affixed to the wall above. These, together with the ones in each of the bell-chamber openings bear heraldic symbols.

In 1902, John Taylor and Co. of Loughborough were commissioned to supply a peal of five bells and to hang them in the new tower of St. Andrew's church. Half a century later, in 1957, they were again entrusted with the casting of a further bell, a new Treble, to augment the peal to six. They are a good example of bell-founding at its best. The six bells are inscribed.

Treble	Centenary Year 1959
	E.J. Lewis, Vicar.
	N. Walker, J.W. Andrews, Churchwardens.
2nd.	They crowned a King when I did ring, 1902
3rd.	O Praise the Lord with one accord.
4th.	At heavens gate be never late.
5th.	A thankful man our chime began.
Tenor	The faithful soul to rest I toll.

The five 1902 bells carry the name of the founder upon the inscription band, whilst on the 1959 treble bell this band is left blank.

The bells have a total combined weight of 2tons. 17cwts. 1qr. 23 lbs. which, with the tenor weighing in at 17cwts. 2qrs.13 lbs. and with a diameter of 46 inches, makes this ring of bells the heaviest peal of six in Derbyshire.

Three great days in the history of Swanwick have been when the church was first built, when the parish became independent and when the tower, complete with its clock and bells, was completed.

On Saturday, April 25th, 1903 the church was full to capacity for the dedication of the tower and bells by the Lord Bishop of Derby. A contemporary news report tells that a shortened form of Evening Prayer was used. Conducted by the Rev. W.H. Draper with the lessons being read by the Rev. W.E. Bradstock and the Rev. R.B. Stoney. The Rev. W.H. Draper next requested the dedication in the following form: "Right reverend father in God, I humbly beseech you to dedicate this gift to the service of Almighty God and in pious memory of her late Gracious Majesty Queen Victoria, for the religious use of the people of this parish." After the production of the Chancellor's faculty, the Bishop, accompanied by the Rural Dean, the Rev. W.H. Draper and Churchwardens, processed to the tower and offered the dedication prayers, and on returning to the chancel besought the Divine blessing on the benefactors of the church. Then followed the hymn, "Thou who has bid all things on earth," and prayer, after which the Bishop delivered an appropriate sermon on Proverbs XVIII, verse 10.

"The name of the Lord is a strong tower: the righteous runneth
into it and is safe".

After the service Mr. and Mrs. Wright entertained the Bishop, clergy and a few friends at The Hayes, whilst six members of the team of bell-ringers from All Saints, Ripley, rang several six-scores of Grandsire Doubles on the bells. The ringers standing as follows; J. Bennett, ringing the treble, H. Day, 2nd. W.H. Frost, 3rd. F. Kay, 5th and H. George conducting the six-scores ringing the tenor. The celebration continued throughout Sunday, with the Rev. W.H. Draper occupying the pulpit morning and evening.

Collections throughout the weekend amounted to a total of £34.16s.9 1/2d. This was put toward the cost of renovating the church and churchyard walls at an estimated cost of between two and three hundred pounds. The greater part of which Mr. Wright had generously promised to repay.

On the last day of the year 1910, Saturday, December 31st, five local ringers rang the first peal of 5040 changes upon the bells in three hours and twenty-three minutes. This peal, of Grandsire Doubles, was a great local achievement as three of the ringers, Leonard Simpson, Charles Walvin and Henry Cartledge were ringing their first ever peal. Thomas Stimpson, ringing the third bell, and Herbert Fretwell, ringing the tenor, had both rung in peals previously at other belfries but on this occasion Herbert Fretwell conducted, making it his first peal as conductor. A plaque to commemorate the peal hangs in the ringing chamber.

Members of the East Derbyshire and Nottinghamshire Association of Change Ringers first visited the tower for a special meeting on Saturday, September 24th, 1904. The Association's minute book records: "The bells, a beautiful ring of five by Taylor's were greatly admired by all present. The best thanks of members are due to Mr. Kay, for making all arrangements. The bells and belfry reflect great credit on him as tower keeper".

No mention is made in the minutes of the Association regarding the ringers of Swanwick affiliating. But, on reading subsequent minutes, one can assume that Swanwick ringers did in fact affiliate to the Association in September 1904. They were certainly affiliated by November that year when members met at Clay Cross, and heard read a letter from the Association's Secretary, Mr. Tom Allibone of North Wingfield, in which Mr. Allibone apologised to the meeting for being indisposed through illness and subsequently missing the special September meeting. This was the first meeting in a period of ten years that Mr. Allibone had been absent from and most probably accounts for the omission of the minute confirming the Swanwick ringers' affiliation.

Among the young ringers learning at St. Andrew's in 1904 was Charles John Walvin. Charles joined the Association in 1905 and served the church and the tower with regular and enthusiastic calling until his untimely death, after a very short illness, at the age of 36 years, in November 1924. He had been tower keeper for four years at the time of his death. Well known as one of the most competent five bell ringers in the district he was greatly missed. As an old comrade said of him "Faithfully and well has he rung his course, till the Conductor called 'stand'."

It is interesting to note that for over ninety odd years since the installation of bells at Swanwick there has always been Association members at the tower. They have always extended a warm welcome on the numerous occasions when Association members have met and rung at the church. On one occasion, Cupid put in an appearance and romance blossomed. This resulted in St. Andrew's gaining, in the course of time, another tower keeper upon whom the minute recorded at the 1904 meeting in Mr. Kay's honour is very apt at the present time. Without in any way wishing to cause any embarrassment, I refer of course to Mr. Eric Sterland, and his charming wife Joan. Joan has the longer connection with the tower of St. Andrew's, for she is a member of the Swanwick bell-ringing family of Walvin, whilst Eric was a member of the young post-war Morton band. It is fitting also to recall that their three children, John, Judith and Helen learned to ring and have served St. Andrew's tower for many years.

Sadly, Judith died at the end of October 1996, at the age of 38 years and is greatly missed. The previous decade saw the death of another young Swanwick ringer, who is also greatly missed, Barry Dye, who met with a tragic accident in 1972. Had fate been kinder, Barry would, without doubt, have become one of the foremost ringers in Derbyshire.

When the peal of five bells were hung in the new tower, space was allocated within the bell-frame for the addition of a treble bell. Exactly one hundred years on from the building of the church this space was filled. The new bell, weighing five hundred-weight, two quarters and one pound was, like the original five, cast by John Taylor & Co. of Loughborough.

On St. Andrew's Day, Monday, November 30th, 1959, the Rt. Rev. George Sinker, Assistant Bishop of Derby, dedicated the bell to mark the centenary of the church. Rev. E.J. Lewis assisted. The cost of supplying and hanging the bell was £360.

In 1967 an appeal was launched to cover the cost of general repairs to the church and renovation of the tower, together with the installation of an electrical winding mechanism, to replace the hand winding gears of the clock, and to illuminate the three external clock dials. It was estimated that some £700 would be needed for the electrical winding gear and to carry out the installation of it, plus the illumination of the clock's three faces. The Alfreton Urban District Council were approached and because the clock was deemed to be a public amenity the committee responsible agreed to pay for the lighting of the clock dials and to make a grant of £100 toward the electrification.

From time to time we read in our newspapers of bell-ringers withdrawing their services. Or as headline seekers seem to prefer "Bell Ringers Go On Strike". For some reason any action taken by a voluntary group of people that is outside the normal practice expected of that group, receives sensational publicity by the media. And especially so if an incumbent is involved. In 1952 such was the situation at Swanwick.

Early January witnessed a clash of opinion between the Vicar and his ringers over attendance at services after ringing. This was picked up by the press and in very quick time opinions were being parleyed about on a national scale. Almost fifty years on, the personal element needs to rest, in spite of its inference still being recalled vividly by some parishioners. But, it is worthy of note, if only because the subject received widespread publicity at the time. It also became the subject of the following editorial in the ringers' weekly publication, The Ringing World, the journal of the Central Council of Church Bell Ringers, and in whose letter columns, for many weeks afterwards, opinions were aired.

The Ringing World. Friday, January 18, 1952.
No2129 Vol. XLVII.

The ringers' 'strike' at Swanwick, Derbyshire, of which many will have read in the newspapers, brings to the forefront once again the vexed question of whether or not a ringer is under any obligation to attend the service for which he has just rung. Most clergymen, no doubt, and many ringers also, will sympathise with the view of the Vicar that all ringers should normally attend the service after ringing; most ringers, surely, will maintain that their obligation to do so is no greater than that of any other parishioner who has been baptised and brought up as a member of the Church of England. Certainly only a very small minority would go so far as to insist that a ringer should be obliged to attend every service for which he rings, whilst most will support the Swanwick ringers in questioning the right of the parson to make such attendance a condition of membership of his ringing band.

Nevertheless, most of us would think little of a parson who did not express a desire that his ringers should go to church with at least some regularity; most of us, indeed although we may be reluctant to confess it, admire those ringers who do attend service regularly. We realise that if they attend two services it means that they give up practically their whole day, a fact that some clergymen may overlook. For in many cases to travel, to ring, to attend service and then to journey home again will occupy three and a half to four hours, and with a repeat performance in the afternoon not much of the "day of rest" will remain.

The whole question arises because of the two-fold nature of bellringing, which is at once a sporting recreation and a form of service to the Church. And the wise parson and the wise ringer alike will recognise that each aspect of bellringing reacts upon the other to their mutual advantage. Most of us take up ringing and almost all of us continue to go ringing, not because we feel an ardent desire to serve the Church, but because we find ringing a fascinating hobby and wish to make progress in our art. But at the same time, since almost all our bells hang in church towers, we should never forget that it is only "by kind permission of the Church" that we are allowed to ring at all, and that whenever we ring we are also willy-nilly rendering a service to the Church. Likewise the wise parson will encourage his ringers, irrespective of their attendance at divine service, to practice their art, since the bells undoubtedly do remind the people around that the Church does still exist. The thoughts of one or two, especially at Easter and Christmas, may be turned to certain events of about 2,000 years ago; very occasionally some may even be tempted to venture inside the sacred building, although it is becoming less and less true to say that the primary purpose of the bells is to call the people to worship. Naturally the ringing of the bells is a convenient indication that a service will shortly take place, but, except in our country villages, there must be hundreds of churches to-day where only a handful if any of the congregation live within earshot of the bells.

In some respects the position of the ringers is comparable to that of the members of the choir. Many choristers, if they are honest, will admit that they belong to the choir primarily not because of their love of the Church, but because they enjoy singing and love music. In other words, the singing of many a choirman is as much a hobby and recreation as ringing is the bell-ringer's. But it is only proper to add that both choirman and bell-ringer should feel some pride and satisfaction that they are enjoying themselves they are also serving the Church or, as the Vicar of Swanwick himself puts it, taking part in an act of worship.

One difference between a choir and a band of ringers should perhaps be pointed out - in most churches a would-be member of the choir has to reach a certain standard before he is accepted, but in far too many belfries people are allowed to ring for Sunday service before they are capable of doing so properly. The resulting noise tends rather to bring the Church into disrepute than to inspire any feeling of respect or veneration. Curiously enough, too, with a few notable exceptions, the most devout of churchmen seem to make very poor ringers!

Our first duty as ringers, surely, is to see that the sound we send forth are worthy of the great institution we serve. And even if we are not obliged to do so, and indeed feel a strong objection to any compulsion in the matter, could not more of us look upon it as a pleasant courtesy occasionally to go inside and listen in turn to those who have been listening to us? Or could we not say that while excessive religious devotion should never become a detriment to our campanological progress, yet our pre occupation with the practical and theoretical development of our art should not be allowed entirely to blind us to its religious associations?   F.E.H.

The whole of F.E.H.'s article was analyzed over the next few weeks by readers, with letters reaching the editor's desk in quantity and from all points of the country, some expressing either a broad agreement or picking up on some poignant detail. One newspaper ran the following; "For the first Sunday for ninety peacetime years the bells of St. Andrew's, Swanwick, Derbyshire, were silent". The tower, you may recall, had only been built fifty years! But, from Cambridgeshire came this little rhyme that had graced the walls of Littleport belfry for a number of years.

"Do not ring and run away,
Leaving other folk to pray,
For when a ringer doeth so,
Hand says 'come', but foot says 'go'."

The East Derbyshire and West Nottinghamshire Association has always been strongly represented at St. Andrew's belfry and over the years several members have held office. In 1917 and again in 1920 the Vicar, Rev. C.G. Everett, was President. Two Association secretaries have been ringers at the tower. Mr. H.G. Fretwell held the office for ten years from 1920 and Mr Eric J. Sterland from 1966 to 1969. As treasurers, Mr. Thomas Stimpson was elected in 1920 and remained treasurer until 1930. Mr. Eric Sterland held the same office in 1968 and followed that with a period as Ringing Master.

In April 1982 Mr Fred Pembleton of Glapwell completed an overhaul of the bells frame and fittings. The old five bells had been hung on plain bearings. These were replaced with ball-bearings, and a new set of clappers, and bell-fittings, were supplied. The local ringers did much in the way of ancillary work under Fred's expert eye. The whole exercise bringing about a considerable improvement to the handling of this heavy peal.

The first peal on the six bells when all the bells were rung as 'working' bells, instead of the tenor bell 'covering' in sixth's place throughout, as in Doubles, was rung on Saturday, February 10th, 1973. It was a peal of 5040 changes, being six extents of Plain Bob Minor, and one of Single Oxford. It took three hours and eight minutes to complete. The ringers were David Palmer, treble; R. John Sterland, 2nd; Harold Franklin, 3rd; Peter H. Wright, 4th; Brynley A. Richards, 5th; and Eric J. Sterland, tenor. The peal was conducted by Brynley A. Richards.

However, following the 1982 overhaul a peal was rung on the bells on Saturday, November 13, 1982 in two hours and fifty-five minutes. Notice to what effect the new ball-bearings had with regard to the length of time this peal, of the same number of changes, took to complete when compared with the previous one. A saving of thirteen minutes.

A Peal of Minor, 5040 Changes,
Being one extent each of London Surprise, Norwich
Surprise, Cambridge Surprise, Kent Treble Bob,
Oxford Treble Bob, Oxford Bob and Plain Bob.

Frederick Pembleton	Treble	Christopher B. Richards	4
J. Stuart Brown	2	Eric J. Sterland	5
R. John Sterland	3	Brynley A. Richards	Tenor.

Conducted by Brynley A. Richards.

When the original five bells were hung it was made possible to chime the bells by means of an Ellacombe chiming apparatus. This was a system whereby hammers placed adjacent the bells could be activated by means of wires and pulleys to strike each bell at the command of one person operating the clavier. In this case, the clavier being a set of five ropes placed side by side, within a small frame. This was situated in the clock chamber. The hammer system was dismantled in 1959 when the new treble was installed.

Fifty years after the foundation stone of the church was laid the ringers rang a quarter peal in commemoration. It took place on Monday, November 30th, 1908, when 1260 changes of Manchester and Plain Bob Doubles was rung by Ben. Walvin, H. Kerry, T.W. Gamble, T Stimpson and F.H. Kay who conducted. In the following year a date touch of 1909 changes of Grandsire Doubles was rung by F. Kay, who composed and conducted the touch, Ben. Walvin, T. Gamble, Charles Walvin and T. Stimpson.

Several items of interest are to be found in the ringing chamber. Two photographs, one of Mr. F. Kay, the first tower captain from 1902 until 1915, and alongside, in a solid piece of stained oak and fashioned in the shape of a bell, is let in a photograph of a group which includes the ringers. It was taken prior to 1925 and includes three members of the Walvin family. A further piece of oak, in the same shape and size, acts as a peal board to record the first peal on the bells in 1910. On the other wall hangs a framed account giving the weight and inscriptions found on the original five bells and recording both the date touch and the quarter peal referred to above. There is also a framed copy of the East Derbyshire Association rules and objectives. These were issued in the early years of the Association to all towers upon affiliation but only a few have survived.

Mention was made at the beginning of the church possessing one bell. This was housed in a fine tall bell-turret built on the west gable of the nave, the west pier sitting on a corbel whilst the south and north piers rested in line with the gable wall of the nave. Tall pointed bell-openings were placed between the piers and rising above a graceful spire led the eye to the ball finial and weathercock. It is believed the turret was taken down at some time during the 1940s, possibly as a result of some damage being effected due to blast caused when a bomb dropped from an enemy aircraft exploded on landing across Derby Road. What happened to the bell is not known.

Finally, as one leaves by the north porch a stone let into the west wall records that the tower and bells were erected in 1902 by Fitzherbert Wright Esq. A legacy which the parishioners of Swanwick can be justly proud.

The Belfry of St. Katherine, Teversal

Molyneux family gift bells. Five bells for over two centuries.
£10 paid for bell-frame in 1737. A fine gilded weathercock.

The building of the church of St. Katherine, Teversal, began during the first half of the 12th century. By 1170, the north arcade and the chancel arch had been added, together with the completed main body of the church, but no tower. It is believed that before the erection of the tower the Norman doorway we see today stood at the western end of that church. The plan of the tower is interesting in that it is built partially over the western bays of the nave arcade. It was completed during the 15th century. By 1552 two bells had been installed and it is known that two more were added before 1740. The gift of a further bell in 1758 augmented the ring to five. These five bells have now been in service together for almost two hundred and fifty years.

The tower is built minus the usual form of diagonal or angled buttresses, instead the tower wall is set back at two stages. The first set-off occurs at the aisle roof level whilst the second is some five feet above the wall of the nave. This gives the impression of it being built in three stages, but on checking the masonry one soon dispels this theory. The parapet rises from the string course at the head of the third section and is built of an entirely different stone, a lighter grey and ashlar in appearance. Let into the parapet on the south and west face of the tower are very plain gargoyles. They make no pretension at being decorative, but, judging from the projection, are admirable at doing their job - that of carrying off rainwater from the tower roof. A fine gilded weather cock, placed centrally on the tower roof, indicates for all to see, from what direction the wind bloweth, and the tower is further adorned by the erection of a flagstaff in the south west angle from which the flag of St. George is proudly raised in commemoration of saints' days, festivals of the church and days of national observance. The stepped battlements are further enhanced by eight small beehive finials. Small, two-light louvered bell-openings are placed high in the upper third of the tower and beneath on the west face is the clock dial. This sits squarely within a rendered panel that admirably serves to highlight the Roman numerals and minute points. There is no west door, but above is a two light window that allows daylight into the ground floor ringing chamber. Immediately above the glazing is a shield bearing a cross. This, through the ravages of time, is now badly weathered, as is the stonework in general upon the lower section of the tower.

Inside, the belfry is entered from the nave via a low doorway opening directly into the ringing chamber. From here a curved stair in the north west corner leads to the gallery while diagonally opposite another stair allows access to the bells. Of recent years the door from the nave into the belfry was replaced and the present door serves as a memorial given in memory of Mrs. Hannah Hallam.

We now come to the five bells which are inscribed:-

Treble   The gift of Sir Charles Molyneux, Bart. 1758.

The inscription is in plain capital letters. the Molyneux family lived for almost two centuries at the Manor House close by the church. An elaborate border circles the crown of the bell.

2nd.   The gift of Sir John Molyneux.
I was new cast and added to in 1758.
I. (Molyneux Arms) M.

This inscription is also of plain capital letters with the second line being inscribed upon the waist of the bell. Beneath this are the initials of Sir John Molyneux, and between them a shield surmounted by the crest, bearing his coat of arms. As with the treble an elaborate border is to be found round the crown.

3rd.   Gloria in Excelsis Deo. 1617.
P.H.

This inscription is in late Gothic capitals with the addition of the initial P.H. on the waist of the bell. These initials are placed upon a plaque that is edged with a square cable border. The 'G' of the word Gloria bears a fylfot cross within. This clearly identifies the casting of the bell with Chesterfield, and the foundry of the Heathcote family of whom a brief history is to be found in another chapter.

4th.   Ex Dono roger Greenal, Armiger,
ORTo SEPTe Ao 1SS1
IHV BEDICTV SIC NOME DM
The mark of Henry Oldfield.

In small Gothic capitals this inscription reads, "From the gift of Roger Greenal, Esquire, 4th September, 1551. Blessed be the name of the Lord Jesus."

This bell was cast by Henry Oldfield. The letters used are of interest as they found their way to the Nottingham foundry from one in Worcester a century earlier, being originally the property of John Rufford, who was casting bells in London about 1370. For some reason Oldfield had no numerals available when casting this bell and so the date 1551 is made up of a capital I and two capital Ss from Rufford's alphabet and a final old English S that looks very much like the figure one when in black lettering.

Tenor   Hec Campana Sacra Fiat
Trinitate Beata. 1683.
T.W.I.C. wardens.
I. (Molyneux Arms) M.

The capitals of this inscription are very fine and ornamented using the symbols of grapes and vine leaves. The H contains a chalice with wine falling from the grapes into it. The other letters are in black-letter type. These letters, neglected and unused for a century and a half, possibly because of Puritan scruples, were revived by George Oldfield II. It is thought that they originated in York.

Teversal Manor, formerly the home of the Molyneux and Carnarvon families was mentioned in Domesday Book, the Saxon owner named Lewric was followed by Ralph FitzHerbert the Norman overlord. It then passed to Galfredus Barry whose

230

descendants held it until the end of the fifteenth century. It then passed into the hands of Radulf Greenhalgh, and eventually to the Molyneux family. It would appear, from the inscriptions upon the bells, that it was through the good offices of the last two of these families that the bells at Teversal were cast and hung in the tower. It is also most probable that the Greenhalghs were responsible for the building of the tower, as they came into the parish at the end of the fifteenth century. Upon Roger Greenhalgh's death in 1562 the Manor passed to the Molyneuxs.

Placed upon the waist of the second and fifth bells is the arms of Sir John Molyneux. The Rev R.F. Wilkinson in his Notes on the church bells of Nottinghamshire, describes the arms of Sir John Molyneux: "The shield is 'Azure, a cross moline quarterly pierced' or, surmounted by a crest "A chapean gules, turned up ermine adorned with a plume of peacock's feathers ppr.' The shield also has a canton the 'sinister hand, gules', the mark of Baronetcy."

Almost four hundred and fifty years ago, two bells hung in the tower. Without doubt the present fourth bell is one of them, but which of the other bells was the second? The present second bell seems to be the most likely one for its inscription tells: "it was new cast and added to in 1758". The third bears the date 1617, the tenor, 1683 and the treble was new in 1758 so these three bells are exactly the same today as they were when new cast all those years ago. The possible reason for adding further metal to the second bell, when it was recast in 1758, would be to alter its note, and thereby put it in harmony with the others. It would be most interesting to learn its true age and by whom it was first cast.

An old volume of the church accounts beginning in 1732 reveals many references to the bells and ringers. Here are a few.

May 27	1732	Pd for oil for the bells	6d.
January 1	1733	Pd for Bellrope	11.0d.
January 25	1737	Pd to Robert Hill for bellframes	£10.0.0d.
July 20		Paid for set of bellropes	11.0d.
October 19		Ale for ringers	6.0d.
April 6	1738	pd for the Bellropes	11.0d.
May 5	1740	Pd for four new bellropes, 25½ pounds	12.6d.
December24	1741	Ale for ye Ringers at Christmas	4.0d.
June 12	1794	For mending bell weels	17.0d.
August 5	1809	New bell ropes	£2.0.0d.
January 10	1812	Pd Jno Thompson on Acct repy bells	£2.10.0d.
March 12		Pd Mr Fox for hoops to bells	15.0d.
November 9	1813	Ringing Ale	7.6d.
October 28	1819	New bell ropes	£2.10.0d.

By comparison, a new bellrope today costs about £100 depending upon whether it is all made from good quality hemp or has a section of synthetic material inserted.

Gone are the days when 250p would purchase more than one rope, but then, earnings are not on the level of 3p for a full day's toil either!

Few peals have been rung on the bells. Probably the first one taking place was rung by members of the Midland Counties Association in 1925.

On Saturday, November 9, 1929, in two hours and thirty nine minutes, a peal of 5040 Changes of Doubles, consisting of 3600 changes of Grandsire and 1440 of Plain Bob was rung by Horace Porter, treble; Hubert Bailey, 2nd; Arthur Smithson, 3rd; Bernard Porter, 4th. and Fred W. Knowles conducting, and ringing the tenor. This was the first peal rung by Horace and Bernard Porter. Fifty years later, on Saturday, July 14, 1979, a peal of 5040 changes of Stedman Doubles was rung on the bells. It was the first peal of Stedman Doubles rung by each member of the band; Brynley A. Richards, treble; J. Neville Parkin, 2nd; David C. Lester, 3rd; Leslie G. Smith, 4th and conducted from the tenor by Adrian Dempster.

For a great many years Mr H.L. Parker has been a ringer at St. Katherine's. A craftsman in wood, Les, as he is known to all his ringing friends, has not only been responsible for the upkeep of the tower and bells but has fashioned a number of furnishings to be found in church. Among them, a marriage prayer desk, oak doors and much in the way of extremely fine repair work to the ancient woodwork.

Inscription on the third bell at St Katherine's Church, Teversal
Cast by Godfrey Heathcote of Chesterfield in 1617.

The letter 'P H' are to be found on the waist of the bell. Each letter being enclosed
in a square cable border. These initials do not relate to a member of the Heathcote family

The Belfry of St. John the Baptist, Tibshelf

Tower clock installed 1901. Several long serving ringers.
Girl of twelve rings peal. Gallery removed from tower arch.

Standing upon the high ridge of land bordering the eastern edge of Derbyshire, the embattled tower of St. John the Baptist, Tibshelf, has been a local landmark for over five hundred years. The ancient tower and part of the chancel are the only survivors of a major rebuilding scheme in 1729. The tower is a fair example of the Perpendicular period and closely resembles the towers at South Normanton and that at South Wingfield. The small west door, standing only a few yards from the busy highway, with the pointed west window, containing three principal lights, above, are framed by diagonal buttresses reaching, in five set-backs, almost to the parapet. The four louvred bell-chamber openings echo the fine arch of the west window and doorway. The battlements have at each angle, pyramidal pinnacles, these again are echoed by four of smaller design, placed centrally upon each cardinal face. There is evidence that these were restored in 1729. An illuminated clock dial, fixed below the bell-openings on the south and north face of the tower, are visible from afar, in clear weather, on account of the white ground beneath the black numerals.

Inside, a narrow arch reaching to the roof of the nave is filled with a fine oak screen. Note how the top of the arch is cut off through insufficient allowance being made with the nave roof elevation. Formerly, this arch was blocked in by a heavy gallery that protruded somewhat into the nave. A door within the oak screen admits directly into the ground floor ringing chamber where the six bell-ropes descend in a tight circle from the six bells hung above. To the right of the tower arch a brass plaque informs that the clock was installed in 1901. It was bought by public subscription and is in memory of Queen Victoria. The bells are inscribed :-

Treble.	1837 V.R. 1897
2nd.	C.& G. Mears Founders London 1848.
3rd.	ihc ma ri a
4th.	C.& G. Mears Founders London 1848
5th.	John Taylor & Co. Founders Loughborough 1868
Tenor.	John Taylor & Co. * Loughborough * 1898

The tenor is tuned to F#. The diameter and weights being:-

Treble	4 cwts 0 qrs 27 lbs.	27¼ inches.
2nd.	4 cwts 1 qrs 1 lbs	28¼ inches
3rd.	4 cwts 0 qrs 0 lbs	29¾ inches
4th.	5 cwts 1 qrs 4 lbs	32¼ inches
5th.	6 cwts 2 qrs 2 lbs	35¼ inches
Tenor	9 cwts 1 qrs 0 lbs	38¼ inches

Until 1868 the tower contained three bells. Cox, writing in 1875, quotes the tower as possessing five bells. The catalogue of John Taylor and Sons, published in

1894, lists the casting of a fourth bell for Tibshelf. (An interesting aside is that they give the tenor's weight at eleven hundredweights.) Cox was of the opinion that Taylor's supplied two bells and that the second was in fact the ancient bell, because he clearly attributes bells one, three and five to have been cast by Mears in 1848. This seems to be unusual. And, if correct, what happened to the third bell of Mears, probably the tenor? Was it re-cast later in 1898 by Taylor's when they cast and installed the tenor bell. If so, it is most unusual not to find Taylor's placing the fact upon the bell when re-casting it, for they are extremely careful of recording such matters. At the moment everything points to Cox's information not being quite correct and that the present third bell was in fact already ringing out over Tibshelf. It is thought this bell dates from about 1520 and is attributed by some to have been cast by Selyoke, a bellfounder of Nottingham. The inscription has long intervening spaces between the letters of the word 'ma ri a' and is preceded by the founder's stamp, a cross pate. Either way it is a very old bell and one of which the people of Tibshelf can be justly proud.

On April 8th, 1899 the new treble was dedicated. The old tenor had been recast, and the other bells re-tuned and rehung on new headstocks with new bearings and wheels. The whole project being a reflection of the lasting public esteem upon the Diamond Jubilee of H.M. Queen Victoria that had taken place two years previously, and in whose honour the treble bell had been cast.

Ten years after the founding of the East Derbyshire Association of Change Ringers the vicar of Tibshelf, Rev. E.A. Morgan, became its third president, the ringers of St John Baptist having affiliated in 1889. Among these early members were the three Draycott brothers, Jos, Harry and Jack who each gave well in excess of fifty years service to the belfry and the church. 1913 saw Major R.P. Leach elected president of the Association and some fifty years on Mr Thomas Radford took office as Honorary Secretary. Tom's untimely death was not only deeply felt within the Association but in the belfry, where he was diligently, and with great success, working at the training of a young band of ringers.

Among the band of ringers who joined the association in 1889 was John William Scott. A native of County Durham John William had begun ringing at Winlayton at the age of twelve in 1858. Moving to work in Tibshelf in 1871 he immediately joined the band of ringers. Upon his death in 1930 at the age of 84 years the following tribute was placed in the Parish Magazine.

"By the death of our friend Mr. Scott, another old standard bearer has been removed from the Church life of our Parish. His figure has been so familiar to us for so long that he will be sadly missed. It is not easy to imagine the fact, but Mr. Scott's association with our Church dates back to the year 1871. Right onwards from that time, he has rendered a service to the Church which will not be readily forgotten. That service has been regular, unstinted, and devoted. For a period of 70 years he was a Bell Ringer, and his love for the art was remarkable. As for a long period

Captain of the Belfry- he was seen, in all weathers, Sunday by Sunday, wending his way to the Church long before the actual time of worship. His hobby of ringing was no mere passing fancy, for he entered into the real spirit of all that it meant, not only calling people to Church - but remaining with them to worship. This practice he continued until quite recently.

Mr. Scott found great joy too, in teaching young men the art of ringing. Scores of students have passed through his training, and one of his great disappointments was that so few continued. Mr. Scott was known over a wide area in the ringing world, and when a younger man he was known to tramp for miles to join a company for peal ringing.

As a village we owe a great debt to Mr. Scott for all the trouble and care he bestowed, for thirty years, on the clock in the Church Tower. It is true to say that he knew every step and turn in the tower - and had spent more time in it than any of his predecessors. And not only so, but much might be said of his willingness to help every branch of Church activity. There was scarcely any meeting at which he was not present. He was formerly a Sunday School Teacher as well as a Sidesman.

And now (Tuesday, August 5th, 1930,) his earthly service is finished. He has entered into Higher Service, to serve God not by faith, but by sight. A memory is left of an honoured and dutiful servant of Christ." " W.F.C."

John William Scott was tower secretary from 1895 until 1929 and was instrumental in teaching a new band of ringers at Ripley and proposing four of them as members of the East Derbyshire Association at a meeting of members held at South Normanton on Saturday, December 7th, 1895. Two years later, on Easter Monday, April 19th, 1897, at the Association's A.G.M. he proposed that the Annual Report be issued each year at Easter. To this day both the Annual Report and the Annual Meeting conform. For another thirty years his name occurs regularly in the minutes either proposing, seconding, taking the chair or giving a vote of thanks. He proposed many new members, among them in 1900 was Tibshelf ringers Mr. W. Ward and the vicar Rev. G.H. Legge. By 1902 he was engaged with a new learner band at Pleasley and in 1903 became Association auditor, an office he held for a number of years.

In 1909 John William proposed that officials of the Association use a badge of office and members a lapel badge. He provided samples for consideration. There is no mention of the proposal taking effect, and it is interesting to note that it is only during the last decade that an Association lapel badge has been available to members. A proposal of his in September, 1914, that the Association send £2 to the Prince of Wales War Fund resulted in a circular being sent to all towers in union asking for a donation. The total amount received was £1.17.0d. which was forwarded to the Ringing World Office on February 16th, 1915.

Saturday, June 19th, 1909 was a great day with the ringers of Tibshelf when the following peal was rung upon the bells by local ringers. Taking two hours and forty minutes to complete, the peal, 5040 changes of Treble Bob Minor in seven methods;

235

New London Pleasure, Violet, Duke of York, Woodbine, Kent Treble Bob, Oxford Treble Bob and College Pleasure was rung by J.W. Scott, treble; W. Holling, 2nd; J. Ward, 3rd; H. Draycott, 4th; F. Lowe, 5th, and C. Lowe, tenor. Charles Lowe conducted the peal and it was the first peal by all the band except J. W. Scott.

With Tibshelf bells half-muffled, as a mark of respect and in thanks of John William Scott's seventy two years of devoted service to bell-ringing, the following peal was rung by six East Derbyshire Association members on the day of his interment, Thursday, August 7th, 1930.

A Peal of Minor, 5040 Changes,
being two extents each of Kent and Oxford Treble Bob
and three extents of Plain Bob.

Arthur Smithson	Treble.	Fred. W. Knowles	4th.
William Swain	2nd.	Harold Fradgley	5th.
Ernest T. Mallender	3rd.	John W. England	Tenor.

Conducted by John W. England.

John W. England, of South Normanton, had been taught to ring by John William Scott as had Frank and Charles Lowe, W. Holling, J. Ward and Harry Draycott who rang in the 1910 peal.

The three Draycott brothers gave well over half a century each in the service of Tibshelf belfry, and when at the age of 87 years, Harry died, in February 1956, a Peal of 5040 Changes of Minor was rung half-muffled on the bells in memoriam. It marked Harry's sixtieth year as a ringer and was conducted by possibly Tibshelf's first resident lady ringer, Miss Doreen Armstrong. The peal consisted of one extent of Single Oxford, and two each of Plain Bob, Kent Treble Bob and Oxford Treble Bob. The ringers being:-

Thomas Radford	Treble.	Frank Bradley	4th.
Doreen Armstrong	2nd.	Wilfred Riley	5th.
George E. Hancock	3rd.	Albert Wheeler	Tenor.

The ringer of the treble bell, Thomas Radford took over as tower captain and for a decade the tower prospered. An enthusiastic and regular Sunday service band, made up of new young recruits, whom Tom taught, and a few older ringers, including Tom Hall and Sydney Holdgate, who both came back to ringing after a few years break, made up this team. It was therefore quite a blow when Tom died prematurely in December 1967. A peal of 5040 changes of Minor was rung with the bells half-muffled in memoriam by members of the East Derbyshire and West Nottinghamshire Association:-

Arthur Smithson	Treble.	Wilfred Riley	4th.
Thelma E. Staples	2nd.	Eric J. Sterland	5th.
Barry Dye	3rd.	Brynley A. Richards	Tenor.

The peal was conducted by Brynley A. Richards and it was the first peal rung by Barry Dye, a young ringer of Swanwick, who just five years later was to meet with a fatal accident.

A decade on and young ringers again enter the Tibshelf belfry scene. Following the death of Tom Radford a long standing ringer of Blackwell, Wilfred Riley, and a regular visitor at the weekly Tibshelf practice was approached and asked if he would be willing to instruct learners at Tibshelf. In his normal quiet manner Wilf undertook the task and in no time at all another young team emerged onto the local ringing circuit. They achieved a very high standard and it is thanks to Wilf's tenacity that at the age of 12 years Elizabeth Hill was able to ring the treble bell in a peal of Plain Bob Minor on Thursday, November 12th, 1977 and on November 18th in the following year Elizabeth's sister Sarah rang the treble bell in a similar peal at the age of 14 years. In both peals the youngsters were accompanied by Frank Bradley, Wilfred Riley, Doreen Armstrong, George L. Hall and Frederick Pembleton. At this period it became a regular occurrence to ring a Quarter Peal prior to evensong and the walls of the ringing chamber carry many cards recording the details of them.

In 1980 a major overhaul was undertaken. The second and fourth bells were quarter turned, and the fifth bell had the gudgeons and bearings renewed. Two bells had their clappers re-bushed and roller rope guides were installed together with the timber frame and the timbers of the bell-chamber floor and ceiling treated. The whole project cost in excess of £600.

Annual Report read Easter 1889

Income and expenditure for the year are as follows.

Income

	£	s	d
Balance brought forward		5	9
Honorary Members subscriptions.			
Canon Massey 10/ Rev. J. B. Nodder 10/ Rev. Jos Oldham 5/ Per Mr Sanderson 5/.	1	10	0
Members Subscriptions			
Clay Cross 4/6 North Wingfield 3/9 Heath 6/ Old Brampton 3/9 Ashover 3/9 South Normanton 5/ Bolsover 6/6 Ault Hucknall 6/3	2	3	3
Annual Tea Subscriptions	2	0	0
Total	**5**	**19**	**0**

Expenditure

	£	s	d
To Mrs Smith providing Tea, Hot Water, &c.	1	14	5
Advertising two local papers		10	0
Post Cards, Stamps, Stationery		5	0
Total	**2**	**9**	**5**

	£	s	d
Income for Year	5	19	0
Expenditure " "	2	9	5
Balance in Treasurers Hand	3	9	7

The Belfry of S.S. Peter and Paul, Warsop

Rector's son gifts clock, 1844. 19c. Bell cast in Mansfield.
Unusual Norman tower arch. Tenor rings in memory of the fallen.

Standing on rising ground the church of S.S. Peter and Paul, Warsop features a broad massive tower. It is, with the exception of its fourteenth century top storey, chiefly Norman. The tower plan shows it to be wider from north to south than from east to west. At an early date the tower must have collapsed, for the south-west angle has been entirely re-built with a Norman buttress to the lower stage and a circular stair within. Early in the nineteenth century immense buttresses have been added on the north west and to the east side. A rounded string-course below the fourteenth century upper stage is curiously finished off at each of the angles by flat disc-like ends, that represent the mould as carried through the angles. Between the renewed west door and the window above is a course of masonry cut and dressed in triangular fashion and bonded together in mosaic. Beneath the clock dial, on the south face, is an original narrow belfry light with an incised splayed-armed cross. This is cut on the stone that forms the circular head of the window.

The clock dates from 1844, a gift of Mr. Francis Martin, the second son of the Rector at that time. A feature of the clock is its mechanism, constructed in such a way as to allow the metal to expand and contract in accordance with the season and without affecting its accuracy of the time keeping. The clock's pendulum swings within the ringing chamber.

Inside, the Norman arch to the nave is unusual in character. It is of two orders, the inner order consisting of a roll soffit on each side of which is worked a series of triangular teeth that point radially inwards. Each point occupies a single voussoir, (wedge-like stone) variable in size. And, as there is no additional ornament cut upon the architrave formed by the flat face of the teeth, the effect is harsh. The arch is supported on half-round engaged shafts with square chamfered abacus and long conical capitals. An early sixteenth century floor-slab, with traces of an incised cross and inscription, is affixed to the tower wall.

Of the present ring of eight bells four are of recent casting and four date from earlier times. The oldest bears the date 1615. In 1913, Messrs John Taylor & Son, of Loughborough, recast the treble bell, second and tenor bell and rehung the peal of four in a new iron frame having completely replaced all fittings. The new frame was supported by massive girders built into the masonry of the tower. During morning service on Sunday, April 27th, 1913, the rector, Rev. R. J. King, conducted the office of dedication.

When the first bell was hung in the tower is not recorded. But it can be assumed, with some degree of certainty, that an important structure such as the tower we find

239

erected at the western end of the church of S.S. Peter and Paul would have been the keeper of at least one bell from shortly after it was built. If for no other reason than to adhere to Church rubric.

Of the four bells hanging in the tower prior to 1812, we find today that they are inscribed:-

A.   S. Midworth, Mansfield. 1812.
      Recast 1913. (The medallion of John Taylor & Son.)
B.   GOD BE OUR SPEED. 1747.
      Recast 1913. (The medallion of John Taylor & Son.)
C.   +UT TUBA SIC SONITU DOMINI CONDUCO
      COHORTES. 1615. (Bell mark of Henry Oldfield.)
      Recast 1947. (The bellmark of John Taylor and Co.)
D.   All you that hear my doleful sound
      repent before yoor laid in ground.
      October 14, 1737.
      Recast 1913   (The medallion of John Taylor & Son.)

These four bells now ring as three, four, five and six in the 1970 octave. With three of these four original bells being recast in 1913 by John Taylor & Son, at their foundry in Loughborough, the belfry was left with one original nineteenth century bell cast in Mansfield hanging in the tower until 1947. It in turn was recast by Taylor's in that year when the two new tenor bells were installed to make a peal of six.

Two of the old bells had been cast in Nottingham by two different founders, but quite probably in the same foundry, and situated in the vicinity of what is now Parliament Street. The bell of 1615 was cast by Henry Oldfield and the bell of 1747 was cast by Thomas Hedderly. Both men came from traditional bell-founding families and prior to Hedderly's ceasing trading, sometime around 1785, a statement was made by them to the effect that they were of the belief that bells had been cast on their site for upwards of three hundred years.

The inscription of Hedderly's 1747 bell, which became the treble to a peal of three bells at the time, is of plain capital letters interspaced with a decorative motif, the whole forming a band encircling the bell. Hedderly had possibly cast the tenor bell of the three ten years previously in 1737 but this is not certain. The inscription, in small black-letters, is one often found on bells destined to be tolled at funerals. Why the date, October 14th, formed part of the inscription, remains a mystery.

"As a trumpet, so by sound I lead together the hosts of the Lord." The Latin inscription of Henry Oldfield is cast in small Gothic capitals on his bell of 1615. It served the faithful parishioners of Warsop for three hundred and thirty two years, calling them to assemble within the church of S.S. Peter and Paul for worship, before it was recast in 1947 in order that it could continue to proclaim and ring out truly within the new octave. Let us hope it continues to do just that for centuries to come.

The 1812 bell was probably one of only four bells cast by Samuel Midworth of Mansfield. The other three known bells of his being at St. Andrew's, Skegby, at Arnold and the original bell hung in the then new tower of St. Peter's, Belper in 1824. Whether, as at Skegby, this bell was an older bell and recast by Midworth is not known. In the Mansfield Directory for 1832 an entry can be found, "Samuel Midworth, Iron Founder and Brass Clock Manufacturer."

The foundry was in Leeming Street where the free library now stands. Midworth lived in Gilcroft House, and the name Blind Lane was later altered to Midworth Street.

Following a survey of the four bells, carried out in 1912, it was found that the frame was in a dangerous condition, and beyond chiming for Sunday services, and that further ringing be strictly prohibited until the bells be rehung. The Midworth bell, the 1747 Hedderly bell and the then tenor bell were all considered in need of recasting. It was agreed that the work recommended should be undertaken during 1913 and the cost, amounting to £167.4.6d, be raised by public subscription.

The four bells were augmented to a peal of six in 1947 and a further two bells, hung as new trebles, were added in 1970 to complete the octave. The local ringers raising £1272 to defray the cost. They are inscribed;

Treble	To the glory of God
	and
	in memory of
	T. Roland Flint 1879 - 1969
	and Reg Lucas 1913 - 1965
	Round the inscription band:
	John Taylor and Company + Founders + Loughborough + 1969 +
Second	To the glory of God
	and
	in recognition of the life long
	service to this parish of
	Fred Blackburn
	and
	H. Lawrence Bray
	1969
	The inscription band is identical with that of the treble bell.

In 1947, at a cost of £1061, two tenor bells had been added to the old four to make a minor peal of six. The six bells were hung on ball bearings. Today, these bells still ring out as the two tenors, but of course they have become bells number seven and eight in the octave. They are inscribed;

Seven	Frank Rolling (1862 - 1944)
	Gave me.
	The inscription band being inscribed John Taylor & Co.
	+ Founders + Loughborough + 1947 +

Tenor The people of Warsop gave me
Ring in memory of the fallen 1939 - 1945
May they rest in peace
The inscription band is identical with that of the seventh bell.
Diameter: 43inches. Weight: 14cwts.2qrs.24 lbs.

An interesting memorandum, dating from 1626, in the Parish Registers records an agreement between the inhabitants of the hamlet of Sookholme to the effect that, in return for seats appointed to them in Warsop church, "the Soukholme men shall paye to the churchwardens of Warsoppe the fourth part of all charges to wind and weather, and to the keeping of the bells in repayre".

The names Herbert Rooke and Warsop are almost synonymous and on Easter Day, April 18, 1976, to commemorate his fiftieth year of service as a ringer at Warsop church, his colleagues, together with Herbert, rang a Quarter Peal in his honour upon the six bells prior to Evensong. Comprising 1272 changes of spliced Kent and Oxford Treble Bob Minor it was conducted by Brynley A. Richards and rung by: J. Hind, treble; H.T. Rooke, 2nd; C.B. Richards, 3rd; R. Hind, 4th; F. Flint, 5th and B. A. Richards ringing the sixth. A contemporary report in the Ringing World had this to say:-

> "Between the two world wars Warsop had four bells, but although the ringers and others at that time had dreams of augmenting them to a ring of eight, it did not materialise. In spite of this, Warsop ringers - assisted by two others - Did after several attempts succeed in winning the Crawford Cup in a striking competition in 1936.
>
> Since then Warsop ringers have had a long string of successes in various striking competitions, and in all of these Herbert has taken an active part as he has with the augmentation of the bells at Warsop.
>
> After the war the two tenor bells were added, and Herbert, freshly "demobbed" took a job with the bellhangers whilst work at Warsop was being done. In 1970 two new trebles (given by the Warsop bellringers) were added to complete the octave and a lot of DIY was done by several willing helpers, including, of course, Herbert!
>
> He is (1976) captain at Warsop and has been as long as one cares to remember. The ringing and achievements of Warsop are in no small part due to the tremendous enthusiasm and standards of ringing that Herbert has shown and gives to others. B.R."

Herbert began ringing in 1926, at the age of 14, and was taught by Roland Flint. He became Tower Captain early in the 1930s and held that Office until ill health intervened in 1977. Herbert died on August 30th, 1982, and on the evening of the Wednesday following, as he was brought into church to lie overnight prior to the funeral service next day, his ringing friends rang a Quarter Peal of Stedman Triples, with the bells half muffled but with the tenor bell left open, as he would have wished.

On a lighter note, Herbert befriended a stray dog he found in distress and abandoned whilst travelling on the motorway. He gave the Border Collie a good home and in return was amply rewarded by the faithfulness of Glen. As a regular visitor to belfries with Herbert, Glen would find a suitable corner to sit or curl up in whilst Herbert was ringing, but immediately the bells came back into ringing rounds at the end of a touch Glen knew and became alert again. The B.B.C. used to broadcast on Christmas morning a short programme known as Christmas Bells which was a recording of bells being rung at selected churches throughout the length and breadth of the country. On Christmas Day, 1975, Warsop bells were broadcast ringing out the Christmas message, but not without Glen getting a mention for very good behaviour in the ringing chamber. In fact, such was the affection bestowed on Glen by Herbert's fellow ringers, that it was suggested that perhaps a new ringing method should be named after them --- "Herbert's Pedigree Chum".

On Saturday, October 29th, 1977, members of the East Derbyshire and West Nottinghamshire Association of Church Bell Ringers met in the Tudor Barn of the Parish Centre to celebrate ninety years of the Association with a Dinner and Social Evening. It was a great success, with the main vote of thanks going to the Warsop team of bell ringers who were the perfect hosts.

Today a very accomplished band of ringers keep the eight bells ringing to a high standard. Mr Fred Flint is tower captain and auditor to the East Derbyshire and West Nottinghamshire Association of Church Bell Ringers. Christopher Richards and his father Brynley are regular members of the band together with Mrs A. Boot, Mrs J. Crosby, Miss M.K. Freeman, J.S. Brown, R. Hind, R. Marshall, N.J. Parkes and John A. Underwood who also serves as treasurer to the Association. Christopher Richards is a trustee of the Association's Bell Repair Fund and Brynley Richards is one of the Southwell Diocesan Guild's representatives on the Central Council of Church Bell Ringers. A regular practice takes place each Monday evening.

The Belfry of All Saints, Wingerworth

Sixteenth Century Sanctus bell? Sun-dial from 1770 on tower wall.
5040 Grandsire Doubles in 1888. Metal bell-frame erected in 1886.

The tower of All Saints Church, Wingerworth was built no later than 1500 and is supported through the lower stages by diagonal buttresses. Below the embattled parapet project, on each cardinal face, a pair of gargoyles of varied design. Those on the west face being in the best state of preservation depict a muzzled bear and an ape. Between these two gargoyles is a small shield, apparently uncharged. The west window, with an obtusely pointed head, together with the four pointed and louvred bell openings of which the two principal lights have cinque-foil heads are good examples of the period. On the south face, above a small window that allows light into the ringing chamber, is a sun-dial bearing the date 1770. The corner stones of the battlements show traces of having supported small pinnacles. Rev Charles Cox writing in 1875 states that the battlements were of considerable height and unusually thin and that at the time of his visit the weather had taken its toll and they could be swayed at the touch. We know that work was carried out on the bells a few years after that visit and so one assumes the battlements were made safe.

Inside, the base of the tower once housed the organ. It may have been used as the ringing chamber previously but that is not within living memory. The underside of the oak floor of the ringing chamber is ornamented with bosses of similar design to the carving on the rood-loft. In the bell chamber, built into the south wall is a circular head of an incised cross, which has originally formed a portion of a coffin lid. This stone is about a foot square and very much worn. Its date is quite as early as the oldest part of the church, says Cox, and he goes on to say how ruthless the builders of the Perpendicular period appear to have been in their selection of materials by using anything suitable and that was immediately to hand.

The tower has since 1886 housed a peal of five bells. Of these three are somewhat old. The present third and fourth bells bear the date 1678, faithfully reproduced by Taylor's when they recast them in 1886. But of the second bell, also recast in 1886, we are not so lucky in identifying its original year of casting. The five bells are inscribed:-

Treble	J: TAYLOR & Co. FOUNDERS LOUGHBOROUGH 1886
2nd.	BENEDICTUM SIT NOMEN ICH
	Recast by J. Taylor and Co. Loughborough 1886
3rd.	IHS NAZARENVS REX IVDEORVM FILI MISERERE
	I.B. I.D. Wardens 1678
	HEN HVNLOKE BAT TYRWIT
	Recast by J. Taylor and Co. Loughborough 1886
4th.	HEC CAMPANA SACRA FIAT TRINITATE BEATAE
	I.B. I.D. Wardens 1678

Recast by J. Taylor and Co. Loughborough 1886

Tenor   J. TAYLOR & Co. FOUNDERS LOUGHBOROUGH 1886

The tenor bell weighs 11cwts.0qrs.9 lbs and is tuned to G.

On the inner south wall of the Narthex, formerly the old nave, hangs the Sanctus Bell. This bell, about eleven inches in diameter and devoid of inscription, dates probably from the 17th century. It seems to have been hung in several places around the church. Originally it hung over the gable at the east end of the nave. Then it was located in the bell chamber, probably in post- reformation days, before being again resited, this time in a cote on the roof of the mausoleum and finally coming inside again to its present position to the right of the door. It is sad that it appears today not to play any part in the worship of All Saints.

The second bell was reputed to be of a particularly sweet tone and although undated carried a founder's mark of a crown over the initials T.R. The inscription, Benedictum Sit Nomen IHC, being executed in fine Lombardic characters.

Of the other two old bells Dr. Cox had this to say: "The brother bells are in a sad condition, one of them being cracked in several places right up to the shoulder, whilst the other has actually lost a fragment from the rim, fully six inches in length. The story runs that many years ago an idiot obtained access to the belfry, and being anxious, of his own unaided self, to produce music from all three bells at once, took with him a sledge hammer. Two yielded to his blows but the stouter metal of the old bell happily held out until he was removed."

The present third bell, which you will recall was first cast in 1678 and given by Henry Hunloke, Bart., had below its inscription a shield bearing the Hunloke arms: "Az., a fesse between three tigers' heads erased, or impaling Tyrwhit, gu., three Tyrwhitts (or lapwings), or." Sir Henry Hunloke, the second Baronet, held the title for sixty seven years and was buried at Wingerworth at Epiphany, 1715.

On Whit-Monday, May 21st, 1888, the Wingerworth Guild of Ringers rang a true and complete peal of Grandsire Doubles. Consisting of 5040 Changes it was conducted by H. Lenthall and took two hours and forty five minutes to complete. The ringers being:- H. Walton, treble; F. Parke, 2nd; T.P. White, 3rd; W. Lentall, 4th and H. Lenthall, tenor. It was the first peal to be rung on the bells and the first peal that each of the ringers had attempted.

The three bells had been recast, and augmented with a new treble and a tenor two years earlier through the generosity of a gift by the Hon. Mrs. Hunloke. The work was undertaken by John William Taylor, Bellfounder of Loughborough who at the same time installed a new iron bellframe.

It is recorded that in 1887, Mr. Herbert Walton, who rang the treble in the above peal, completed fifty years as a ringer in the service of Wingerworth belfry.

1964 members of the East Derbyshire and West Nottinghamshire Association of Church Bell Ringers were approached and asked to ring for the dedication of the new church building. This was organised by Mr. Arthur Smithson of Blackwell. Among the alteration taking place was that the medieval nave became a vestibule, the chancel became the Lady Chapel and the Hunloke Mausoleum a vestry.

Almost a century after the five bells were installed a major overhaul took place. Mr. Frederick Pembleton was engaged to rehang the five bells on new ball races. He also provided new gudgeons, housings, clappers, crown staples and replaced the pulleys.

No. 1. Vol. I.   FRIDAY, MARCH 24th, 1911.   Price 1d.

The Ringing World is a weekly journal which, as was stated in the very first issue dated March 24th, 1911, aims at recording faithfully and promptly the doings of those engaged in the pursuit of Bell-ringing.

Founded by John Sparkes Goldsmith who remained as editor for 31 years. Five editors on, it is still published weekly and is the Official Journal of the Central Council of Church Bell-Ringers. The current Editor is Tina Stoecklin and the cover price £1.15.

7 THE DECADE NEXT BEFORE THE MILLENNIUM

Augmentations. Belfry improvements. Computer ringing. Ringers' of the future.

The previous chapters have been but a brief glimpse into past events. Earlier, it was mentioned that history is always in the making and that it is to be expected, that no sooner does the ink become dry than out of the masonry and the woodwork of our three dozen belfries will emerge change. This change can effect both structure, the art of Change Ringing and of course the ringer.

Again as previously mentioned, this work came about through the East Derbyshire and West Nottinghamshire Association of Church Bell Ringers reaching the centenary of its founding in 1987. Ten more years have now passed and for the greater part of this period the author was not in circulation as an active bellringer. This absence was unavoidable as my wife, Susan, was in need of liver and kidney surgery. Whilst waiting this necessitated Susan undergoing renal dialysis three times each week over several years, before finally being offered a combined liver and kidney transplant. This life saving operation, the first combined liver and kidney transplant to be carried out at the hospital, was nothing short of a miracle. It was carried out at King's College Hospital, London, in March 1992 by Dr. K.C. Tan of the Institute of Liver Studies, together with Mr. Michael Bewick head of the Dulwich Hospital Renal Unit and their respective medical teams.

Three years later I became the candidate for heart surgery and in need of a replacement aortic valve. This was carried out at Glenfield Hospital, Leicester in March 1996. Thankfully, we are both able to tell the tale and what you have read is my tale.

Instead of undoing and re-writing each chapter in an effort to bring each belfry's history up-to-date, and in so doing still run the risk of not including something of importance, I have decided to add this last chapter of belfry happenings of the past decade.

This, I think, will add greatly and stand as a timely reminder to all readers that no belfry is forever dormant. Like the church it serves, our belfries ought to be forever forward looking. They ebb and flow with activity as custom changes. But, the fact that most have already served the community for several centuries acts as a timely reminder that we as individuals are custodians only for a brief spell in time.

My decision to write this final chapter came about quite unexpectedly. During just one week I came across two new-cast bells, a new ringing chamber, talk of a second chamber being installed and a tower where the ringers have decided to move back and ring in a rather decrepit first floor ringing chamber. To keep apace with such change I would need to re-write the whole book. Add to this the expected upsurge in the popularity of ringing as we approach the millennium and my task could take on the impossible.

247

All this of course is wonderful news for the exercise as a whole and for local towers in particular. It also illustrates and gives a timely illustration of how vibrant bell-ringing could become by the new millennium.

Ashover belfry has become a tower with ten bells. As I write the dedication of two new treble bells is about to take place. A few days ago I had the pleasure of seeing the two bells before they were hoisted aloft and installed in the new alloy frame that accommodates all ten bells on one level. They carry inscriptions, which I have inserted within the chapter about All Saints belfry in order to give a more complete picture of the bells.

However, such a project cannot be undertaken without much in the way of planning, fund raising and sheer hard graft on the part of the local ringers and the church's congregation. The rector, Rev. Tom Johnson, has given his wholehearted support throughout which culminated in a Service of Thanksgiving and Dedication of the Bells and Bell-frame by the Rt. Rev. Jonathan S. Bailey, M.A. Bishop of Derby, on the morning of Sunday, December 7, 1997.

The two new trebles were cast at Loughborough by John Taylor and Company. The eight old bells have been refurbished with new fittings and a new frame to accommodate the ten bells has been made using galvanised steel. The whole contract being carried out by Hayward Mills Associates of Radford, Nottingham.

The whole project cost is in excess of £64,000 of which the Central Council of Church Bell Ringers was able to award a grant of £24,035. This was awarded from the first batch of awards granted to individual projects under the Millennium Commission's umbrella scheme, "Ringing in the Millennium".

In addition there is the generous donation of the two bells. The new Treble bell kindly donated by the Misses Elisabeth and Sara Katherine Bassett in memory of their family. Both Miss Elisabeth and Miss Sara were ringers at All Saints for many years until shortly after the Second World War. The new second bell is given by friends of All Saints Church to mark the Golden Jubilee of the Derby Diocesan Association of Church Bell Ringers which was celebrated in 1996. The first Ashover ringer to become a member of this Association was Mr. Edwin Hopkinson who was elected prior to ringing the seventh bell to a Peal of Plain Bob Major, 5024 Changes. The peal was rung upon All Saints bells on Saturday, May 1, 1948 in two hours and fifty five minutes and was conducted by Herbert E. Taylor of Darley.

Taking twenty-four from sixty-four leaves forty, and forty thousand pounds was the amount needed to be raised locally if the project was to succeed at all. But, first bear in mind that three years ago no one knew about the Millennium Commission so in fact it was to be the full £64,000 that was needed to be raised. To the Rector, the P.C.C. and to the ringers of Ashover this was a daunting sum to try and find. Albeit that the initial project was to simply overhaul the bells and frame. To tower captain,

Jim Heading, and his fellow ringers the need to get the bells put into a good state of repair was of the utmost importance and so with the backing of the Rector, P.C.C. and the parishioners in general an appeal was eventually launched. The usual round of parish events were organised and slowly the fund started to build. With no ringing taking place at All Saints Jim Heading set about organising practices at other church belfries in order to keep the All Saints band of ringers together. Eventually Jim was approached and asked to look after the ringing at Chesterfield parish church for one year to help them out of a difficult period. With no bells able to be rung at Ashover for the time being he accepted the invitation. His wife Wendy was duly elected as caretaker tower captain at Ashover and with her usual flare for organisation continued apace with the money raising projects and, when it was launched, taking the initial step toward the obtaining of a grant from the Millennium Fund.

At this juncture fund raising was going apace and outside help was at hand. Also, outside help suggested increasing the number of bells to ten. This being based upon the fact that by now it was known that a new bell-frame was required for the eight bells in any case, and that to add space for two more bells would in fact add little cost. What was more, the new galvanised steel frame proposed takes up less space, which in turn would make it possible to place the ten bells on one level within the belfry. All very practical and sound advice in favour of augmenting to ten bells, but, without thinking through the practicality of maintaining a strong enough band of bell ringers, in such a small populated parish as Ashover, to enable the ten bells to be rung regularly for service.

In the event it was decided to augment by the addition of two fine treble bells. The new frame enabled the ten bells to be hung on one level and at this juncture a band of new ringers is being trained by tower captain Philip Mahew.

In order to remove the bells from the tower, and to return them, it was necessary to remove the oak tower screen. This has given an idea for a further plan. To return the screen but at the same time to build a new ringing chamber on a level with the top of it. This could give the advantage of providing the church with a kitchen and catering area if required. An interesting idea as we find at St. Mary's, Denby.

A recent visit to a ringing meeting at Denby revealed the installation of a new ringing chamber. This apparently happened in 1993 when it was felt there was a need for installing facilities for the preparation of refreshments within the church. The ringers were removed from the ground floor and installed on a new floor erected in line with the springing of the tower arch into the nave. The placing of the new floor at this level is most pleasing. The arch being filled with glass allows the ringer to be closeted and yet have a direct view into the nave. In return this has the effect of bringing ringer and church congregation together. In keeping with all the woodwork found in the tower the new floor is made of oak and is suspended within the small square of this ancient belfry. It does not extend into the arch or the west window opening, there being on these two sides a fine balustrade fashioned by local craftsmen. Access is gained via a trap door atop a small but finely executed oak stair.

Lifting the ringers to this level has brought an initial problem with regard to bell-handling. Because of the short fall of rope the sally (the coloured woollen hand grip) now disappears of necessity through the holes in the floor above, whereas before, the sally when at its topmost point of its cycle was at a short distance below these holes and therefore the position was of no consequence. Now, because each sally travels through its hole there is a temporary loss of sound within the ringing chamber at each pull of the bell. The overall effect of this is that the sound becomes muffled in a random way which is a little off-putting until the ringer becomes accustomed. In order to acquire a good circle of the six bell-ropes within the ringing chamber some channelling has been undertaken. This has to a slight extent created drag when ringing certain bells but on the whole the new arrangement is an improvement. Especially when considered in context with the facilities it has allowed to be incorporated on the ground floor.

The clock at St. Helen's Church, Darley, has been out of repair for some years but thanks to the Parish Council a grant of £2500 has been allocated for its refurbishment. Restoration work is being undertaken by the Holloway firm, Traditional Tower Clock Services. The mechanism has already been overhauled and restoration of the three-clock dials is to follow.

Tibshelf belfry has become very active of recent months (1997) with an upsurge of interest from parishioners of all ages. No fewer than ten people wishing to learn to ring attend a regular weekly practice. Initially they are being taught by several local ringers.

A weekly practice at Pentrich is well attended, but Mr. Robin Gentle, who is tower captain, could do with support for Sunday service ringing and would very much welcome the return of those who learned to ring at the tower immediately after the bells were augmented to six. Other towers are also in need of establishing a resident band of ringers.

The Golden Wedding Anniversary of H.M. The Queen and H.R.H. The Duke of Edinburgh was celebrated throughout the land on Thursday, November 20, 1997 by the ringing of church bells following the Service of Thanksgiving at Westminster Abbey. Nowhere was it heralded more sincerely than by the ringers of a peal upon the six bells at Morton. For, four of the band of ringers, Peter Wright, Eric Sterland, Brynley Richards and Glyn Holdgate, who, as members of the resident band of ringers at Morton fifty years earlier, had taken part in a peal on the bells to commemorate the actual wedding. And who had again in 1972 taken part in a further peal on the bells in honour of Her Majesty's Silver Wedding Anniversary. It was therefore quite exciting and a great privilege for them to be able to take part in a further peal on the bells in celebration of the Golden Wedding Anniversary, and in so doing honour H.M. The Queen's fiftieth year of marriage to H.R.H. The Duke of Edinburgh.

Holy Cross Church, Morton.
East Derbyshire and west Nottinghamshire Association
of Church Bell Ringers.
On Thursday, November 20, 1997, in 2 hours and 40 minutes,
A PEAL OF TREBLE BOB MINOR, 5040 CHANGES;
being two extents of Oxford Treble Bob, and three of Kent
Treble Bob, and two of Oxford and Kent treble Bob Spliced.

David Palmer	Treble	R. John Sterland	4
E. Glyn Holdgate	2	Eric J. Sterland	5
Peter H. Wright	3	Brynley A. Richards	Tenor.

Conducted by Brynley A. Richards.

A year ago several retired ringers started meeting for practice on the afternoon of the second and fourth Friday in each month. It was not long before they were joined by younger ringers who happen to be free on some of the Friday afternoons. Everyone with basic method ringing skill is most welcome. The object being to offer method ringing to individual bellringers who happen to be isolated. Either by being the only method ringer at their belfry and therefore busy training a team of learners the rudiments of bell handling and basic changes. Or sadly, those who happen to be the only experienced ringer at a tower and are unable to keep up their own practice. The ability to ring touches of Plain Bob is the starting point but in fact plain courses and touches of many plain, treble bob and surprise methods are rung.

The computer has, I understand, opened up new change ringing techniques. It enables those interested to take part in the ringing of changes to a variety of methods - minus the handling of the bell. A fantastic breakthrough as an aid to learning the theory. A wonderful toy in which to indulge. It has already proved indispensable in proving composition and new methods have been recently introduced at a rapid rate. All this is good but please do not let it be forgotten that bellringing is belonging to a team. The joining together with other like minded people to ring the bells of our parish churches to the glory of God and for the civic occasions of our nation. It would be such a pity if modern technology be allowed to outdo our English tradition.

The one hundredth and tenth annual report of the East Derbyshire and West Nottinghamshire Association of Church Bell Ringers has just dropped through my letter box as I write. Upon perusal I find that this year's A.G.M. is to be held at St. Bartholomew's, Clay Cross and at All Saints Church, Wingerworth on Easter Monday. The President, Mr Terrance A. Jeffrey and his daughter Karen, Ringing Master, are both ringers at St. Bartholomew's. The Honorary Secretary is Mrs Jane Aked of Mansfield Woodhouse and the Honorary Treasurer is Mr John A Underwood, a regular ringer at Warsop. Mr Adrian Dempster of St. Helen's, Selston, is the representative on the Central Council of Church Bell Ringers. Mr Eric J. Sterland of Swanwick and Mr Brynley A. Richards of Warsop are Vice

Presidents. The four Executive Committee members are Mrs Wendy Heading of Ashover, Mrs Pam Jeffrey of Clay Cross, Mr Tim Simmons of Blackwell and Mr Tom Stocks of Sutton Scarsdale, whilst Mr Christopher B. Richards, Warsop and Mr Eric J. Sterland are Trustees of the Bell Restoration Fund. Mr Fred Flint of Warsop has served as Honorary Auditor for many years.

Membership has decreased by one to a total of seventy two which is lower than one would wish for, but quite healthy when compared with past years. The Association has assets of almost £1500. This is after donating £200 towards the Sutton in Ashfield tower project during the year. A further £700 is earmarked, £500 for Ashover and £200 for Clay Cross, so whilst the value of the Association's grants may appear small by comparison with present day costs they are most generous when taken in pro rata of membership. Not forgetting of course that it is the same members who are responsible and active contributors to their own belfry funds. In fact, it is a repetition of what has been taking place down the centuries in the belfries of the churches. The unselfish dedication, determination and generosity of bellringers to keep just a few of England's bells ringing out over country and town as they have down the ages of time.

My intention was to conclude now with a brief reference to the coming millennium, but before I do, it has become appropriate to include a brief account of just one item from the annual general meeting of The East Derbyshire and West Nottinghamshire Association of Church Bell Ringers, held on Easter Monday, 1998. It was, after all, the celebration of the centenary of this Association in 1987 that sowed the germ of an idea to write about its member towers, bells and ringers so it would be quite appropriate to now include and welcome the ringers and belfry of St. Mary's Church, Sutton Scarsdale whose affiliation to the Association was elected at that meeting. Not only does the affiliation illustrate how the world of the bellringer is a live and integral part of church life, constantly ebbing and flowing as life goes on, but clearly and aptly it also shows why it is necessary for a cut-off point to this story is essential.

So, in welcoming St. Mary's, Sutton Scarsdale, let us take a brief look at their fine belfry and its four ancient bells.

The embattled west tower of St. Mary's is a well proportioned example of the Perpendicular style of the fifteenth century and is supported by diagonal buttresses. With the exception of that on the north-east angle the four crocketed pinnacles are of much later construction, possibly about 1807 when the Church underwent considerable repair. The tower stands cheek by jowl with the ruin of Sutton Scarsdale Hall, erected in the seventeenth century and remodelled about 1724. So close was the north face of the tower to former outbuildings that it was used as a support. A century ago it was in fact utilized to form one side of a red-brick chimney to the outhouses.

Six years after the restoration of Charles II the second bell was cast and hung in the tower to make a ring of four bells and they have rung out over this rural parish to this day. But, the oldest bell, the third, was ringing out over Sutton in the Dale, as the parish was formerly known, for a century and a half before its younger companion was cast. These few facts alone make St. Mary's peal of bells singularly unique. They are inscribed:-

Treble	IN HONORE IHS RE SONABO
	The legend is not very legible with part being in Lombardic and part in Gothic characters. It was cast in Chesterfield by either Ralph Heathcote or his son George. George took over the business in 1558 on his father's death and the bell is thought to have been cast at that period. It is an extremely rare bell.
2	GOD SAVE THE KING 1666
	This bell was cast by George Oldfield, Nottingham, and no doubt in grateful thanks for the restoration of the monarchy.
3	N HONORE SCE GABRIELIS
	+ (RC) 1490-1510
	This is the oldest bell and cast in Nottingham by a member of the Selyoke family, possibly Richard.
4	GOD SAVE THE CHURCH (PH) 1623
	The founder's mark, a quartered shield, in the upper quarters of which are the initials P.H., and in the lower two sprigs of foliage. This is the work of Paul Hutton a founder with the Oldfields of Nottingham.
	Weight: 7cwts.2qrs.0lbs.

The four bells hang in a spacious chamber and are in good working order. They are under the loving care of Tom Stocks who over a number of years has promoted St. Mary's belfry through his enthusiasm and readiness to travel to other towers in order to gain experience in change ringing on five to ten bells. Minimus methods being the limit of ringing at St. Mary's. It is therefore fitting that after eleven decades since the founding of the Association in 1887 its members can promote and welcome the ringers of St. Mary's Church, Sutton Scarsdale. Who knows, the next millennium may witness an augmentation of the four bells now hanging in St. Mary's belfry?

In 1695 Ralph Heathcote became rector and remained at St. Mary's until 1710 when he was appointed rector of Morton where he remained until his death in 1739. Ralph Heathcote was a direct descendant of the Chesterfield bellfounding family.

Returning once again to the Association's report and another feature to be found therein. It is headed: "Ringing in the Millennium". For those who are not quite sure what the aim of this much publicized statement means it is simply to attempt to ring every church bell, before and as part of a fifteen minute service which will commence at noon on New Year's Day, 2000 A.D.

A wonderful idea! An awe-inspiring challenge! An opportunity to ensure the bells of England ring out for years to come as a timely reminder to all who hear them that God is ever present.

Let us finish by recalling a part of just one inscription to be found among the two hundred and forty bells hanging in the belfries of East Derbyshire and West Nottinghamshire that have been lovingly cared for by local bellringers down the centuries. The four lines were added to the inscription already placed upon the tenor bell cast in 1610 for the Church of S.S. Peter and Paul, Mansfield, when it was recast in the third year of the Atomic Age. And that was fifty years ago, in 1948;

" A day of doubt -
Men's hearts failing them for fear
Still we ring out
That all the voice of God may hear."

Acknowledgement

It is my profound wish to place on record and to thank my many ringing colleagues and friends for the help they have given me, throughout many years, by letting me see and use their personal records and data. Especially with regard to peal ringing, belfry notes, personal anecdotes, photographs, etc., etc.

I would also like to thank all members (past and present) of the East Derbyshire and West Nottinghamshire Association of Church Bell Ringers, together with its Executive Committee, for allowing me to draw information from the account books and minutes. It was having access to this complete dossier, whilst I served as Honorary Secretary, that originally gave me the idea to write this book and which subsequently formed its framework.

I am indebted to my wife Susan for her unstinting encouragement over many years of compiling, writing, re-writing and the general upheaval she has endured at home. Also to our son Andrew for his ready help with elementary computer problems which somehow don't fit in naturally with my age group.

My sincere thanks go to Mr. Gladwyn Turbutt for so readily agreeing to read my manuscript and whose ensuing comments, and suggestions, have been most valuable.

My grateful thanks to Robert Gent and Ruth Gordon of the Derbyshire County Library Service for their help and encouragement and to John Moorley and Peter Newberry of Moorley's Print and Publishing, Ilkeston. Their patience and practical help with the publishing, especially in the initial stages, assured me that the project was feasible.

Finally, my grateful thanks to you the reader for choosing to pick up a copy. I trust you will obtain much enjoyment from your read and that the contents will be found fascinating.

Glyn Holdgate.

Bibliography & Acknowledgements

The author gratefully acknowledges the following sources of reference and the co-operation of those listed below.

The Parish Records, Magazines and numerous guide books and leaflets made freely available.

The complete records of the East Derbyshire and West Nottinghamshire Association of Church Bell Ringers.

The Ringing World. The official weekly journal of the Central Council of Church bell Ringers.

The Bell News and Ringers' Record. The Bellringer.

Notes on the Churches of Derbyshire by J. Charles Cox. 1875.

Thoroton Society Transactions - Rev. Canon R.F. Wilkinson, 1929 and 1931.

Journals of Derbyshire Archaeological and Natural History Society, years 1879, 1880, 1896, 1897 and 1917.

Old Nottinghamshire (1881) and Curiosities of the Belfry (1883) by John Potter Briscoe.

The Derbyshire Times, Ripley and Heanor News, Mansfield Chad, Chronicle Advertiser.

The Family of Heathcote by E.D. Heathcote, 1899.

The Saints and Sinners of Ashover.

The Inns and Outs of Ashover.

A History of Shirland and Higham by Gladwyn Turbutt.

Smiths of Chesterfield by Philip M. Robinson, 1957.

Church Bells of Lincolnshire and Leicestershire, North.

Nottinghamshire Spires (1912) by Harry Gill.

Extracts taken from notes kindly loaned by former bell-ringers, the late Thomas Hopson, William Swain, Arthur Smithson, Wilfred Riley, Thomas Radford, Frank Ashman, Sam. Scattergood, William Wain, Wilson Dobb, Thomas Jennings, John W. England, Robert Mason, Cyril Jaques and Frederick Adcock.

I am indebted to Mr Gladwyn Turbutt for so readily agreeing to read my manuscript and whose ensuing comments and suggestions have proved most valuable. To Mr John Moorley and Mr Peter Newberry of Moorleys Print & Publishing Ltd., Ilkeston, whose practical help and expertise have been invaluable.

Information has been taken from a few other sources where it has not been possible to trace the respective author or photographer before publication. This has been inspite of considerable searching, enquiry and effort. To these few it is very necessary to thank them for their unwitting contribution and to recognise their valuable work.

Finally, the use of anecdotes and notes taken from the records of ringing colleagues and friends over many years and who unfortunately space does not allow to be listed here. However, many of them will be found mentioned in the text.